Trails of

Also by Michael Haynes

Hiking Trails of Montréal and Beyond
Hiking Trails of Mainland Nova Scotia, 9th edition
Hiking Trails of Cape Breton, 2nd edition
Hiking Trails of Ottawa, the National Capital Region and Beyond
Trails of the Halifax Regional Municipality, 2nd edition

MICHAEL HAYNES

Trails of
PRINCE EDWARD ISLAND

GOOSE LANE

Edited by Charles Stuart.
Cover and interior photographs by Michael Haynes
(unless otherwise noted).
Maps prepared by Digital Projections.
Cover and page design by Julie Scriver.
Printed in Canada.
10 9 8 7 6 5 4 3 2

Goose Lane Editions
500 Beaverbrook Court, Suite 330
Fredericton, New Brunswick
CANADA E3B 5X4
gooselane.com

Library and Archives Canada Cataloguing in Publication

Haynes, Michael, 1955-, author
    Trails of Prince Edward Island / Michael Haynes.

Includes bibliographical references and index.
Issued in print and electronic formats.
ISBN 978-0-86492-048-5 (pbk.).
ISBN 978-0-86492-727-9 (pdf)

1. Trails--Prince Edward Island--Guidebooks.
2. Hiking--Prince Edward Island--Guidebooks.
3. Prince Edward Island--Guidebooks. I. Title.

GV199.44.C22P75 2015   796.5109717
C2014-906840-9   C2014-906841-7

Goose Lane Editions is located on the traditional unceded
territory of the Welastekwiyik whose ancestors along with
the Mi'kmaq and Peskotomuhkati Nations signed Peace and
Friendship Treaties with the British Crown in the 1700s.

Goose Lane Editions acknowledges the generous financial
support of the Government of Canada, the Canada Council
for the Arts, and the Province of New Brunswick.

Following this capsule description, you will find more details on how to reach this particular trail, as well as a detailed explanation of the route being profiled This detailed trail outline is divided into the following sections:

Access Information: How to drive to the trail's starting point from convenient and consistent landmarks.

For routes in the **Prince County** region, the western portion of the **Queens County** region, and for western routes of the **Confederation Trail**, driving directions begin from the junction of Granville Street and Highway 2 in Summerside.

For routes in the eastern **Queens County** region, PEI National Park, and central sections of the Confederation Trail, driving directions begin from the junction of Highway 1 and Highway 2/Malpeque Road in Charlottetown.

Directions to all routes in the **Kings County** region, two routes in Queens County, and some sections of the Confederation Trail begin from the junction of Grafton and Water Streets in Charlottetown, crossing the Hillsborough Bridge.

Introduction: Background about the trail, possibly including historical, natural, or geographical information, as well as my personal observations or recommendations.

Route Description: A walk-through of the hike, relating what I found when I last travelled this route. In every case I describe junctions and landmarks from the perspective of someone following the trail in the direction I have indicated. If travelling in the opposite direction, remember to reverse my bearings.

SCENIC NOTES

Scattered throughout the book are fifty capsule descriptions of some of the plants, animals, geological features, and human history that you might encounter on the various trails. These are intended to be brief samples to whet your curiosity about the world through which you are hiking/biking, and to encourage you to learn more. An index of all scenic notes is found on pp. 341-342.

USER TIPS

Unless you are an experienced hiker/ biker, you might not know how much water to carry on your hike, or why wearing a helmet when biking is both a good idea and a legal requirement on PEI. Twenty-five helpful hints are sprinkled among the trail descriptions. An index of these can be found on p. 341.

NOVICE WALKERS—
GETTING STARTED

New or occasional walkers should begin by selecting routes with a difficulty rating of 1 or 2. These are likely to be completed within one or two hours by people of almost any fitness level. With experience, trails with a higher difficulty level can be attempted. Level 1 routes should be comfortable for most children; level 2 routes, which can be as long as 10 km (6.25 mi), should only be considered with children once you are familiar with their capabilities.

Clothing and footwear are extremely important. For shorter walks in comfortable weather, there is little need for specialized gear. However, as distance and time walked increase, comfort and safety will be substantially improved by wearing hiking shoes and outfits specially designed for outdoor activity. There is a bewildering array of products available, more than enough for a book on its own, and choosing the right gear is also dependent upon individual preferences. I, for example, like to hike in sandals, while friends often wear heavy boots. Once you have decided that hiking is a regular part of your lifestyle, you can visit outdoor stores and find what works for you.

However, there are a few items that should always be carried, even if you are only going for a short hike.

Doing so may help make every hiking experience an enjoyable and safe one.

Water: Nothing is more important than water. You can survive up to two weeks without food; you may die in as few as three days without water. I carry one litre (1 qt) per person on a hike up to 10 km (6.25 mi), more if the distance is greater, if the day is particularly hot or humid, or if I am taking children with me. Dehydration occurs rapidly while hiking, and the accompanying headache or dizziness diminishes the pleasure of the experience. Drink small sips of water often and do not wait until you are thirsty to do so. Portable water filtration systems are available in any outdoor store and are worth carrying, especially on hot summer treks.

Map: I consider a topographical map valuable, whether paper or electronic. With a map, I have an idea of the terrain through which I will be hiking. Is it swampy? Are there rivers? If I become misdirected, in what direction do I find people? I prefer the National Topographic System of Canada 1:50,000-scale map of the area, and for each route I provide the appropriate map listing.

Food: Though not essential on a day hike or bike ride, I always carry something to snack on while I walk, and

Helmet

Wearing a helmet while cycling is the law in Prince Edward Island for both children and adults. Besides, it just makes good sense. A suitable helmet should fit snugly yet keep your head relatively cool. Look for plenty of vents and easy-to-adjust straps to ensure a comfortable fit.

who doesn't enjoy a picnic? Apples, trail mix, bagels; anything like this is good. Chocolate bars, chips, and other junk food are not the best choice and should be saved for after the trip.

Whistle: If you are lost and want to attract attention, a whistle will be heard far better than your voice, and is less likely to wear out from continuous use. Test it out: take one outside the house and give a couple of blasts. See how much attention you attract. (Spoiler alert: too much, probably.)

First Aid Kit: When in the woods, even minor injuries can be a serious problem. At the least, they can distract from an otherwise pleasant experience. A small first aid kit, with bandages, gauze, tape, moleskin, etc., permits you to deal with blisters and bruises that require attention.

Garbage Bag: You should always carry your trash out: food wrappers, juice bottles, and even apple cores should go into the bag. (And if you find litter left behind by others, take a moment to put as much as you can into your own garbage bag.)

Warm Sweater and/or Rain Jacket: Weather is highly changeable, especially in spring and fall. Cold rains and high winds can create uncomfortable, even life-threatening, conditions. No matter how fine the weather seems to be, always carry some protective clothing, especially when walking on exposed beaches.

Backpack: You need something to carry everything, so I recommend that you invest in a quality day pack. It should have adjustable shoulder straps, a waist strap, a large inner pouch, and roomy outer pockets. The equipment listed earlier will fit easily inside a good pack and will sit comfortably on your back. After one or two trips, wearing it will become just another part of your walking routine. I rarely hike without my pack.

Blue Jeans

Great in the city, but not so good in the outdoors. Not only are blue jeans constricting, but when they get wet they can triple in weight! And they take forever to dry. Choose something else to wear on your walk.

Optional (but recommended) Equipment: Sunscreen, hat, bug repellent, camera, binoculars, field guides, extra socks, bandana, and toilet paper.

HAZARDS

Prince Edward Island contains little in the way of hazards. There are no bear, moose, or even deer, and local coyotes are so shy that there is very little chance of sighting one. Because there are no big game animals, there is no period in the fall when hunters with high-powered rifles wander the woods. (Hunters pursue waterfowl, but this is far less of an impediment to recreational hiking/biking.)

Nor does PEI have much in the way of rugged terrain or isolated wilderness. A few of the "Destination Trails" are located in areas as remote as possible, but you are never more than a kilometre or two from the nearest road. However, that does not mean you should be cavalier about preparing for a recreational outing. On every walk and bike ride, I carry my backpack, which contains food, water, first aid kit, navigation (compass and GPS), and other equipment.

Accompanying each route description are specific **cautionary notes**, provided in one- or two-word descriptions. Following is a more detailed explanation of what each one of these means.

Road Crossings: If your route must cross a public road, I will list this to remind you to watch for traffic when you must cross. All Confederation Trail routes require multiple crossings, and often on roads where the speed limits are 80 or 90 kph (50 or 55 mph).

Motorized Vehicles: ATVs, snowmobiles, and other vehicles sometimes share the trail with walkers and bikers. This is true on all of the Scenic Heritage Roads, where automobiles, trucks, and farming equipment might also be encountered. Drivers of these vehicles will not necessarily be expecting pedestrians or cyclists; be attentive.

Cliffs: Although only a few trails take you next to cliffs, remember that the soft soils of PEI erode very quickly, and the edges are usually undercut and unstable, particularly in the spring .

Poison ivy/giant hogweed: These skin-irritating plants are too often found along the edges of many trails and fields. Managed trails will usually post warning signs, but as both plants are spreading and extending their range, they could be almost anywhere. Best way to avoid them: stay on the path.

First Aid Kit
When you are out in the woods, even small problems can become very important. A basic first aid kit with bandages, gauze, tape, moleskin, etc., can permit you to deal with the blisters, scratches, and bruises that require attention. Keep your kit in your backpack always, no matter what distance you are walking or cycling.

Navigation: Some routes, such as the Beck Trail and Strathgartney Provincial Park, are occasionally challenging to follow, either because they are very winding and complex, or because their signage is limited. Do not attempt these unless you are comfortable with the possibility of being uncertain of your exact location, and confident that you can navigate your way back if you are.

Wind and Waves: On a sunny, summer day, a walk on a long, sandy beach must be one of the most relaxing experiences available. However, visit that same beach when a late-fall gale is lashing it, and you might be forgiven if you thought you were undertaking an Arctic expedition. There is no shelter on a beach, no buffer to shield you from the full force of nature's power. A surging rogue wave, created by high winds and strong currents, can be several times larger than the usual, and will be strong enough to knock the strongest person off their feet, and possibly pull them out to sea. I most enjoy beach walks during fall and winter, but I walk above the high-water mark.

Hunting: I listed this as a hazard for only one route: Pigot's Trail, which circles the Allisary Creek Impoundment. The surrounding marshes are very popular with waterfowl hunters.

***

Congratulations! You have completed the instructions and should be able to use this book to its full potential. You are ready to begin your ambulatory and cycling discovery of Prince Edward Island. I hope you enjoy your explorations as much as I did mine.

Share your pictures of your hikes on the *Trails of Prince Edward Island* Pinterest page at www.pinterest.com/hikerhaynes.

53. Gulf Shore Way West

Etiquette

Many trails support more than one use, such as walking and cycling. Here are a few simple rules that make "sharing the trail" safer:

- Be friendly and courteous.
- Ride, walk, or run on the right, pass on the left.
- Cyclists yield to horses, runners, and hikers. Keep your bike at a safe speed.
- Runners and hikers yield to horseback riders.
- Downhill traffic should yield to uphill traffic.
- When in doubt, give the other user the right of way.
- Dogs should be kept on leashes and under control.
- Pack out your litter, including dog waste.
- Respect private property.
- Stay on the trail. Creating your own route creates erosion, damages habitat, and causes new trails that can't be maintained.

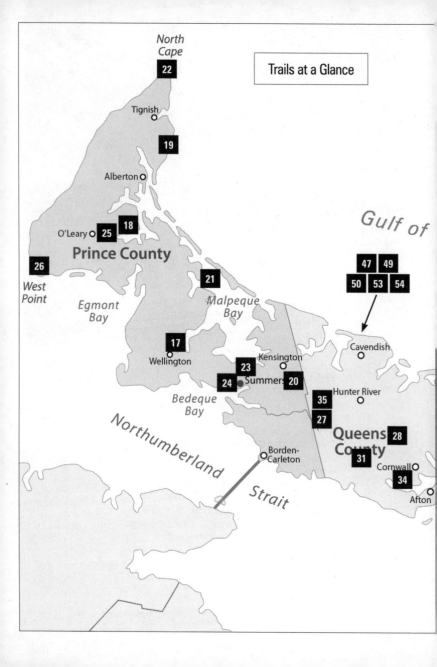

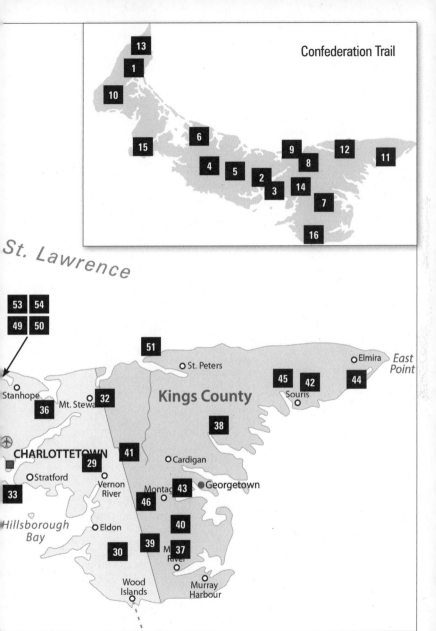

Confederation Trail

St. Lawrence

Kings County

East Point

Elmira

St. Peters

Souris

Stanhope

Mt. Stewart

CHARLOTTETOWN

Stratford

Vernon River

Cardigan

Georgetown

Montague

Hillsborough Bay

Eldon

Murray River

Wood Islands

Murray Harbour

TRAILS AT A GLANCE

Trail Name	Difficulty level 1-5	Length km (mi)	Time to complete (hours)	Permitted Uses (No snow)	Permitted Uses (Snow)	Dogs	Page
				Features			

Uses (no snow): W = Walking, B = Biking, A = ATVing, H = Horseback Riding, I = Inline Skating
Uses (winter): S = Snowshoing/Walking, X = Cross-Country Skiing, Sm = Snowmobiling
Uses (dogs): P = Dogs prohibited, L = Dogs permitted on leash, O = Dogs permitted off leash
* = Permitted on some sections of the route, but not all

CONFEDERATION TRAIL (difficulty and time indicate bicycle use)

Trail Name	Difficulty level 1-5	Length km (mi)	Time to complete (hours)	Permitted Uses (No snow)	Permitted Uses (Snow)	Dogs	Page
1. Alberton to O'Leary	3-B	46 (28.75)	3+	W, B	Sm	L	29
2. Charlottetown to Mount Stewart	5-B	70 (43.75)	5+	W, B	S*, X*, Sm*	L	35
3. Charlottetown to Vernon River	4-B	60 (37.5)	4+	W, B, I*	S*, X*, Sm*	L	41
4. Emerald to Borden/Carleton	3-B	38 (23.75)	2.5+	W, B	Sm	L	47
5. Hunter River to Charlottetown	4-B	61(38.25)	4+	W, B	S*, X*, Sm*	L	53
6. Kensington to Hunter River	4-B	64 (40)	4+	W, B	Sm	L	59
7. Montague to Georgetown	2-B	35 (22)	2.5+	W, B	Sm	L	73
8. Mount Stewart to Cardigan	3-B	64 (40)	4+	W, B	Sm	L	77
9. Mount Stewart to St. Peters	3-B	53 (33.25)	3.5+	W, B	Sm	L	83
10. O'Leary to Wellington	5-B	92 (57.5)	6+	W, B	Sm	L	89
11. Souris to Elmira	3-B	50 (31.25)	3.5+	W, B	Sm	L	97
12. St. Peters to Souris	5-B	72 (45)	5+	W, B	Sm	L	103
13. Tignish to Alberton	2-B	43 (27)	2.5+	W, B	S, Sm	L	109
14. Vernon River to Wood Islands	5-B	73 (45.75)	5+	W, B	Sm	L	113
15. Wellington to Kensington	4-B	64 (40)	4+	W, B	Sm	L	119
16. Wood Islands to Murray Harbour	3-B	46 (28.75)	3+	W, B	Sm	L	127

Trail Name	Difficulty level 1-5	Length km (mi)	Time to complete (hours)	Permitted Uses (No snow)	Permitted Uses (Snow)	Dogs	Page
PRINCE COUNTY (difficulty and time indicate walking use)							
17. Camp Tamawaby Woodlot	1	1.9 (1.2)	.5+	W	S, X	O	135
18. Hackney Scenic Heritage Road	1	5 (3.1)	1+	W, B, A, H	S, X, Sm	O	145
19. Jacques Cartier Provincial Park	3	11.5 (7.2)	3+	W	—	L*	149
20. John Hogg Kensington Public Forest	1	4.5 (2.8)	1+	W, B*	S, X*, Sm*	L	151
21. Lennox Island — The Path of Our Forefathers	2	10 (6.25)	3+	W	S	O	155
22. North Cape/Black Marsh Nature Trail	1	5 (3.1)	1+	W	S	L	159
23. Rotary Friendship Trail	2	6 (3.75)	1.5+	W, B	S, X	L	163
24. Summerside Baywalk	3	13 (8.1)	3+	W, B, I*	S*, X*	L	167
25. Trout River	2	7 (4.4)	2+	W	S	O	171
26. West Point Beach	2	9.5 (6)	2.5+	W, A*	—	L*	175
QUEENS COUNTY (difficulty and time indicate walking use)							
27. Breadalbane Nature Trail	2	7 (4.4)	2+	W, B*	S, Sm*	L	181
28. Brookvale Nordic	2	6.5 (4.1)	1.5+	W, B	X	L	185
29. Dromore Woodland Trails	4	16 (10)	4+	W	S, X	O	189
30. Gairloch Road	2	7.5 (4.7)	2+	W, B	S	O	193
31. McKenna Scenic Heritage Road	2	9.5 (6)	2.5+	W, B, A, H	S, X, Sm	O	197
32. Pigot's Trail	1	5.3 (3.3)	1+	W, B*	S, X, Sm*	L	201
33. Port-la-Joye — Fort Amherst National Historic Site of Canada	1	4.25 (2.7)	1+	W	S	L	205

Trail Name	Difficulty level 1-5	Length km (mi)	Time to complete (hours)	Permitted Uses (No snow)	Permitted Uses (Snow)	Dogs	Page
				Features			
34. Strathgartney Provincial Park	4	9 (5.6)	2.5+	W, B*, H*	S	L	217
35. Warburton Scenic Heritage Road	2	10.5 (6.6)	2.5+	W, B, A, H	S, X, Sm	O	223
36. Winter River	2	6 (3.75)	1.5+	W, B*, A*	S, X*, Sm*	O	227
KINGS COUNTY (difficulty and time indicate walking use)							
37. Beck Trail	4	10 (6.25)	2.5+	W, B	S, X	O	235
38. Boughton River Trail	2	9 (5.6)	2.5+	W	S, X	O	239
39. County Line Scenic Heritage Road	1	5 (3.1)	1.5+	W, B, A, H	S, X, Sm	O	243
40. Harvey Moore Sanctuary	1	2.5 (1.6)	1+	W	S	L	247
41. Mooneys Pond	1	1.9 (1.2)	1+	W, B	S	L	259
42. New Harmony Scenic Heritage Road	2	7.5 (4.7)	2+	W, B*, A*, H*	S, X, Sm*	O	265
43. Roma	2	4.5 (2.8)	1+	W	S, X*	L	269
44. Singing Sands Beach	3	11 (6.9)	3+	W	—	O*	273
45. Souris Striders Trails	2	6.25 (3.9)	2+	W, B	S, X	P	277
46. Valleyfield Demonstration Woodlot	1	1.7 (1.1)	1+	W	S	O	281
PRINCE EDWARD ISLAND NATIONAL PARK (difficulty and time indicate walking use, unless otherwise stated)							
47. Balsam Hollow / Haunted Wood	1	2.5 (1.6)	1+	W	S	L	287
48. Bubbling Springs/Farmlands	1	4.5 (2.9)	1+	W, B	S, X	L	291
49. Cavendish Beach	3	11 (6.9)	2.5+	W		L	295
50. Clark's Lane	2	5.25 (3.3)	1.5+	W, B	S, X	L	299
51. Greenwich Dunes	2	8 (5)	2+	W, B*	S, X*	P*	305

Trail Name	Difficulty level 1-5	Length km (mi)	Time to complete (hours)	Permitted Uses (No snow)	Permitted Uses (Snow)	Dogs	Page
52. Gulf Shore Way East	5-W 4-B	25 (15.6)	6+ W 2+ B	W, B, I	S, X	L	309
53. Gulf Shore Way West	5-W 2-B	17 (10.6)	4+ W 2+ B	W, B, I	S, X	L	313
54. Homestead	2	8.5 (5.3)	2+	W, B	S, X	L	317
55. Reeds & Rushes/Woodlands	2	7.5 (4.7)	2+	W, B*	S, X*	L	329
56. Robinsons Island	1	4 (2.5)	1+	W, B	S, X	P*	333

Sunscreen
Critical when you are regularly active outside, especially on those sunny, Island summer days on the mostly shadeless Confederation Trail. Use a sunscreen rated SPF 15 or higher, renewing every two hours, even on overcast days, and particularly at peak times: 1100 to 1500 hours. Keep children well protected. When cycling, use "sport" sunscreens.

5T. Greenwich Dunes

9. Mount Stewart to St. Peters

CONFEDERATION TRAIL

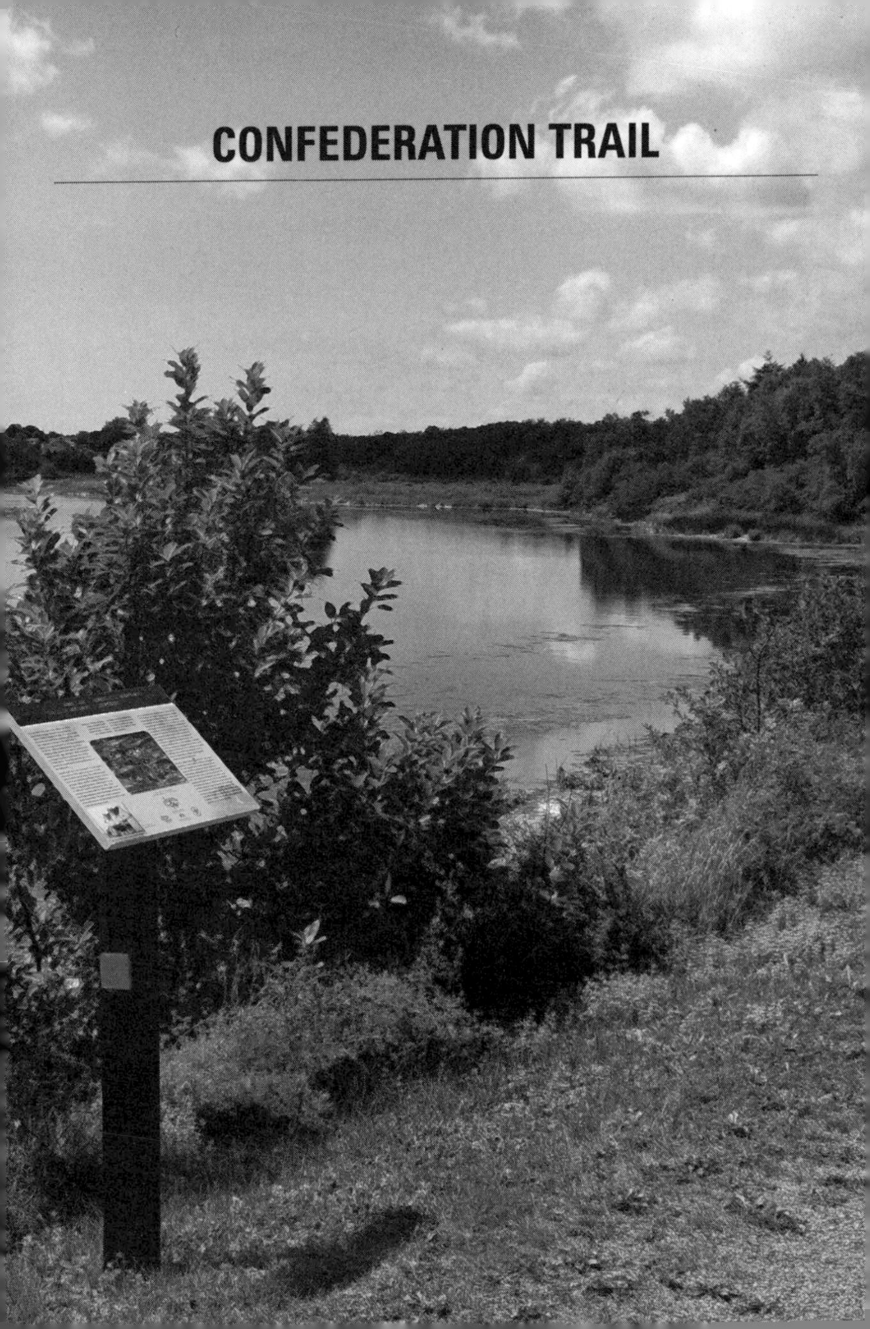

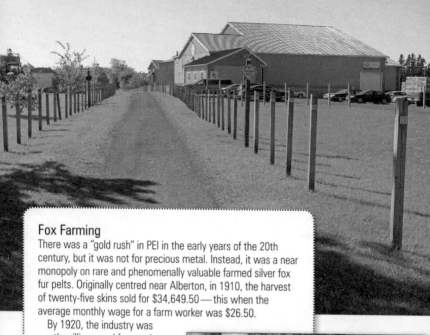

Fox Farming

There was a "gold rush" in PEI in the early years of the 20th century, but it was not for precious metal. Instead, it was a near monopoly on rare and phenomenally valuable farmed silver fox fur pelts. Originally centred near Alberton, in 1910, the harvest of twenty-five skins sold for $34,649.50—this when the average monthly wage for a farm worker was $26.50.

By 1920, the industry was worth millions, and fox ranches were springing up all over the island. But overproduction, declining quality, and other factors ended this fabulous era, where so many fortunes were made. In 1946, there were 3,729 ranches with 99,269 foxes; by 1955, only 189 ranches with 3,293 foxes remained. Many farmers let their animals loose when they became too expensive to feed, which is why wild silver foxes are still occasionally spotted.

1. Confederation Trail — Alberton to O'Leary

◄ - - - ► 46 km (28.75 mi) rtn

⏱: 3+ hrs (biking)

🚴: 3-B

Type of Trail: crushed stone

Uses: walking, biking, snowmobiling

⚠: road crossings

🔧: adequate throughout

Facilities: benches, garbage cans, interpretive panels, picnic tables, washrooms, water

Gov't Topo Map: 21I16 (Tignish), 21I09 (O'Leary)

Trailhead GPS: N 46° 57.095' W 64° 2.140'

Access: From the junction of Central Street and Highway 2 in Summerside, follow Highway 2 west for 81 km (50.6 mi) to the community of Tignish. Turn left onto Railway Street, and follow for 180 m/yd. The parking area is directly ahead.

Introduction: When the Prince Edward Island Railway was first constructed, in the 1870s, its western terminus was Northport, the community adjacent to Alberton. The line was extended to Tignish in the 1880s. Alberton's railway station was one of only two on the island built entirely from stone. It is now home to the tourist information centre.

O'Leary's prosperity as a community grew from its convenient position on the main line of the railway, and at a location where there was a side rail and spurs, off the main line, for loading and unloading of cars. O'Leary quickly became the most important trade and service centre for West Prince.

The Confederation Trail connecting these two communities is a pleasant ride with facilities available at both ends of the route. If you like to fish, the Mill River, which the trail crosses, is a popular destination for anglers.

Route Description: In Alberton, the trail begins in Stone Station Park, a large grass field with picnic tables, interpretive panels, and even a playground. The crushed stone track passes through a gate, and reaches a junction 250 m/yd from Church Street. The sign there directs you left, stating that O'Leary is 24 km (15 mi) away.

The trail reaches another junction 250 m/yd later; keep straight (left), crossing Prince William Street 100 m/yd further. For the next 850 m/yd,

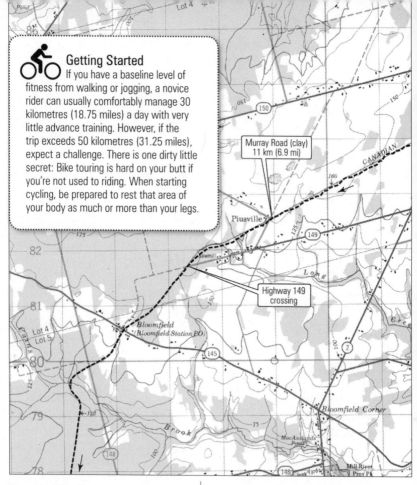

Getting Started
If you have a baseline level of fitness from walking or jogging, a novice rider can usually comfortably manage 30 kilometres (18.75 miles) a day with very little advance training. However, if the trip exceeds 50 kilometres (31.25 miles), expect a challenge. There is one dirty little secret: Bike touring is hard on your butt if you're not used to riding. When starting cycling, be prepared to rest that area of your body as much or more than your legs.

Murray Road (clay)
11 km (6.9 mi)

Highway 149
crossing

forest borders both sides of the trail, but then there are cultivated fields adjacent. At least two benches along this stretch provide an opportunity to rest.

About 2.9 km (1.8 mi) from the start, the trail moves to within 25 m/yd of Highway 150, and continues alongside it for the remainder of the

distance to Elmsdale. As a result, automobile traffic noise will be constant, and there are many driveways that must be crossed. At the km 24 (15 mi) marker, there is a sheltered table and an interpretive panel.

At 4 km (2.5 mi), the trail crosses Highway 150 at a particularly dan-

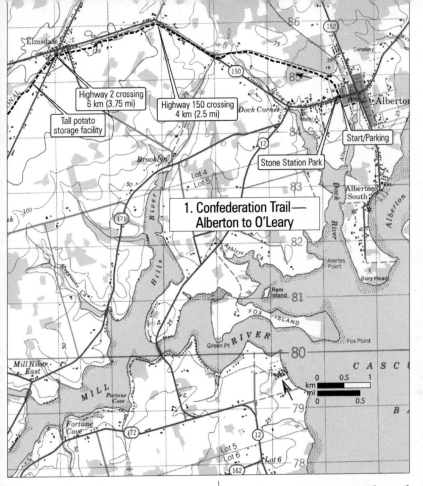

Tall potato storage facility

Highway 2 crossing 6 km (3.75 mi)

Highway 150 crossing 4 km (2.5 mi)

Start/Parking

Stone Station Park

1. Confederation Trail— Alberton to O'Leary

gerous spot, in a curve, just before Oliver Road connects to the Highway. I recommend dismounting to cross, as I do when crossing Highway 2 later.

Once across, the trail continues parallel to Highway 150, with no barrier between them until a small stand

of trees at 5.4 km (3.4 mi). The trail then runs behind a number of houses in Elmsdale, crosses Butcher Road 350 m/yd later, and reaches Highway 2 about 250 m/yd after that. Adjacent to Highway 2 is a trailhead, with a bench, picnic table, several panels, and a boulder—something unusual

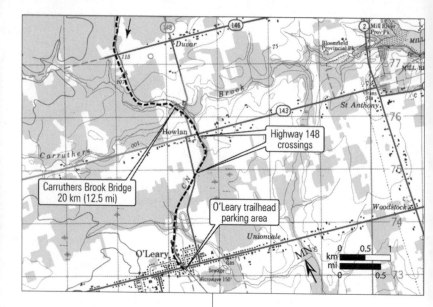

Carruthers Brook Bridge
20 km (12.5 mi)

Highway 148
crossings

O'Leary trailhead
parking area

for PEI. There is also a convenience store next to the road crossing.

On the far side of Highway 2, the trail curves left, passing between rows of wooden posts intended to separate the trail from Griffin Farms, which has large buildings on both sides of the pathway. About 750 m/yd from Highway 2, there is a tall concrete and steel potato storage facility immediately beside the trail.

For 2 km (1.25 mi), until the km 29 (18.1 mi) marker, the trail remains close to Highway 2, though gradually moving away. Then it curves right, angling off about 45°. An extended straight section follows, mostly with cultivation bordering both sides of

the path, until shortly after crossing Murray Road at Piusville, some 11 km (6.9 mi) from Alberton.

Fields are soon left behind, and the route heads into a remote wooded area for the next 3.5 km (2.2 mi), relieved only by the crossing of Highway 149 and infrequent curves. As usual on the Confederation Trail, there are frequent benches, and the occasional sheltered picnic tables. At Bloomfield, where the trail crosses Highway 145/O'Halloran Road, there is a trailhead parking area, a picnic table, and an information panel.

From Bloomfield, the trail definitely appears to be gently descending, and it also becomes more curving.

About 1 km (0.6 mi) further, the clay surface of Highway 148 is crossed, then the trail turns left and reaches the bridge over small Cains Brook 500 m/yd further, 16 km (10 mi) from Alberton.

Once over the brook, the trail begins to climb quite noticeably, while continuing its curving route. The forest on both sides of the path remains unbroken. Just 600 m/yd later, at the concrete remains of one of the former watering stations for the railway, there is a sheltered picnic table, and one of the rare solar-powered outhouses on the Confederation Trail. I have always found these facilities to be both clean and well-stocked.

This is another remote section, remaining so until fields come into sight, shortly before reaching clay-surfaced Highway 146, 2.5 km (1.6 mi) from Cains Brook. The trail stays straight for another 900 m/yd before making a quite tight (for a former rail line) left turn. Fields soon replace forest, the trail curves right, and at 20 km (12.5 mi) from Alberton, it reaches the bridge crossing Carruthers Brook, where there is another picnic table and an information panel—this one about beavers.

Less than 200 m/yd from the bridge, the trail crosses Highway 148, and 500 m/yd after that, Highway 143. There are many houses near the trail through here, especially to the right, though the trail enters a small, but thick, stand of trees soon after crossing Highway 143.

After a gently curving 900 m/yd section, Highway 148/Gaspe Road must be crossed again; there are large potato fields on the right. Soon back into a wooded area, 800 m/yd from Gaspe Road the trail passes next to the active Charles F. Willis Memorial Racetrack (for horses), which is to the left.

Only 500 m/yd of forested pathway remains before the trail emerges, just after the km 44 (27.5 mi) marker, to run between a number of large agricultural buildings and enter the community of O'Leary. About 300 m/yd further, the trail crosses North Street, then runs between more large buildings to finish at Highway 142/Main Street, where there is the former train station, a parking area, interpretive panels, a picnic table, and a community signpost.

Retrace the trail back to Alberton when ready.

2. Confederation Trail—
Charlottetown to Mount Stewart

◄--- ► 70 km (43.75 mi) rtn

🕐: 5+hrs (biking)

🚲: 5-B

Type of Trail: crushed stone

Uses: walking, biking, snowshoeing*, cross-country skiing*, snowmobiling*

⚠: road crossings

🚾: adequate throughout

Facilities: benches, garbage cans, interpretive panels, picnic tables, washrooms, water

Gov't Topo Map: 11L03 (Charlottetown), 11L06 (North Rustico), 11L07 (Mount Stewart)

Trailhead GPS: N 46° 14.420' W 63° 7.150'

Access: The trailhead is in Joseph A. Ghiz Memorial Park, 450 m/yd east of the intersection of Highway 1 and Grafton Street (Hillsborough Bridge) in Charlottetown. Turn right onto Edward Street, and park there or on Kent Street. The trail begins at Grafton Street.

Introduction: The salt marshes on the Hillsborough River near Mount Stewart are extensive and rich with bird life, and this section of the Confederation Trail features almost 2 km (1.25 mi) where the wetlands border both sides of the pathway. The Hillsborough River Eco-Centre contains a museum, natural and cultural history displays, a library, and even a snack shop.

Snowmobiling is the only permitted winter use on the main Confederation Trail. However, from

Royalty Junction to Joseph A. Ghiz Memorial Park, only non-motorized uses are permitted year-round.

Route Description: From the trailhead in Joseph A. Ghiz Memorial Park, ride the 8 km (5 mi) through Charlottetown to Royalty Junction (for a detailed description, see pg. 53), where a sign indicates that Mount Stewart is 27 km (16.9 mi) and York is 6 km (3.75 mi) further, to the right.

It is only 1.1 km (0.7 mi) to the crossing of Highway 15/Brackley Point Road, and the route is mostly wooded. At the other side of the junction, there is the first bench, and two interpretive panels: the first of many. The km 177 (110.6 mi) marker is only 100 m/yd from the junction.

On the opposite side of Highway 15 is a large trucking facility, and the trail divides the parking area, so be

---

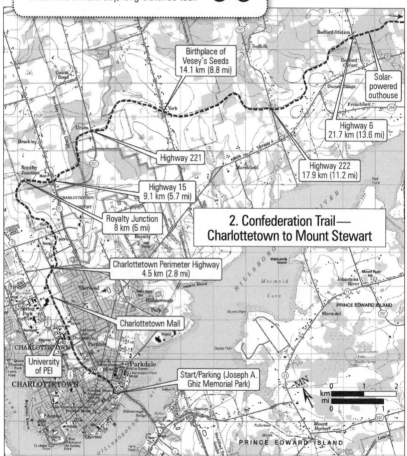

Birthplace of Vesey's Seeds
14.1 km (8.8 mi)

Solar-powered outhouse

Highway 6
21.7 km (13.6 mi)

Highway 221

Highway 222
17.9 km (11.2 mi)

Highway 15
9.1 km (5.7 mi)

Royalty Junction
8 km (5 mi)

2. Confederation Trail— Charlottetown to Mount Stewart

Charlottetown Perimeter Highway
4.5 km (2.8 mi)

Charlottetown Mall

University of PEI

Start/Parking (Joseph A. Ghiz Memorial Park)

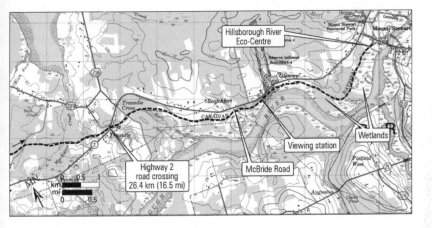

cautious. However, after 250 m/yd the path is bordered by large fields, and 450 m/yd further it enters the forest, about where it crosses a small stream, and where there are bordering fences. After a pleasant curving path, much of it beside cultivated fields, the trail reaches Highway 221. The terrain is similar for the 2.8 km (1.75 mi) to York, although there is a shelter with an information board at about km 181.2 (113.25 mi), and an attractive pond and wetland about 300 m/yd before reaching Highway 25.

York boasts a community signpost, a gazebo with a picnic table, and an interesting panel describing the origins of Vesey's Seeds, founded in York. The next 3.75 km (2.3 mi), to Highway 222, continues gentle and rural, with alternating field and forest, punctuated by the occasional bench or sheltered table. And from there to

tiny Bedford Station and Highway 6, where there is a solitary interpretive panel, it is a further, comparable 3.8 km (2.4 mi).

About 400 m/yd past Highway 6, the trail skirts a large bog, and just past the km 191 marker, 800 m/yd from Highway 6 and about 22.5 km (14.1 mi) from your start in Charlottetown, there is a sheltered picnic table, flanked by five information boards, and one of the Confederation Trail's rare solar-powered self-composting outhouses.

The land bordering the trail is mostly forested, with only infrequent and smaller fields encroaching. When the Corrigan Road is crossed, 1.4 km (0.9 mi) from the outhouse, it is one of the uncommon locations where there are no houses nearby. This area appears quite remote, with nothing but thick forest for a considerable distance. It is only as the trail approaches Highway 2, which the trail crosses 2.5 km (1.6 mi) from Corrigan Road, that fields and residences reappear.

This can be an exceptionally dangerous crossing, as the speed limit is 90 kph (55 mph) and it is near a curve in the Highway. Exercise particular caution here.

Once across, the trail plunges back into forest, although there is a horse-racing track on the right in 300 m/yd, and the crossing of Highway 218 only 200 m/yd later. But then the route heads into an area of more bogs, where the adjacent trees are spruce, larch, and fir. Although no houses can be seen, Highway 2 is still quite close, and you will almost certainly hear traffic.

Trail and highway approach each other, and when cultivated fields resume, on the left, you should be able to see traffic on the higher road. They are running roughly parallel, though the trail conforms more to the contour of the slightly undulating slope. About 100 m/yd beyond the km 198 marker is an interpretive panel about a unique group of immigrants, the Glenaladale Settlers.

By the time the trail crosses McBride Road, it is almost a sidewalk of Highway 2. Some 400 m/yd past here is a side trail, cut for snowmobilers, and a sign directing to a restaurant just across the highway. Soon, the Hillsborough River and its extensive bordering wetlands come into view, on the right.

At the next sheltered table, 1.2 km (0.75 mi) from McBride Road, there is a relevant interpretive panel. You are also just across Highway 2 from a service station/store. And 300 m/yd further, there is another panel on the trail, and a connecting walkway to a tourist information point for motorists. From here, there are completely unrestricted views of the river, and the path runs along the edge of the salt marsh.

The view does not last long, as the trail moves behind a hill about 500 m/yd later, and into some thick hardwood forest. It also begins to move away from Highway 2, crossing several private driveways. Then, about 1.5 km (0.9 mi) from the sheltered

table, the trail comes out of the forest and into a quite large wetland area.

The trail becomes a causeway through a sea of cattails. Expect to see many waterfowl, even on the trail itself, as well as muskrat and beaver. Red-winged blackbirds will scold you as you intrude into their territory. This area, known as Carrs Point, is a protected wetland and is rich with interesting flora and fauna.

You have nearly 2 km (1.25 mi) before the trail moves onto higher, and drier, ground. Then, only 300 m/yd remains before you reach the community of Mount Stewart, and the Hillsborough River Eco-Centre, the end of your trip.

Retrace the route to return to Charlottetown.

Canada Goose

Canada geese are easy to identify: large, plump birds with black heads and necks and contrasting white throats. They are noisy, constantly making low honking sounds that rise in volume considerably when they become airborne. Their long V-formations, often heard before seen, are a biannual reminder of nature's changing seasons.

On trails near water, geese are frequently a hazard, both because of their violent territorial defence when approached, especially near their nests or in the company of their young — they show little fear of humans — and their extravagant and abundant droppings (bikers beware!).

Hillsborough Bridge

Tunnel

Trail ends (temporary)

Pippy Road trailhead

Shakespeare Drive

Future trail

Start/Parking (Joseph A. Ghiz Memorial Park)

Road detour

Road detour

Mount Hebert Road

3. Confederation Trail—
Charlottetown to Vernon River

3. Confederation Trail—
Charlottetown to Vernon River

◄---► 60 km (37.5 mi) rtn

🕐: 4+hrs (biking)

⛷🚴: 4-B

Type of Trail: asphalt, concrete, crushed stone

Uses: walking, biking, inline skating*, snowshoeing*, cross-country skiing*, snowmobiling*

⚠: road crossings

🚰: adequate throughout

Facilities: benches, garbage cans, interpretive panels, picnic tables, washrooms, water

Gov't Topo Map:11L02 (Montague), 11L03 (Charlottetown)

Trailhead GPS:N 46° 14.420' W 63° 7.150'

Access: The trailhead is in Joseph A. Ghiz Memorial Park, 450 m/yd east of the intersection of Highway 1 and Grafton Street/Hillsborough Bridge in Charlottetown. Turn right onto Edward Street, and park there or on Kent Street. The trail begins at Grafton Street.

Introduction: The final section of the Confederation Trail, between Stratford and Iona, was to be completed in 2014-2015. A length of this section, between Mount Albion and Uigg, had previously been developed, but there were significant challenges that prevented its development through the more developed urban areas.

Officially, this section opened on September 12, 2014. However, when I visited on September 25-26, a considerable amount of work remained.

No crusher dust had been laid from Mount Hebert to Mount Albion, there was a blockage near Lake Verde where a cattle passageway was being built, and neither signage, benches, nor sheltered tables had been placed through most of this route.

By mid-summer 2015, all remaining work should be finished, and this section will be completed, except for two road detours where land issues currently remain unresolved. Because it will be available for use, I have included this in the book. Unfortunately, I am not able to provide the same level of detail found on the other portions of the trail.

Route Description: Ghiz Park to Stratford, 1.8 km (1.1 mi): No trail links the trailhead at Ghiz Park, where there is a Trans Canada Trail pavilion, with the beginning of the off-road

---

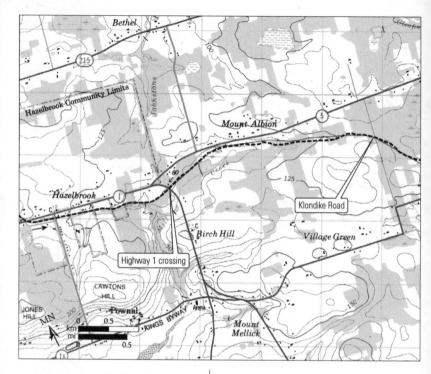

pathway in Stratford on the opposite side of the Hillsborough Bridge. However, there is a paved shoulder, so cyclists should be able to safely ride across the bridge. The off-road pathway begins on the Charlottetown Bay side of the road, shortly after the end of the guardrail.

Stratford start to Shakespeare Drive, 2.5 km (1.6 mi): A wide crushed-stone pathway skirts the edge of the bay for about 400 m/yd to a sheltered picnic table, where there is a plaque commemorating the opening of the Stratford to Iona section. The path turns left 90° and heads 250 m/yd to Stratford Road, where it turns right and follows the sidewalk; watch for directional arrows on nearby poles.

After 125 m/yd, the route crosses Stratford Road and continues alongside Glen Street on a crushed-stone track for 250 m/yd. Turn left, and cross Glen Road at the crosswalk. On the opposite side, a concrete pathway (sidewalk) passes between several buildings and, in 200 m/yd, passes underneath Highway 1.

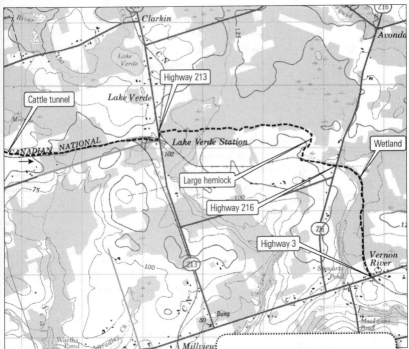

From there, the trail becomes an asphalt surface, keeping straight at an intersection 120 m/yd later, turning right at another intersection 40 m/yd further. (This is in a pleasant green space, with benches and mowed lawns.) After 50 m/yd, the trail reaches Shakespeare Drive, which it parallels on a crushed-stone pathway for 1 km (0.6 mi), ending at the intersection with Jubilee Road.

Shakespeare Drive to Mason Road, 1 km (0.6 mi): The crushed-stone pathway on Shakespeare Road ends

Ride Defensively Crossing Roads
The Confederation Trail frequently crosses busy highways, including some where the speed limit is 90 kph (55 mph). Quite a few of the crossings are diagonal, and some require travelling a short distance on the side of roads. Stop at all crossings and assure yourself that there is no oncoming traffic. Always ride under the assumption that drivers don't see you. Make eye contact with drivers. Cross as quickly as possible.

beside a large Petro-Canada station. In the future, the off-road pathway will cross Jubilee Road and continue straight. Until this is built, trail users must turn right and cross Highway 1 at its intersection with Jubilee Road. Once across, turn left and cycle on the wide paved shoulder—there is no sidewalk—the 800 m/yd to Masons Road. There are neither street lights nor sidewalks at this intersection, so extreme caution must be undertaken turning left onto Masons Road. In less than 100 m/yd you will reach Hollis Avenue, where the trail resumes on the right side of the road.

Hollis Avenue to Reeves Boulevard, 1.5 km (0.9 mi): The crushed-stone pathway parallels Hollis Avenue for 300 m/yd, continuing straight through hardwood forest when the road ends. (The wooded section was under construction and closed to the public when I was there.) It emerges

after about 1 km (0.6 mi) at the end of Macintosh Drive. From here the pathway continues alongside the road to its end, and then back into the forest, where it is possible to travel nearly another 1.5 km (0.9 mi). However, it then reaches a section where it is blocked because of an ongoing property dispute.

Consequently, only 200 m/yd after reaching Macintosh Drive, trail users must begin another, quite long, road detour when they reach Reeves Boulevard.

Reeves Boulevard to Pippy Road trailhead, 3.4 km (2.1 mi): Upon reaching Reeves Boulevard, where there is a signpost, turn right and head to Highway 1, about 250 m/yd. Cross and turn left. Follow it for 1.5 km (0.9 mi) to Mount Hebert Road, where you turn left. Cycle along this for 1.7 km (1.1 mi) to its intersection with Pippy Road. A trailhead parking area is just across the street.

Pippy Road to Mount Albion, 6.1 km (3.8 mi): This entire section was unfinished when I visited, so I could not travel it. However, it follows the bed of the former railway, so it will be surfaced in crushed stone, wide, and almost level. It does have to cross busy Highway 1 about 3.7 km (2.3 mi) from Pippy Road, and again at a corner in Mount Albion. However, except for the occasional house, the

Gloves

Long-distance walking may produce blisters on your feet; long-distance cycling may cause chafing to your hands. Cycling gloves protect them from rubbing and minimize impact if you fall. Gloves for warmer weather are usually half-fingered, while colder conditions require full coverage.

trail travels through wooded terrain bordered by numerous cultivated fields.

Mount Albion to Vernon River, 13.4 km (8.4 mi): This segment is entirely on an excellent crushed-stone pathway. The first 3.6 km (2.25 mi) is through a mostly forested area, though the trail comes quite close to Highway 5 at times. After crossing the clay-surfaced Klondike Road, the trail moves into a more remote area, mostly wooded but with some farmland.

About 650 m/yd from Klondike Road, the trail climbs slightly to cross a newly constructed cattle tunnel, then curves gently left shortly afterwards. Continuing mostly straight, it reaches Highway 213 about 7.2 km (4.5 mi) from Mount Albion.

Little more than 50 m/yd past Highway 213, the trail turns sharply left, and in another 100 m/yd turns sharply right and onto one of the rare sections of the Confederation Trail not built on the route of the former railway. For the next 2.1 km (1.3 mi), the trail is straight, but it rises and falls depending on the elevation of the land. (After the carefully graded former rail line, this is almost disconcerting!)

After 2.1 km, the trail turns sharply right, in 225 m/yd reaching a towering hemlock tree where the trail splits to pass on both sides. Both a bench and a sheltered table have been situated there. The trail continues another 850 m/yd, descending noticeably, before emerging from the forest in a series of tight turns next to some cultivated fields. About 350 m/yd alongside the fields, the trail reconnects to the former railbed, where there is a bench, and it turns 90° left.

In 400 m/yd, the trail crosses Highway 216, and then returns to thickly forested terrain. In 250 m/yd, the pathway curves right; a large wetland is on the left. After a further 350 m/yd, it settles into a long, straight section, which lasts for slightly more than 1 km (0.6 mi). The final 400 m/yd is a gentle curve to the left, emerging from the forest just before reaching Highway 3. The Vernon River trailhead sign is on the opposite side.

Turn around at this point and retrace your route to the trailhead.

Monarchs and Milkweed

Probably the most well-known North American butterfly, the monarch also undertakes the longest migration of any of the continent's insects. Starting from northern Mexico and the southern United States in the spring, these fragile butterflies, each one weighing only 0.5 grams, travel thousands of kilometres to Canada, where several generations reproduce in the summer and early fall.

The health of this beautiful butterfly's population depends on the availability of milkweed plants. The monarch caterpillar will only eat milkweed because it produces a toxin that defends them from predators, and adult monarchs lays their eggs on the underside of milkweed leaves.

In recent years, PEI naturalists have been planting milkweed in an effort to boost the monarch butterfly population on the island.

4. Confederation Trail— Emerald to Borden-Carleton

◀----▶ 38 km (23.75 mi) rtn

🕐: 2.5 + hrs (biking)

🚲: 3-B

Type of Trail: crushed stone

Uses: walking, biking, snowmobiling

⚠: road crossings

🚻: adequate throughout

Facilities: benches, garbage cans, interpretive panels, picnic tables, washrooms, water

Gov't Topo Map: 11L05 (Summerside)

Trailhead GPS: N 46° 21.685′ W 63° 32.860′

Access: From the junction of Granville Street and Highway 2 in Summerside, follow Highway 2 east for 19.6 km (12.25 mi). Turn right onto Highway 8, following for 1.3 km (0.8 mi), then turning left onto Highway 232. Continue for 3.4 km (2.1 mi), crossing the trail then turning right onto Highway 113/Nodd Road. The parking area is on the right in 250 m/yd.

Introduction: The Emerald to Borden-Carleton branch trail is particularly important because it connects the main Confederation Trail with the principal means of access to PEI, the Fixed Link (or Confederation Bridge, as it is officially named).

At 38 km (23.75 mi), I found this a relatively short and pleasant day trip for a bike ride. I also walked it in three sections: Emerald to Kinkora, Kinkora to Albany, and Albany to Borden-Carleton.

Route Description: From the parking area, cross the large grass-covered field to the trail, and head left, in the direction of Summerside. After 350 m/yd, the trail reaches the junction where the route to Borden-Carleton splits to the left. At the trailhead, and near the junction, there are seven interpretive panels, some Trans Canada Trail Discovery Panels, others designed especially for the Confederation Trail. They require almost too much time to read!

At the junction, head left; a sign there indicates that Kinkora is 6 km (3.75 mi) distant. The path curves left, and at 750 m/yd it crosses Highway 113. As usual, at every road crossing there are metal gates on the trail on either side.

The path descends gently for 600 m/yd to a bridge crossing the Dunk River, where there is another information panel. From here, the

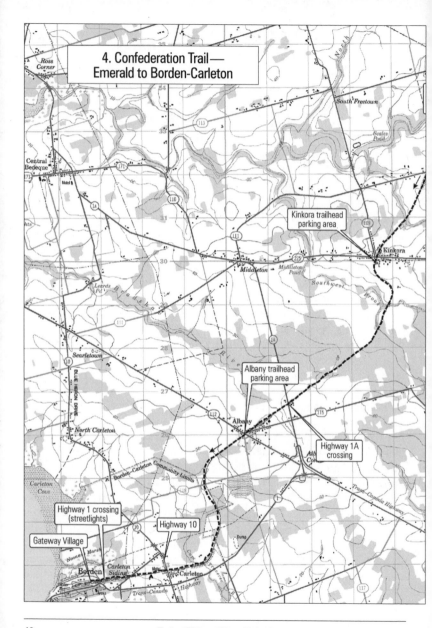

4. Confederation Trail—
Emerald to Borden-Carleton

Ross Corner

South Freetown

Scales Pond

Central Bedeque

Motel

Kinkora trailhead parking area

Kinkora

Middleton

Middleton Pond

Southwest

Brook

Leards Pd

Bradsha

River

Searletown

BLUE HERON DRIVE

Albany trailhead parking area

North Carleton

Albany

Highway 1A crossing

Alb Cr

Trans-Canada Highway

Carleton Cove

Borden-Carleton Community Limits

Highway 1 crossing (streetlights)

Highway 10

Gateway Village

Nooras Marsh

Borden

Carleton Siding

Carleton

Trans-Canada Highway

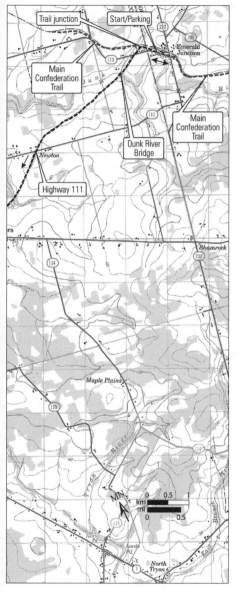

trail gradually climbs, although very modestly. Potato fields are visible on both sides of the trail, except for the wooded area near the river, and the gently rolling terrain enables extended views to the right. About 550 m/yd from the river, the trail crosses clay-surfaced Greenan Road, and before that you will pass the km 1 (0.6 mi) marker. As this is measured from the junction, you will have travelled a bit further.

For the next 1.7 km (1.1 mi), it is a pleasant ride, the trail usually bordered by lines of trees, but with cultivated fields visible to either side. Driveway crossings for farm equipment are frequent, and posted with warning signs. At 3.6 km (2.25 mi), there is the first sheltered picnic table and another interpretive panel. About 400 m/yd further, the trail crosses Highway 111.

Just 300 m/yd from the road, there is a solitary interpretive panel on the left. It is about milkweed, and was positioned at this spot because that plant, so vital to monarch butterflies, grows alongside the trail here. From there it is a pleasant 1.1 km (0.7 mi) though field and forest until the trail emerges from the trees to run alongside two large ponds of a water treatment facility.

The community of Kinkora is visible ahead, across the open

1A is reached, about 400 m/yd past the km 10 (6.25 mi) marker.

The next 1.1 km (0.7 mi) to the Albany trailhead is open, passing large agricultural buildings, but then both Highway 115 and 112 must be crossed in little more than 100 m/yd. After that, it is a climbing, curving 1.6 km (1 mi), bordered by fields, to the next crossing, at clay-surfaced Highway 118. (The trail might actually be in better shape.)

The next section passes through some gorgeous, largely maple forests, where there are even places with an overhead canopy of leaves. There are two sheltered picnic tables, one at the km 14 (8.75 mi) marker, and another—with an interpretive panel—600 m/yd further.

But soon the trail emerges from this forest, into more fields, and curves to the right. Maybe 250 m/yd to the left, Highway 1 should be visible. The trail crosses a number of driveways—including one that is sunken a little and has gates on the path—then arrives at Highway 10, and the village of Carleton, about 200 m/yd past the km 16 (10 mi) marker.

There is a Borden-Carleton community trailhead sign here, but this is not the end. Continue over Highway 10. For 1 km (0.6 mi) the trail runs behind houses and a campground, then it arrives at a tricky intersection.

fields, but it is 500 m/yd before the first building is reached, and a further 450 m/yd before the trail reaches Highway 225. On the far side, there is a community signpost, a picnic table, and even a children's playground. The trail is grass-covered for a few metres/yards.

Within 200 m/yd of crossing Highway 225, the trail curves left and leaves the buildings behind, passing the km 6 (3.75 mi) marker about 100 m/yd past the gates. The next 4.5 km (2.8 mi) are pleasant, with the trail bordered by rich agricultural lands on both sides for the first 1.5 km (0.9 mi), before heading into an area primarily of hardwoods. This is a remote-feeling section, with no road crossings until busy Highway

First it crosses Industrial Avenue; immediately it turns right, and crosses Dickie Road. It then turns left again and continues alongside Dickie Road, as close to it as a sidewalk is normally.

For 550 m/yd, the trail runs alongside Dickie Road, heading toward an upcoming intersection with traffic lights. Just before reaching the light, it crosses the wide entrance to a trucking facility then passes two interpretive panels and a map showing trail distances between Borden-Carleton, Kensington, and Hunter River.

Fixing a Dropped Chain

If your chain falls off while you're riding, adjust your shifter to the position for the small chain ring. Get off your bike, stand on the side with the chain, then pull the chain towards the front of the bike and drop it back onto the smaller chain ring. Lift your rear wheel and use your hand to cycle the pedals through a few rotations until it settles into gear. (Yes, you will get your hands very dirty.)

You cross the road (Highway 1), dismounting to use the crosswalk. On the far side, the track continues a further 400 m/yd, ending in the Gateway Village, where there is a wide variety of shops and services. When ready, retrace your route back to Emerald.

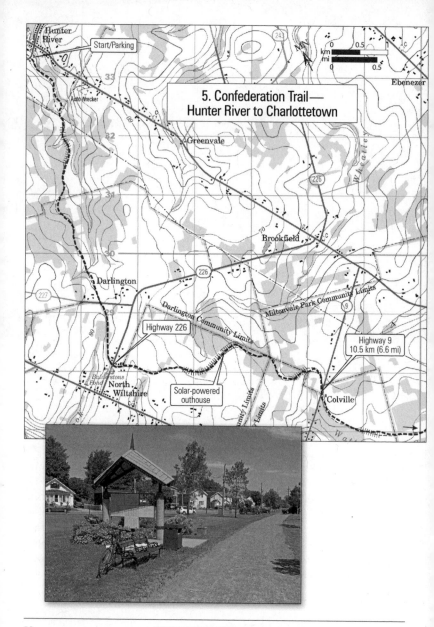

Start/Parking

Hunter River

Ebenezer

33

Auto Wrecker

32

Greenvale

226

Wheatle...

5. Confederation Trail—
Hunter River to Charlottetown

km
mi

0   0.5   1

0   0.5

31

30

70

Brookfield

Darlington

226

226

227

Miltonvale Park Community Limits

Darlington Community Limits

9

Highway 226

Highway 9
10.5 km (6.6 mi)

Beaverstone Pond

North Wiltshire

Solar-powered
outhouse

Colville

Wa...

5. Confederation Trail—
Hunter River to Charlottetown

◀- - -▶ 61 km (38.25 mi) rtn

⏱: 4+hrs (biking)

🚴: 4-B

Type of Trail: crushed stone

Uses: walking, biking, snowshoeing*, cross-country skiing*, snowmobiling*

⚠: road crossings

🚻: adequate throughout

Facilities: benches, garbage cans, interpretive panels, picnic tables, washrooms, water

Gov't Topo Map: 11L06 (North Rustico), 11L03 (Charlottetown)

Trailhead GPS: N 46° 21.180' W 63° 20.970'

Access: From the junction of Highway 1 and Highway 2/Malpeque Road in Charlottetown, follow Highway 2 west for 18.2 km (11.4 mi). Turn left onto Highway 13. The parking area is on the left in 220 m/yd.

Introduction: This route begins in the rolling, wooded hills around Hunter River and ends in the centre of Charlottetown, the largest community and capital of PEI. It provides perhaps the most varied terrain of any single day trip: wooded hillsides, large cultivated fields, and commercial, industrial, and residential urban areas. No route will provide more opportunities to access restaurants and other services.

Snowmobiling is the permitted use in winter on the main line of the Confederation Trail. However, from Royalty Junction to Joseph A. Ghiz

Memorial Park, only non-motorized uses are permitted year-round.

Route Description: For the first 3.5 km (2.2 mi), the trail follows a lovely, sinuous track through rolling terrain, with the land to the left generally somewhat lower. Stands of luxuriant hardwoods alternate with fecund farmers' fields, making summer and fall glorious with nature's richness.

Then the trail straightens, and over the next 1.2 km (0.75 mi), to Highway 227, cultivated lands gradually replace forested tracts, though trees still line the pathway. From here, the trail curves slightly, working along the sloping ground the 1.1 km (0.7 mi) to Highway 226.

The next section is quite charming, with many curves. For 1.5 km (0.9 mi), fields edge the trail. Then it enters an area of quite wonderful hardwoods, where 100 m/yd later a wooden fence lines both sides of the pathway. This is because the trail is elevated quite high, with steep-sided banks above the adjacent ground. For 400 m/yd the fence acts as a guardrail, before trail and terrain are the same level again. And 100 m/yd further, there is a covered picnic table and a nifty solar-powered outhouse (with a fan, and very clean).

The trail resumes its winding way through field and forest. About 2 km (1.25 mi) from the outhouse is the next shelter, one accompanied by an interpretive panel. And 500 m/yd beyond that is the next road crossing, at Highway 9. You have travelled 10.5 km (6.6 mi) so far; this would be a good spot to turn around if you were doing a long hike from Hunter River.

This is a diagonal road crossing, so be particularly cautious. The km 165 marker is about 200 m/yd further, and there is another bench 100 m/yd after that. From here to the Loyalist Road — Highway 256 — is about 3.5 km (2.2 mi), and the trail is straighter and the nearby ground lower, so this should be a quick section to bike. At the km 168 marker there are two interpretive panels beside a picnic table, and 600 m/yd later you reach Highway 256.

From there, it is a fairly straight ride the 850 m/yd to the bridge cross-ing North River, where there is a pic-nic table and six information panels. The trail curves right, almost touch-ing busy Highway 2 before cross-ing another bridge 750 m/yd later. Another 300 m/yd brings you to the trailhead parking area at Highway 248 at Milton Station.

This area is quite open, with broad grass-covered borders alongside the trail. About 500 m/yd from Highway 248, two more information panels flank a bench — right at the km 171 marker. The path curves left, and about 800 m/yd later it crosses Coles Creek on a high embankment bor- dered by wooden railings. And 300 m/ yd beyond the bridge are three more information panels. (There is lots of reading on this route!)

The trail curves left, passing the PEI Firefighters Association Training Centre, then into an urban area, Winsloe, where you cross the High-way 236, 2 km (1.25 mi) from Coles Creek. For the next 500 m/yd, the path runs between rows of houses, some-times with fence or vegetation sepa-rating trail and yard. This section is quite pleasant, sharing the space with adjoining families.

When you arrive at Highway 2, you have travelled slightly more than 20 km (12.5 mi) from Hunter River. Just to the right is the Trailside B&B, should you wish to stop for the day, and 100 m/yd down Highway 2 is a

Prince Edward Island Railway

The railway fever of the late 1800s did not bypass PEI. In 1871, the then-independent colony began construction of the PEI Railway. Unfortunately, the government had not specified either maximum length or precise route, so the contractors built a sinuous track that avoided hills and streams, resulting in a railbed almost one-third of which consists of curves. Further, every community demanded its own station, resulting in one being built for every 4 km (2.5 mi) of track.

The soaring costs of construction brought down the government and forced Prince Edward Island to reconsider joining the Dominion of Canada, which it had rejected in 1867. It did so in 1873, but only on condition that the federal government assume the island's crushing railway debt.

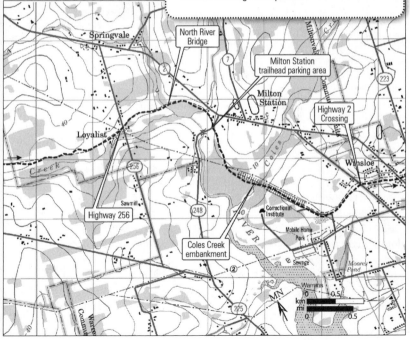

Springvale

North River Bridge

Milton Station trailhead parking area

Milton Station

Highway 2 Crossing

Loyalist

Winsloe

Sawmill

Highway 256

Correctional Institute

Coles Creek embankment

Mobile Home Park

Sewage

Moores Pond

Warrens

MN

Tim Hortons. A sidewalk connects both with the trail. Dismount, and wait for traffic to halt, before crossing Highway 2.

There are 300 m/yd more of urban area. Then—after another interpretive panel—the trail crosses Highway 223. It continues another 1.5 km (0.9 mi), bordered by trees but flanked by cultivated fields, until it reaches Royalty Junction, where a sign indicates that Charlottetown is to the right, 9 km (5.6 mi) further.

So keep right; in 350 m/yd this path reaches the other side of the junction, where there is an information panel and directional signs. A further 250 m/yd and the trail crosses Royalty Junction Road, where there is a km 1 marker. It continues on a curving route, still in rural surroundings, for another 1.4 km (0.9 mi). After that, it moves into an area where, on the right at least, there is considerable industrial activity.

About 2.5 km (1.6 mi) from Royalty Junction, the trail crosses Sherwood Road, where there is a crosswalk. There is also another information panel here. Charlottetown Airport is less than 1 km (0.6 mi) to the left. The trail continues, with businesses on both sides, to Macaleer Drive, 700 m/yd further. After another 400 m/yd, it reaches Highway 1, the controlled-access Charlottetown Perimeter Highway. The path turns sharply right, and heads 150 m/yd to cross first Mt. Edward Road, then Highway 1, at an intersection with traffic lights and crosswalks.

Once across this hectic intersection, the trail heads into the urban area of Charlottetown, though immediately proximate to the path there will be considerable green space for a little longer. From Mt. Edward Road/Highway 1, the route is a long sweeping curve that descends to a tricky road crossing 900 m/yd later at an entrance to Charlottetown Mall, which is on the right.

From there, it is a pleasant 1.6 km (1 mi) almost straight section that runs between the University of PEI and a large field. There are many benches along this stretch, and you can expect to encounter many walkers and cyclists. At Belvedere Avenue, a very busy street, there is a crosswalk with signal lights controlled from the path.

On the far side, there is a very interesting sculpture, and the farmer's market is just off the trail on the right. Continuing past a small pond, the trail reaches several panels and a bench 550 m/yd later, as the trail passes through the Experimental Farm grounds. However, once the path reaches Allen Street 300 m/yd later, the green space ends.

Only 1.2 km (0.75 mi) remains, passing between rows of houses and across several streets, before the trail reaches Joseph A. Ghiz Memorial Park, where the trail ends at Grafton Street, near a Trans Canada Trail Pavilion. Retrace the route to return to Hunter River.

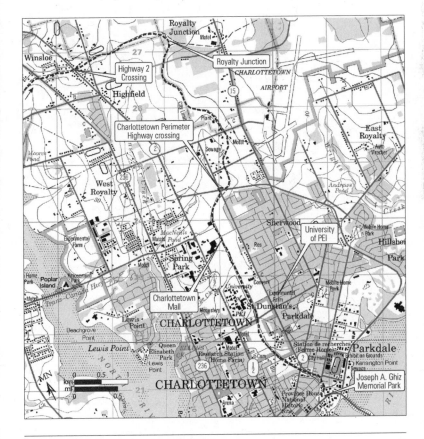

Trails of Prince Edward Island

6. Confederation Trail — Kensington to Hunter River

◄---► 64 km (40 mi) rtn

🕐: 4+hrs (biking)

🚲: 4-B

Type of Trail: crushed stone

Uses: walking, biking, snowmobiling

⚠: road crossings

🚻: adequate throughout

Facilities: benches, garbage cans, interpretive panels, picnic tables, washrooms, water

Gov't Topo Map: 11L05 (Summerside), 11L06 (North Rustico)

Trailhead GPS: N 46° 26.220' W 63° 38.420'

Access: From the junction of Granville Street and Highway 2 in Summerside, follow Highway 2 east for 11.4 km (7.1 mi) to the community of Kensington. Turn left onto Commercial Street. The parking area is on the right in 110 m/yd.

Introduction: This is one of my favourite sections of the Confederation Trail. The hilly landscape between Breadalbane and Hunter River provides scenic views reminiscent of some European valleys. In addition, the trail is rarely straight for very long, curving constantly to conform to the rolling terrain.

The former train station at Kensington is one of only two stone stations built on PEI, and now enjoys the distinction of being a restaurant and pub. Also in Kensington, on display, is the only railway engine remaining on the island, #1762.

Route Description: There are a number of shops and an art gallery located in a cluster of buildings known as Kensington Station at the start. There is also the former railway station, now a pub. The area has quite a number of interpretive panels profiling the history of the PEI Railway, which was so important to the community.

Starting from Engine #1762, head in the direction of Charlottetown (east). Your route passes the former train station, and in the next 1 km (0.6 mi) travels through the community, crossing several streets, reaches more interpretive panels and the km 123 (76.9 mi) marker, and arrives at Highway 2.

Once across the road, there are initially some buildings on the left, but the trail soon leaves the urban area and returns to rural, agricultural central PEI After another 1 km (0.6 mi),

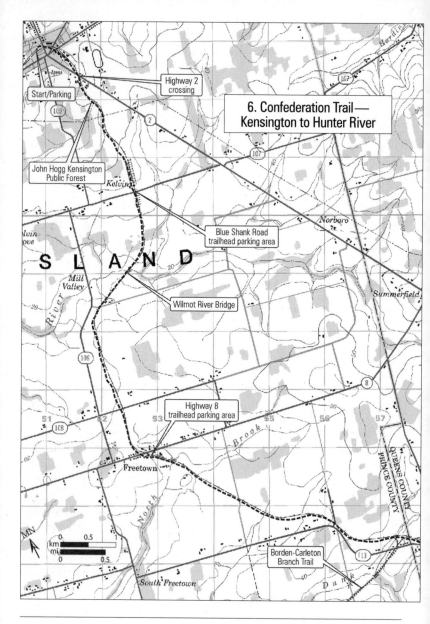

6. Confederation Trail—
Kensington to Hunter River

Highway 2 crossing

Start/Parking

John Hogg Kensington Public Forest

Kelvin

Blue Shank Road trailhead parking area

Norboro

Wilmot River Bridge

Summerfield

Mill Valley

Highway 8 trailhead parking area

Freetown

Borden-Carleton Branch Trail

South Freetown

km
0   0.5
mi
0   0.5

MN

QUEENS COUNTY
PRINCE COUNTY

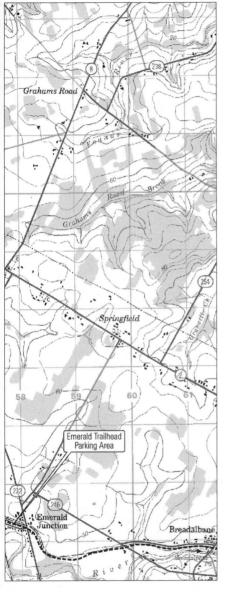

you reach the trailhead for the John Hogg Kensington Public Forest (see p. 151), which is on the right.

With cultivated fields on both sides, the trail continues, gently descending, to reach the trailhead at Highway 107/Blue Shank Road, 3.4 km (2.1 mi) from your start. From here, the path continues downhill another 1.5 km (0.9 mi) to a bridge crossing the Wilmot River. There is a sheltered table here, with an interpretive panel.

From here the trail climbs, and for the next 3.3 km (2.1 mi), cultivation borders both sides of the trail, with only a thin barrier of trees separating trail from farm. Large machinery frequently operates close by—beware the manure spreaders! There are two more minor road crossings, and several more benches, but 8.2 km (5.1 mi) from the start is another picnic table, complemented by two information panels. The trail is descending again, and turning left.

Just 300 m/yd further and Highway 8, at Freetown, is reached. There is a trailhead parking area. Some 500 m/yd beyond that is another small bridge, this one over North Brook. From here until the junction near Emerald, 4.7 km (2.9 mi) away, your route is always flanked by fields, and often without fringing trees. This often enables expansive views, par-

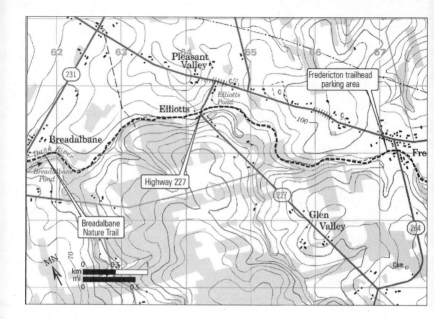

ticularly over areas so extensively cultivated.

About 700 m/yd after the km 135 (84.4 mi) marker, you reach a junction, where the trail splits. To the right is Kinkora, 6 km (3.75 mi) away. Keep left, where the sign says that Hunter River is 18 km (11.25 mi) distant. In 300 m/yd, the trail reaches another junction, where there is a cluster of interpretive panels. Keep straight, passing a gate and two more panels. In 200 m/yd, the path emerges to a large grass-covered field, where the former train station sits, now used by the Bedeque Bay Environmental Association. It is a further 400 m/yd across this field to the crossing of Highway 232.

From here, the path curls around the slightly higher ground on the left, and in 2 km (1.25 mi) arrives at Highway 246, which it crosses. From here until it reaches Breadalbane, the trail tracks alongside Holmes Road (on the left) and the Dunk River (to the right). When you reach the crossing at Highway 231, in Breadalbane, you have travelled 17.9 km (11.2 mi). There is a trailhead here, and interpretive panels in the small park adjacent to the pathway.

Just 200 m/yd after crossing the road is the first of several entrances

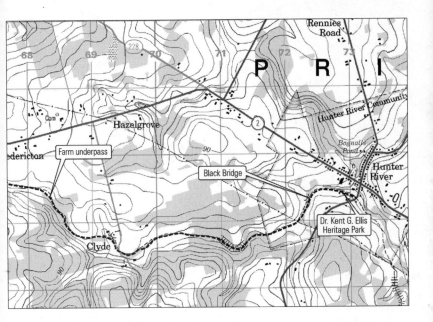

to the Breadalbane Nature Trail (see p. 181). The route also changes, with the terrain through which it is passing becoming much hillier, and as a result, the trail curves much more often, and more tightly. The trail follows the course of the Dunk River, which is to the right, and lower, although the trail runs near the bottom of this valley. There are also more trees around the pathway than at any time since leaving Kensington.

The next road, Highway 227, is crossed 3.3 km (2.1 mi) from Breadalbane, next to a cattle farm. From here to Fredericton, 3.6 km (2.25 mi) distant, the winding trail follows a rapid-ly dwindling Dunk River through a steeper-sided valley. It is quite scenic, in a pastoral sense. You might even spot cars on the ridge to the left at one spot; this is Highway 2.

The trail climbs to reach Fredericton and cross Highway 264, about 300 m/yd past the km 147 (91.9 mi) marker. Highway 2 is less than 200 m/yd to the left. The trail, however, turns sharply (for a former rail line) right, and moves to enter another valley; the Hunter River will now be on the right.

At the km 148 marker, there is a bench and an interpretive panel that speaks about "Rolling Hills." The

view from this spot is quite attractive. The next panel, about 400 m/yd after the km 149 marker, explains "Farm Underpasses." Not coincidentally, the trail crosses one 300 m/yd later.

It is a winding, remote route, with only infrequent farmhouses and fields to disturb the forest blanket. It is also almost entirely descending the entire 6.35 km (4 mi) from Fredericton until the trail crosses the Hunter River. On the far bank is a sheltered table with a panel, explaining that this was once known as the Black Bridge. Today, of course, it is painted in the same shade of purple as all the other railings on Confederation Trail bridges.

Only 850 m/yd remains. The trail curves right, climbing, and reaches a staircase and bridge, on the left, that descends the embankment and crosses the Hunter River, 300 m/yd from the bridge. About 100 m/yd beyond that is the km 154 (96.25 mi) marker.

Houses are visible now on the left, and there is a large common, the Dr. Kent G. Ellis Heritage Park, on the right. The trail arrives at Highway 13; you have travelled 32 km (20 mi), and after a visit to the "By the River" Bakery & Café, retrace your path back to Kensington.

1. Confederation Trail—
Alberton to O'Leary

Stone Station Park

Confederation Trail

2. Confederation Trail —
Charlottetown to Mount Stewart

3. Confederation Trail—
Charlottetown to Vernon River

5. Confederation Trail—
Hunter River to Charlottetown

5. Confederation Trail—
Hunter River to Charlottetown

7. Confederation Trail—
Montague to Georgetown

7. Confederation Trail—
Montague to Georgetown

8. Confederation Trail—
Mount Stewart to Cardigan

8. Confederation Trail—
Mount Stewart to St. Peters

9. Confederation Trail—
Mount Stewart to St. Peters

Showy Lady's Slipper

A rare orchid species, this lovely flower grows in only one place along the entire Confederation Trail, and then only blossoms in late June or early July. Moreover, it may require up to sixteen years for one of these plants to mature to the point that it can produce a flower.

The showy lady's slipper grows best in a fen, a type of wetland characterized by pH-neutral or alkaline water saturated with high mineral levels but few other plant nutrients. Habitat loss has resulted in this beautiful orchid disappearing over much of its original range.

Look, enjoy, photograph, but do not pick. Doing so will kill the plant, which cannot recover from the interruption of its life cycle. Attempted transplantations almost never succeed.

11. Confederation Trail— Souris to Elmira

16. Confederation Trail—
Woods Islands to Murray Harbour

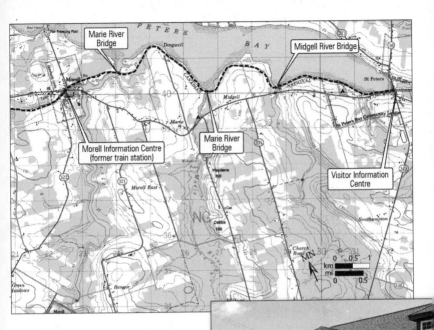

Marie River
Bridge

Midgell River Bridge

Morell Information Centre
(former train station)

Marie River
Bridge

Visitor Information
Centre

yd beyond the house, and an interpretive panel 300 m/yd after that.
The next 2.7 km (1.7 mi) are thickly
wooded, interspersed with frequent
patches of boggy ground.

Just past the km 213 marker, the
trail opens up onto fields, climbing
quite markedly by rail-trail stan-
dards. There are even two commu-
nication towers nearby on the left.
At the crest, 600 m/yd later, the trail
crosses clay-surfaced Macewan Road:
10 km (6.25 mi) from Mount Stewart.

The path heads downhill now, past
large blueberry fields. Some 900 m/
yd from Macewan Road is an elaborate rest area, with bench, sheltered

table, and three interpretive panels.
In a further 400 m/yd, the trail crosses
Kenovan Road and re-enters lovely
hardwood forest. About 700 m/yd
later, you reach MacKinnons Pond,
which the trail crosses on a high embankment.

The trail then crosses two roads, Macvarish 250 m/yd from the pond, Settlement 550 m/yd after that, followed by another 1km (0.6 mi) of thick forest. Then beaver ponds fill the forests on the left for the remaining 400 m/yd to Coffin Road. Two more panels are positioned beside a bench 300 m/yd beyond. The final 850 m/yd into Morell are a pleasant, level ride, with houses and lawns progressively replacing the trees bordering the pathway. And there are several more information boards.

At the Highway 2 crossing sits the former train station, which is now an information centre, café, and outdoor activity centre. In the summer and early fall, this can be quite a busy spot, catering to the many walkers and cyclists. Other businesses are nearby, should you wish to explore the community.

The trail crosses Red Head Road just 150 m/yd from Highway 2,

where the km 219 marker is located. Leaving Morell, the path enters a long wooded straightaway, though in 800 m/yd you gain unhindered view of the Morell River Estuary. At the km 220 marker, there is an interpretive panel, then 400 m/yd later you arrive at the Morell River Bridge; at 235 ft (72 m), the longest structure on the Confederation Trail. There is an information panel on both sides.

The trail returns to a forested area, where it remains another 1 km (0.6 mi); there is another panel further on, at a clay-surfaced road crossing. Yet another panel is found 300 m/yd after that, near a sheltered picnic table. Now, however, the trail is running close to the ocean at St. Peters Bay, where it will remain for the remainder of the route, except for a few times when thick trees will interpose.

About 3.5 km (2.2 mi) from Morell, the trail crosses Dingell Road, after which nothing but cultivated fields cover the low hills on the right. It is 1.6 km (1 mi) further to the bridge over the Marie River, where there are two more information panels, and another one 200 m/yd beyond the bridge.

The trail turns left, conforming to the curve of the land, and climbs slightly. Trees block the view of the ocean, though with frequent breaks. Cemetery Road is crossed 1.3 km (0.8 mi) from the bridge; you have

beautiful views in both directions. Some 800 m/yd further, and there is a picnic shelter with two more interpretive panels, and a special bronze plaque commemorating Adam Mermuys, a trail volunteer.

The third bridge, crossing the Midgell River, and where there is another panel, is reached 500 m/yd later. For the remaining 3.65 km (2.3 mi), the trail runs alongside St. Peters Bay. Wide views up and down the inlet, and across to the hills opposite, are possible. For the final 850 m/yd, the path is squeezed between Highway 2 and the ocean, as it enters the community.

The trail crosses Highway 2—there is no crosswalk—and reaches the at-

Cellphones

Carrying a cellphone for emergency purposes is a good idea. But if you do, start the hike with it fully charged and leave it turned off. Cellphone batteries — particularly those for smartphones — have an extremely short life. Battery strength fades quickly with use or in areas with poor service, where the phone continually searches for a signal. If you can, carry a freshly charged spare battery as a backup.

tractive Visitor Information Centre, which has bike racks and washrooms. A boardwalk and bridge leads from there to the stores and services of St. Peters.

Turn around here, and return to your car at Mount Stewart.

Abandoned Railroads

Railroads were the autoroutes of the late 19th and early 20th centuries, the only practical method to move goods and people over land before the invention of the automobile. Every community vied for a railway connection: having a rail station meant prosperity and growth; being passed by meant decline and economic stagnation.

By the end of World War II, however, railroads were unmistakably in decline, and all but the most profitable routes were abandoned. Yet their role in transportation is not over, for in the past two decades thousands of kilometres of rail lines have been converted to recreational trails for walking, cycling, and cross-country skiing.

10. Confederation Trail — O'Leary to Wellington

◀---▶ 92 km (57.5 mi) rtn

⏱: 6+hrs (biking)

🚲: 5-B

Type of Trail: crushed stone

Uses: walking, biking, snowmobiling

⚠: road crossings

🔱: adequate throughout

Facilities: benches, garbage cans, interpretive panels, picnic tables, washrooms, water

Gov't Topo Map: 21I08 (Cape Egmont), 21I09 (O'Leary), 11L12 (Malpeque)

Trailhead GPS: N 46° 42.430' W 64° 13.495'

Access: From the junction of Granville Street and Highway 2 in Summerside, follow Highway 2 west for 51.7 km (32.3 mi). Turn left onto Highway 142 and continue for 4.8 km (3 mi) to the community of O'Leary. Turn right into the parking area beside the former train station, just after the road crosses the trail.

Introduction: This is the longest single-day route profiled in the book, at more than 90 km (56.25 mi). I have chosen to do so because there are few communities with services between O'Leary and Wellington, and most of this section of the trail passes through a fairly remote area.

For experienced cyclists 90 km (56.25 mi) is not an excessive distance, but those who consider this too much for one day should turn back at Ellerslie, approximately 27 km (16.9 mi) from O'Leary, and complete the remaining 18.8 km (11.75 mi) to Wellington on another day.

Route Description: From the parking area next to the former train station in O'Leary, the trail crosses Highway 142, where a large sign invites you to visit Leards Pond Park, directly ahead. O'Leary's buildings are soon left behind, replaced by forest on the left and large fields on the right. The km 45 (28.1 mi) marker is only 200 m/yd from the road.

The trail begins arrow straight, passing picnic tables and benches. At the km 47 marker, there is a bench with two adjacent interpretive panels. This is also where the first curve appears, the trail turning left slightly. About 200 m/yd later, a sign and side path direct you right, across a road,

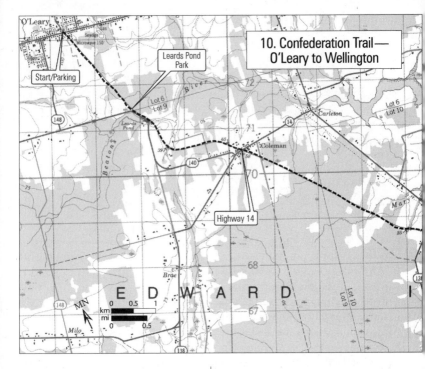

10. Confederation Trail—
O'Leary to Wellington

to Leards Pond Park, where there are benches next to a small pool. And 300 m/yd further, the trail crosses the bridge over Beatons River. On the right is bright red Leards Mill.

The next section is quite attractive, with fields often on both sides and hardwoods bordering the trail. At the km 48 marker, there are two more interpretive panels, and the trail curves left. The first road crossing, of clay-surfaced Thompson Road, occurs 4.3 km (2.7 mi) from O'Leary, and 800 m/yd later, the trail reaches the

community of Coleman, and crosses Highway 14.

For the next 450 m/yd, until the trail crosses Terry Boylan Road, there are houses and fields near the pathway. Once across the road, the trail heads into thick forest, though there are occasional nearby cultivated fields. About 1 km (0.6 mi) from the road, a large power line connects from the left, then runs alongside the trail for the next 2 km (1.25 mi).

This is another straight section, bordered by dense forest, and often

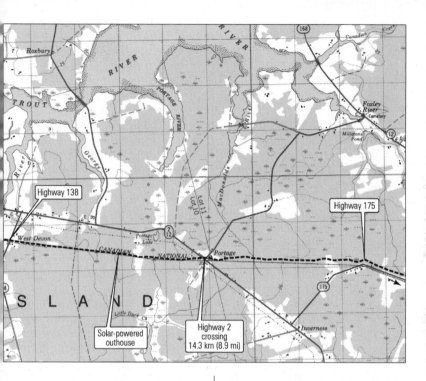

Highway 138

Highway 175

West Devon

CANADIAN — NATIONAL

Portage

Solar-powered
outhouse

Highway 2
crossing
14.3 km (8.9 mi)

Inverness

S L A N D

soggy ground. Shortly after the km 53 marker, there is a bridge, and 350 m/yd after that the power line veers right. Fields soon appear next to the trail, and another small bridge is crossed, just before the km 54 marker. About 400 m/yd later, the trail crosses Highway 138, where there is a cluster of houses, including the collapsing remains of a former railway station.

About 100 m/yd after crossing the road, the power line rejoins the trail, which resumes another extended straight section. It is 1.5 km (0.9 mi) to

the next crossing: Beaton Road. And 500 m/yd beyond that, there is an extensive wetland, with open water on both sides of the trail.

Barely 100 m/yd after the km 57 marker, there is a solar-powered outhouse, to the right, with a bench flanking it. Only 2 km (1.25 mi) remain before the trail reaches the dangerous crossing at Highway 2, in Portage. Just before it does, the power line once again separates and veers right, away from the path.

At Portage, where there is trail-

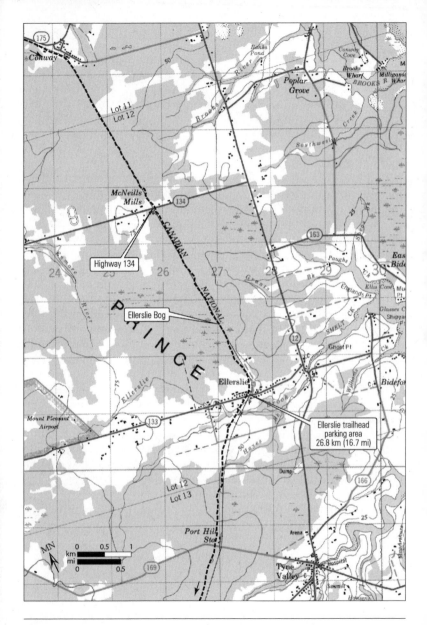

head parking, picnic tables, and information panels, you have travelled 14.3 km (8.9 mi). After leaving Portage, the path continues in a straight line for 3.5 km (2.2 mi), until it crosses Highway 175. There are extensive wet areas whenever the ground is low. Then, for the next 1.9 km (1.2 mi), the route runs alongside the road, passing over several driveways. The trail then plunges back into remote forest, in which it remains until it crosses Highway 134, where there are a few houses, 2.2 km (1.4 mi) later.

Another remote section follows, though relieved somewhat by a boardwalk onto an observation deck in the large Ellerslie Bog, 2.4 km (1.5 mi) from Highway 134. Then there is more forest — including some quite nice stands of hardwoods, at times — until the trail reaches the community of Ellerslie, about 12.5 km (7.8 mi) from Portage.

Ellerslie boasts a trailhead parking area, table, and four interpretive panels. The post office is just across the road, and signs point towards both washrooms (400 m/yd away) and a restaurant, about 1 km (0.6 mi) away. There is also a sign indicating that O'Leary is 24 km (15 mi)

back in the direction from which you have ridden, and that Wellington is 19 km (11.9 mi) further. (These distances disagree with mine, and with some other published figures. When in doubt, it is always safest to plan for the longest distance.)

The next 900 m/yd to Dystant Road is very pleasant. There are fields nearby and good views. At 350 m/yd, the trail crosses small Trout River, and a staircase descends the embankment so you may view the concrete culvert/ bridge, dated 1922.

From Dystant Road, there are perhaps 700 m/yd with more cultivated fields, then the trail plunges back into thick woods, where it remains for the next 4.5 km (2.8 mi). After this, a road—Highway 178—comes adjacent to the trail, and accompanies it almost the entire remaining 1.4 km

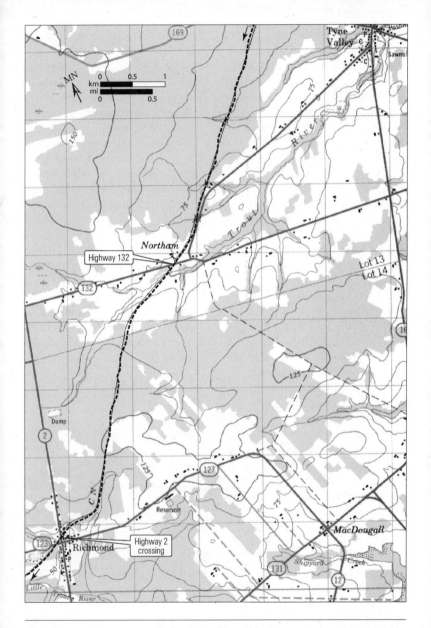

Highway 132

Northam

Highway 2 crossing

Richmond

MacDougall

Tyne Valley

Lot 13
Lot 14

Reservoir

Dump

Shipyard

Little Trout River

Trout River

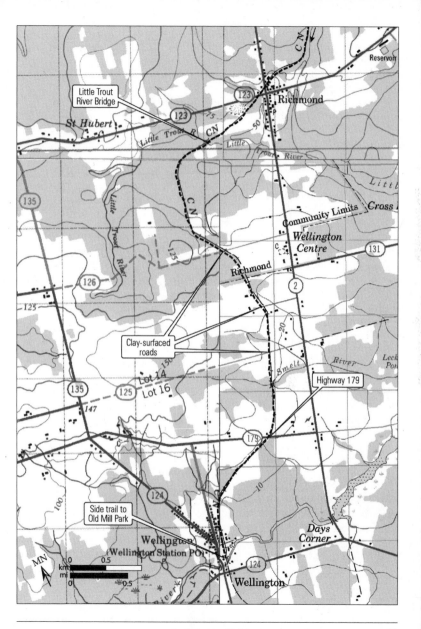

Little Trout
River Bridge

123

St Hubert

Little Trout R. CN

Little

Little Trout River

Richmond

Little

Trout River

Little

Cross

135

Community Limits

Wellington
Centre

131

126

125

Richmond

2

Clay-surfaced
roads

Smelt

River

Leck
Po

Lot 14

Highway 179

135

125

Lot 16

147

179

100

Side trail to
Old Mill Park

124

Wellington
(Wellington Station PO)

Days
Corner

MN

km
0   0.5

124

Wellington

mi
0   0.5

(0.9 mi) to Highway 132 at Northam, where there is another trailhead parking area. At this point your are 33.5 km (21 mi) from O'Leary.

From Northam to Richmond is 4.7 km (2.9 mi) of alternating sections of field and forest. But when the trail arrives at Highway 2, there are many houses, a trailhead parking area, panels, and a table. And just to the right, not 30 m/yd away, is a coffee shop/restaurant.

As the speed limit here is only 60 kph (37.5 mph), this is a less dangerous road crossing. Nevertheless, consider walking across. In just 100 m/yd, Highway 127 must be crossed, then the trail leaves the built-up area and returns to mostly forest, crossing Little Trout River 1 km (0.6 mi) later.

Slightly more than 6.5 km (4.1 mi) remain until Wellington. It is a pleasant section of trail, with a number of fields and farming buildings near the path, once it emerges from the forest section near Little Trout River. At the km 87 (54.4 mi) marker, there are two interpretive panels about tree species that line the trail. The route crosses several small clay-surfaced roads, then Highway 129 less than 2 km (1.25 mi) from Wellington.

This final section, which is wooded, passes quickly. At the km 90 marker, Wellington is in sight. About 200 m/yd further, and the trail crosses Riverside Drive beside the fire hall. Continue another 200 m/yd, to the junction with the side trail to Old Mill Park, where there is a picnic shelter and several interpretive panels.

You have travelled approximately 46 km (28.75 mi) from O'Leary; retrace this route to return.

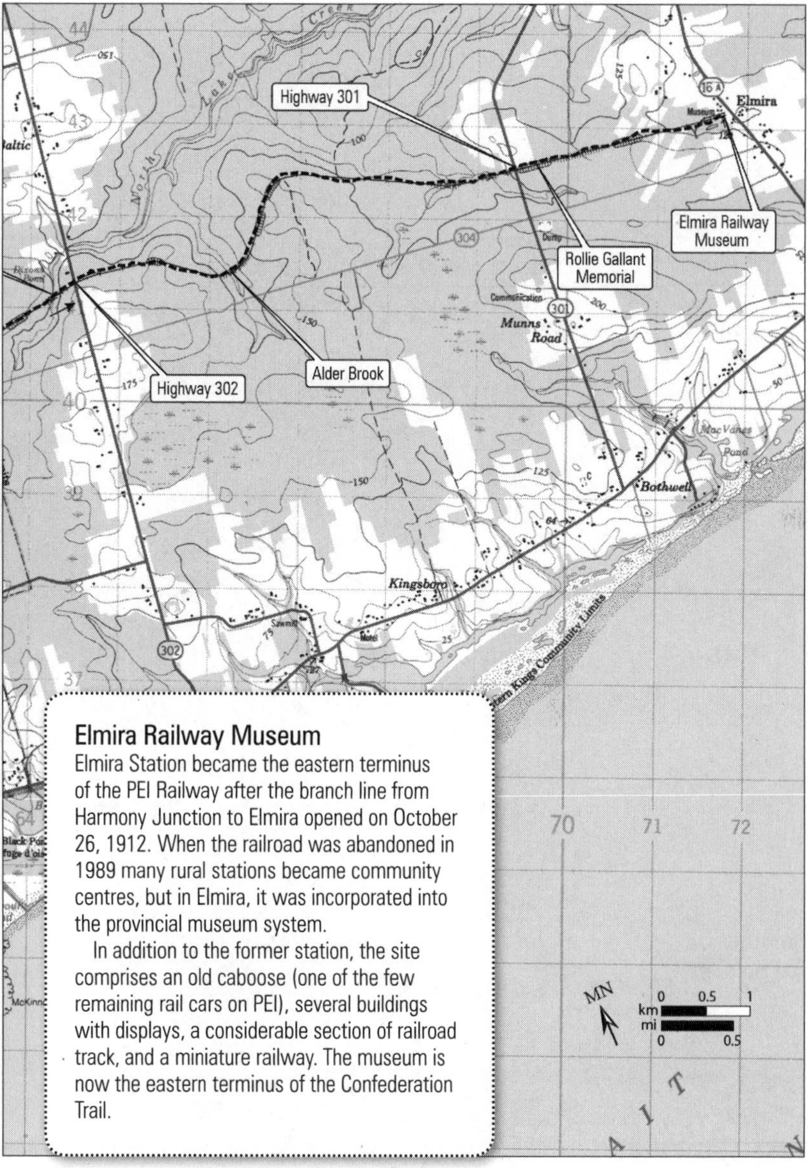

Highway 301

Elmira

Elmira Railway
Museum

Rollie Gallant
Memorial

Alder Brook

Highway 302

Munns
Road

MacVanes
Pond

Bothwell

Kingsboro

Elmira Railway Museum

Elmira Station became the eastern terminus
of the PEI Railway after the branch line from
Harmony Junction to Elmira opened on October
26, 1912. When the railroad was abandoned in
1989 many rural stations became community
centres, but in Elmira, it was incorporated into
the provincial museum system.

In addition to the former station, the site
comprises an old caboose (one of the few
remaining rail cars on PEI), several buildings
with displays, a considerable section of railroad
track, and a miniature railway. The museum is
now the eastern terminus of the Confederation
Trail.

MN

0   0.5   1
km
mi
0   0.5

12. Confederation Trail — St. Peters to Souris

◄--- ► 72 km (45 mi) rtn

🕐 : 5+hrs (biking)

⛛ : 5-B

Type of Trail: crushed stone

Uses: walking, biking, snowmobiling

⚠ : road crossings

📱 : adequate throughout

Facilities: benches, garbage cans, interpretive panels, picnic tables, washrooms, water

Gov't Topo Map: 11L07 (Mount Stewart), 11L08 (Souris)

Trailhead GPS: N 46° 24.910' W 62° 34.795'

Access: From the junction of Highway 1 and Highway 2/Malpeque Road in Charlottetown, follow Highway 1 east for 3.3 km (2.1 mi). Turn left onto Highway 2, then drive for 48.3 km (30.2 mi) to the community of St. Peters and the intersection with Highway 313. Keep straight. Parking is at the Visitor Information Centre.

Introduction: This is one of the longer routes profiled, essentially because it runs through a fairly thinly populated region of PEI. However, it is a quite attractive section, particularly in the fall, when the many hardwoods become a vivid palette of colour.

Both St. Peters and Souris have numerous shops and services. In between, there is nothing close to the trail.

Route Description: From the Visitor Information Centre, you can see the first bench, which is flanked by three interpretive panels. The first 350 m/yd is open ground, with the river to the left. Just after the trail enters the trees, the ponds of the water treatment plant are on either side.

About 700 m/yd from the start is the km 231 marker, and about 100 m/yd further the trail crosses the wide St. Peters River. From here, it is a straight 2.1 km (1.3 mi) to Mill Road, which is lower than trail level, creating a small hill on either side. Just 300 m/yd later you reach a dangerous crossing, of Highway 2, where the speed limit for vehicles is 90 kph (55 mph).

Once safely across, you may read the interpretive panel 200 m/yd later, at the sheltered picnic table. There are cultivated fields alongside the trail through here, but in 350 m/yd, after crossing clay-surfaced Five Houses Road, the trail begins an extended stretch through a forested tract.

For nearly 1.5 km (0.9 mi), it is a pleasant ride bordered by thick woodlands. Then the trail reaches a large pond and surrounding wetland, where an interpretive panel on Cow River Wetlands describes the area. From here, it is back among the trees, and another 1 km (0.6 mi), to the crossing of clay-surfaced Barry Road.

For the next 4 km (2.5 mi) to the crossing of Highway 357, the trail's hardwood tree edging is only occasionally broken by a few wetlands and some boggy areas where black spruce predominate. It is a further 1.2 km (0.75 mi) to Highway 309, though with some fields visible on the left. Just 100 m/yd from this road, a sign states that St. Peters is 12 km (7.5) back, while Harmony Junction is 15 km (9.4 mi) ahead.

Just 800 m/yd from Highway 309 is a lovely spot, where the trail crosses Larkins Pond. There is a sheltered table with an information board, but there is also a separate observation deck. Oddly, 200 m/yd from the bridge, there is cluster of two panels and a bench sitting by themselves in the woods. During the next 2.2 km (1.4 mi) to Highway 308, the trail curves a few times and climbs, the forest transforming into maple and beech. There is a large field on the left for the last 1 km (0.6 mi) to the road crossing.

It is 3.4 km (2.1 mi) to the next road, Highway 307, where a sign states that it is 9 km (5.6 mi) to Harmony Junction. This is mostly forested, except near the highways. At 1.9 km (1.2 mi) from Highway 308, the trail crosses a large wetland; this is actually the Bear River.

After Highway 307, there are fields near the trail for several hundred metres/yards before it returns to thick forest. There are several bogs and wet areas, but many fine hardwood stands, especially as the path climbs. About 1.1 km (0.7 mi) from the road, there is a sheltered table positioned next to an outhouse, one of the Confederation Trail's solar-powered self-compacting facilities. About 600 m/yd beyond that, the trail crosses a large bog that encompasses both sides of the trailbed.

About 1.5 km (0.9 mi) from the bog, the trail crosses Highway 306, New Zealand Road, where a sign declares that 5 km (3.1) remain to Harmony Junction. This section is remote, staying in forest until it nears Harmony Junction. There are occasional benches, but the only information panels are beside a shelter about 400 m/yd past the km 255 marker, and barely 100 m/yd from the junction, beside a small pond.

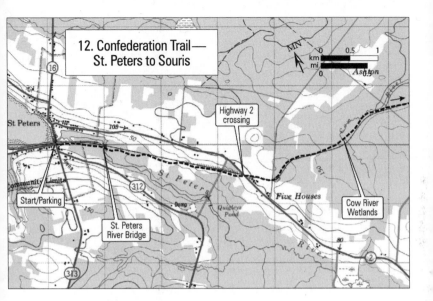

12. Confederation Trail—
St. Peters to Souris

The junction is directly ahead. To the left, it is 50 m/yd to Highway 305, where there is a trailhead parking area. However, to the right, a sign indicates that Souris is 8 km (5 mi) further. You have biked 27 km (16.9 mi) to this point.

This final branch trail is quite attractive. It begins by crossing the Souris River in a long curve to the right. Some 350 m/yd from the junction, the trail of the Souris Striders Cross-country Ski Club crosses, and there are interpretive panels here. Your route continues on its winding path, and the next interpretive panel, about 650 m/yd later, is positioned beside a km 1 (0.6 mi) marker.

The trail is bordered by lush hardwoods, only broken by clay-surfaced Highway 304 at 2.2 km (1.4 mi). At 4.25 km (2.7 mi), cultivated fields replace the forest, and Park Road is crossed at 5.1 km (3.2 mi). Then the route returns to forest for another 1.1 km (0.7 mi), before emerging with large fields to the right and buildings visible ahead.

The next interpretive panel is 7.1 km (4.4 mi) from Harmony Junction, and is on the left, next to a cemetery and church on the hillside to the left. From there, it is only 250 m/yd to Souris River Road, and the beginning of the urban portion of the trail.

Once across the road, the trail

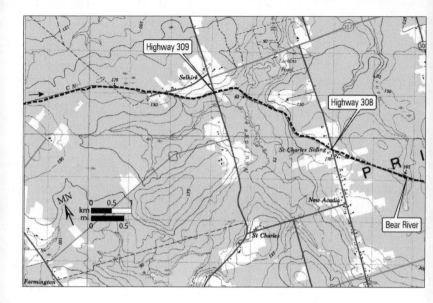

curves left and crosses Chapel Avenue 250 m/yd later, into a small park where there are benches, a sheltered table, and one information panel. It continues past several large agricultural buildings, and crosses Church Avenue 450 m/yd later.

There is one more street crossing, then the path reaches Highway 2, where there is a community signpost, bench, and interpretive panel, 200 m/yd from Church Street. However, this is not the finish. The trail crosses Highway 2, continues another 80 m/yd with a park area on the left, crosses small Bloomsbury Street, then heads into a charming cut, where the ground is higher on

both sides and there is a canopy of tree branches overhead. About 350 m/yd later, the trail passes underneath the next street through a metal culvert, then curves right and finishes 350 m/yd later at the trailhead parking area at Breakwater Street. This is only 150 m/yd from the ferry terminal—and even closer to a nice little restaurant.

You have ridden 36 km (24.5 mi); return to St. Peters along the same route.

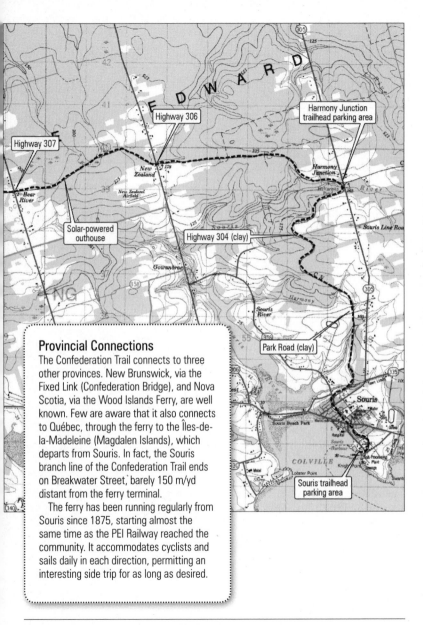

Highway 307

Highway 306

Harmony Junction
trailhead parking area

Solar-powered
outhouse

Highway 304 (clay)

Park Road (clay)

Souris trailhead
parking area

Provincial Connections

The Confederation Trail connects to three
other provinces. New Brunswick, via the
Fixed Link (Confederation Bridge), and Nova
Scotia, via the Wood Islands Ferry, are well
known. Few are aware that it also connects
to Québec, through the ferry to the Îles-de-
la-Madeleine (Magdalen Islands), which
departs from Souris. In fact, the Souris
branch line of the Confederation Trail ends
on Breakwater Street, barely 150 m/yd
distant from the ferry terminal.

The ferry has been running regularly from
Souris since 1875, starting almost the
same time as the PEI Railway reached the
community. It accommodates cyclists and
sails daily in each direction, permitting an
interesting side trip for as long as desired.

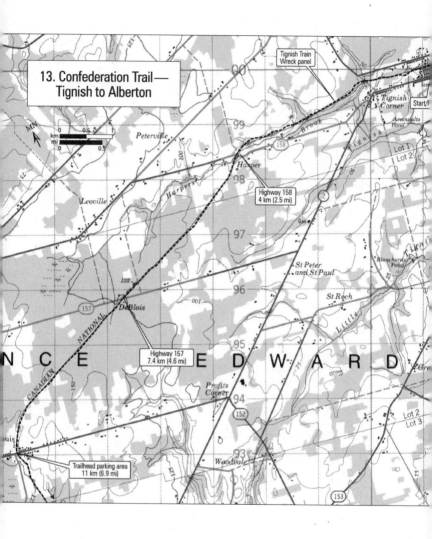

13. Confederation Trail—
Tignish to Alberton

Tignish Train
Wreck panel

Tignish
Corner   Start/F

Areradults
Pond

Peterville

Harper

Highway 158
4 km (2.5 mi)

Gas

Leoville

St Peter
and St Paul

Blanchards
Pond

St Roch

DeBlois

Highway 157
7.4 km (4.6 mi)

Profits
Corner

Woodvale

Trailhead parking area
11 km (6.9 mi)

Lot 2
Lot 3

N C E   E D W A R D

CANADIAN   NATIONAL

13. Confederation Trail—
Tignish to Alberton

◀----▶ 43 km (27 mi) rtn

🕐: 2.5+hrs (biking)

🚴: 2-B

Type of Trail: crushed stone

Uses: walking, biking, snowshoeing,
snowmobiling

⚠: road crossings

🚱: adequate throughout

Facilities: benches, garbage cans,
interpretive panels, picnic tables,
washrooms, water

Gov't Topo Map: 21I16 (Tignish)

Trailhead GPS: N 46° 57.095' W 64° 2.140'

Access: From the junction of Central Street and Highway 2 in Summerside, follow Highway 2 west for 81 km (50.6 mi) to the community of Tignish. Turn left onto Railway Street, and follow it for 180 m/yd. The parking area is directly ahead.

Introduction: Tignish is Kilometre Zero of the main branch of the Confederation Trail, the start of a connected pathway system that exceeds 450 km (281.25 mi) in length. As such, Tignish is most commonly the starting place for those wishing to travel "End-to-End," the 274 km (171.25 mi) Main Trail.

The section from Tignish to Alberton is heavily used by ATVs, though they are not legally permitted on the Confederation Trail. Caution should be taken at dawn/dusk and in poor lighting conditions. This is also a fairly remote portion of the trail, passing no services or nearby stores along the route.

Route Description: The Kilometre Zero Park in Tignish is quite a large field, with picnic tables, garbage cans, and a playground. There is also a cluster of five interpretive panels beside the community sign next to the gate. The path is a uniform 3 m/yd wide and surfaced in crushed stone. Usually, there is a grass border, wide enough for a walker, on either side.

Within 100 m/yd, you are outside the park, and in another 200 m/yd into forest and hidden from most houses. The trail is quite straight, and the first bench is within 500 m/yd of the park. The first road crossing, the Old Western Road, occurs 950 m/yd from the start, and you will notice that there are gates on both sides of the road. On the far side is the km 1 marker. The trail curves gently left now, crossing the first bridge, unusually, over a road, 300 m/yd later. There is a nice house and property on the left, but the trail soon returns into forest.

At about 1.9 km (1.2 mi), the trail reaches the first sheltered picnic table. Beside it are two more interpretive panels, and a large signboard detailing the Tignish Train Wreck, one of the worst ever on PEI. About 700 m/yd beyond that, the trail crosses a large culvert that drains a pond on the right; watch for beavers. The next shelter is 200 m/yd later, and is situated next to the remains of a railway water/sanding station.

The trail crosses Highway 158 exactly at the km 4 marker. This occurs on one of the Confederation Trail's rare hills, where the railway embankment was removed, requiring the path to descend to road level, then climb back to the elevation of the roadbed. These are never steep, simply uncommon and unexpected.

After this, it is almost 3 km (1.9 mi) to the next road crossing, the clay-surfaced Joe Pete Road, then about 400 m/yd to the more dangerous crossing of the asphalt-surfaced Highway 157. Between Highways 158 and 157, the trail passes mostly through forest, occasionally bordered by cultivated fields. There are both benches and picnic tables.

After crossing Highway 157, there follows another remote section of 3.5 km (2.2 mi). The trail then emerges to cross Highway 152. On the far side is a sign for the community of Saint Louis, and a trailhead parking area. There is also a small park, just at the km 11 (6.9 mi), with benches and picnic tables.

Very quickly, the trail returns into a wooded fastness, relieved only, from time to time, by either a bench, a picnic table, a kilometre marker, or by a neighbouring field—although there are more of these in the final kilometre. At 14.5 km (9.1 mi), the trail crosses Highway 151, and just 500 m/yd after that reaches busy Highway 2 with its high-speed traffic. (I recommend dismounting to cross.)

The trail curves behind a Department of Transportation facility, and on the left, running parallel, is the Cheese Factory Road. As a result, over the next 400 m/yd there are several driveways to cross and you will be cycling through people's front yards.

However, road and trail diverge just before the km 16 marker. At this point, the trail appears to be descending, gently but distinctly. About 500 m/yd later the path curves quite markedly to the left, then even more tightly at km 17.3. Just 300 m/yd later, the trail cross a bridge fairly high over the Huntley River and its deep abutting ravine.

Once across the bridge, the trail

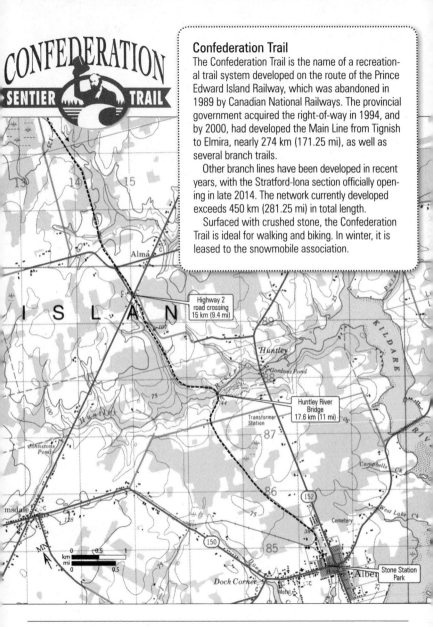

Confederation Trail

The Confederation Trail is the name of a recreational trail system developed on the route of the Prince Edward Island Railway, which was abandoned in 1989 by Canadian National Railways. The provincial government acquired the right-of-way in 1994, and by 2000, had developed the Main Line from Tignish to Elmira, nearly 274 km (171.25 mi), as well as several branch trails.

Other branch lines have been developed in recent years, with the Stratford-Iona section officially opening in late 2014. The network currently developed exceeds 450 km (281.25 mi) in total length.

Surfaced with crushed stone, the Confederation Trail is ideal for walking and biking. In winter, it is leased to the snowmobile association.

Highway 2
road crossing
15 km (9.4 mi)

Huntley River
Bridge
17.6 km (11 mi)

begins to climb, and on the left a large quarry soon comes into view. And just 100 m/yd beyond the km 18 marker, are the gates and crossing at the Oliver Road. As usual, there are houses beside or close to the road crossing.

On the far side of Oliver Road, the trail makes a gentle curve left, and then settles into a straight section more than 1 km (0.6 mi) long. Then there is a barely noticeable bend left, followed by a further extended straight section, mostly through forest and field.

The trail reaches a right-hand turn, and 200 m/yd after starting that reaches a junction, where there is a directional sign. Elmsdale and O'Leary are to the right; Alberton is 500 m/yd directly ahead—you can see a set of gates and buildings in the distance.

The trail passes another junction just after these gates, in 250 m/yd. Then you are in the community of Alberton, with buildings on both sides of the path and wide grass fields. There is a large playground, on the right, and the old train station, which is now a tourist bureau. (Washrooms and water are available when it is open.)

The trail ends when it reaches Highway 12/Church Street, beside the community signpost and opposite a service station and a convenience store. There are also picnic tables, bike racks, and a cluster of information panels.

This is a good place to have a snack and take a break. Retrace the route back to Tignish when ready.

14. Confederation Trail—
Vernon River to Wood Islands

◄---► 73 km (45.75 mi) rtn

🕐: 5+hrs (biking)

🚴: 5-B

Type of Trail: crushed stone

Uses: walking, biking, snowmobiling

⚠: road crossings

🚾: adequate throughout

Facilities: benches, garbage cans, interpretive panels, picnic tables, washrooms, water

Gov't Topo Map: 11L02 (Montague), 11E15 (Pictou Island)

Trailhead GPS: N 46° 12.450′ W 62° 49.970′

Access: From the junction of Grafton and Water Streets in Charlottetown, cross the Hillsborough Bridge, and drive 17.2 km (10.75 mi). Turn left onto Highway 3, and continue for 8 km (5 mi). The trailhead is on the right. You can park in the grassy field beside the trail. (A formal parking lot is planned for construction in 2015.)

Introduction: The branch trail to Wood Islands was one I rather enjoyed, both because it was often more remote than most of the Main Trail and it works through some of PEI's most rolling landscape. I also like that it ends at the Plough the Waves Centre, where there is a variety of services and food options. The section between Wood Islands and Wood Islands Junction is particularly interesting because it is one of the few places on the entire Confederation Trail that does not follow a former railway line.

When I travelled this route, in late September 2014, work was under way to complete the trail between Stratford/Charlottetown and Wood Islands. However, between Uigg and Iona, most of the crushed stone surface had not been laid, nor were benches, sheltered picnic tables, or interpretive panels installed. Further, the distance markers currently in place from Vernon River will be changed once the full trail is complete. I did not reference them in the route description.

Route Description: At the start, there is a signpost listing several distances. Most important to you is that Wood Islands junction is 33 km (20.6 mi) away. From the community, where there are many farmed fields bordering the trail, it quickly heads into a wooded area, and crosses the Vernon River, 900 m/yd from the trailhead.

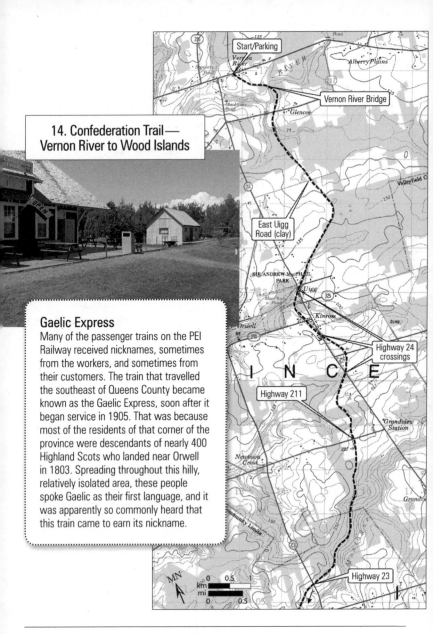

Start/Parking

Vernon River Bridge

14. Confederation Trail— Vernon River to Wood Islands

East Uigg Road (clay)

Highway 24 crossings

Highway 211

Highway 23

Gaelic Express

Many of the passenger trains on the PEI Railway received nicknames, sometimes from the workers, and sometimes from their customers. The train that travelled the southeast of Queens County became known as the Gaelic Express, soon after it began service in 1905. That was because most of the residents of that corner of the province were descendants of nearly 400 Highland Scots who landed near Orwell in 1803. Spreading throughout this hilly, relatively isolated area, these people spoke Gaelic as their first language, and it was apparently so commonly heard that this train came to earn its nickname.

Then, making a long, climbing turn to the right, the path crosses Highway 212 just 650 m/yd later.

At 2 km (1.25 mi), the trail crosses another brook then climbs through a thickly wooded area, to cross the clay-surfaced East Uigg Road after another 1.4 km (0.9 mi). With cultivated fields visible to the right, the path makes a curve right, and descends noticeably to reach Highway 24, in the village of Uigg, 2.9 km (1.8 mi) later.

Over the next 2.5 km (1.6 mi), the trail makes large sweeping curves, first left, then right, making multiple road crossings: first Highway 210, then Highway 24, next Highway 210 again, and finally Highway 24, for the third and final time. The trail curves quite a bit, as the terrain becomes hillier, and the former railroad line attempts to maintain as close to level a track as possible.

The next 6.3 km (3.9 mi) are quite enjoyable. The trail is mostly wooded, though cultivated fields are common, especially near Highway 24. However, you will see few houses, other than the occasional farmhouse and barn, and the rolling terrain keeps the trail always curving. Highway 211 is crossed 1.7 km (1.1 mi) from Highway 24, and after a densely wooded 3.6 km (2.25 mi), Highway 23 is reached.

A further 950 m/yd, and the trail arrives at Highway 206, and the Iona trailhead parking area, where there are three trailhead interpretive panels and a signpost which asserts that it is 20.9 km (13.1 mi) to Wood Islands. (This is also where the trail has been open since 2005, so facilities are in place.)

The forest cover continues, the trail a crushed-stone laneway between tall trees which provide good shade, though no overhead cover. There is a sheltered picnic table, sitting beside two Trans Canada Trail panels, 1.8 km (1.1 mi) from Iona, then clay-surfaced Highway 205 at 3.2 km (2 mi). This section of the trail is somewhat straighter.

The next 3.7 km (2.3 mi), to Gairloch Road, is unbroken trees, with only the occasional bench or sheltered table. This is one of the most remote sections of the entire Confederation Trail. When you reach Gairloch Road, this is the trailhead for one of the Island Trails "Destination Trails" (see p. 187).

The thickly forested surroundings continue to Highway 207, 2 km (1.25 mi) further, where there is a dangerous diagonal road crossing. Just 150 m/yd from the road, you cross a large bridge over the deep gorge of the Flat River. There is an interpretive panel on the far side. Some 100 m/yd later the trail emerges to cross Highway 261 among a cluster of houses, where there is a bench, picnic table,

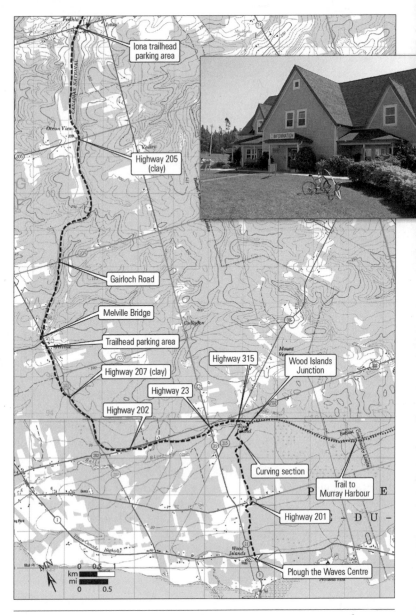

Iona trailhead
parking area

Highway 205
(clay)

Gairloch Road

Melville Bridge

Trailhead parking area

Highway 207 (clay)

Highway 23

Highway 202

Highway 315

Wood Islands
Junction

Curving section

Trail to
Murray Harbour

Highway 201

Plough the Waves Centre

km
0   0.5   1

mi
0   0.5

parking area, and six more information boards!

The trail quickly plunges back among the trees. About 1.25 km (0.8 mi) from the parking area, there is an excavated area on the left, lower than the trail, and an extended fence to prevent the inattentive from falling into the hollow. After 500 m/yd the trail crosses the (now) clay-surfaced Highway 207.

Once again, the trees bordering the trail block any longer views, except occasional glimpses of a road to the right. You might notice more pine through here, especially on higher ground. About 2 km (1.25 mi) from the last road crossing, the next interpretive panel sits beside a sheltered table. Just 500 m/yd further, the trail crosses Highway 202 at one of these unfortunate diagonal intersections.

For the next 1.1 km (0.7 mi), trail and road are close, and there are numerous driveways. These stop after the trail crosses clay-surfaced Munns Road, and the next 1.3 km (0.8 mi) to Highway 23 are forested. Once across this road, there is a large pool to the right, and a shelter with two benches, plus an information board, 250 m/yd later.

Just 600 m/yd further, and the trail crosses Highway 315, where there is another panel. The path crosses the Belle River, 150 m/yd from the Highway, and 100 m/yd from that, you reach Wood Islands Junction, where a signpost indicates that Wood Islands is 3.9 km (2.4 mi) to the right.

As this segment was not a former rail line, it has a few hills, such as the one right at the start. It then makes some surprisingly sharp turns, passing some magnificent hemlock and towering white pine, to arrive at Highway 201, nearly 2.5 km (1.6 mi) from the junction. Turn right, and ride on the road for 100 m/yd; the off-road pathway resumes across the road on your left.

The trail works around a field, making two 90 turns while doing so, then heads through a forested area to a small pond, 750 m/yd from the road. Beside the water is a sheltered table with three information panels; 100 m/yd further, there is another panel.

The trail winds its way another 800 m/yd, reaching a gate that boasts a rather whimsical signpost: Vancouver 6,000 km (3,750 mi). Ken's Trail, also mentioned in this book, is a short footpath around a pond. Keep straight; the woods give way to grass-covered lawns, benches, more information panels, and an overhead gateway for the trail. Ahead are the replica historical buildings of the Plough the Waves Centre.

Continue to the Visitor Information Centre. You have biked 36.5 km. Rest a while, then return to Vernon River retracing your route.

Trans Canada Trail

One of the most ambitious recreational developments in the world is the construction of a Canada-spanning, multi-use pathway connecting all ten provinces and three territories. When completed, the Trans Canada Trail (TCT) system will eventually exceed 18,000 km (11,250 mi).

In Prince Edward Island, the Confederation Trail is this province's portion of the TCT, and the first provincial component to be completed. There are two TCT pavilions, honouring donors, on the Confederation Trail in PEI, and a special sculpture in Summerside to commemorate the province's singular contribution to the success of this exciting national project.

15. Confederation Trail — Wellington to Kensington

◀ - - - ▶ 64 km (40 mi) rtn

🕐: 4+hrs (biking)

🚲: 4-B

Type of Trail: crushed stone

Uses: walking, biking, snowmobiling

⚠️: road crossings

🚻: adequate throughout

Facilities: benches, garbage cans, interpretive panels, picnic tables, washrooms, water

Gov't Topo Map: 21I08 (Cape Egmont), 11L05 (Summerside)

Trailhead GPS: N 46° 27.120′ W 63° 59.975′

Access: From the junction of Granville Street and Highway 2 in Summerside, follow Highway 2 west for 15.7 km (9.8 mi). Turn left onto Highway 124 and continue for 1.7 km (1.1 mi) to the community of Wellington. Turn right onto Highway 124/Mill Road. The parking area is on the left in 110 m/yd at Old Mill Park. The access path to Confederation Trail is on the opposite side of the road between houses #16 and #24.

Introduction: This route begins in the small village of Wellington, population less than four hundred, passes through Summerside, the second largest community in PEI, and finishes in the town of Kensington: population fifteen hundred. In Wellington, there is a CN caboose repurposed as a home; in Kensington, the last train engine on PEI sits on display.

Summerside is a special community in the story both of the Confederation Trail and of the Trans Canada Trail, because one of the first meetings to launch the project was held there in 1993. To commemorate the community's significance, a special sculpture incorporating a plaque has been mounted near the library, close to the Trans Canada Trail pavilion.

Route Description: Starting from the sheltered picnic table next to the side trail to Old Mill Park, cross the bridge over the broad Grand River. A sign indicates that it is 19 km (11.9 mi) to Summerside. Running behind houses in the community, the trail crosses Highway 124 just 250 m/yd from the start.

For the first 1 km (0.6 mi), as the path curves gradually left, there are

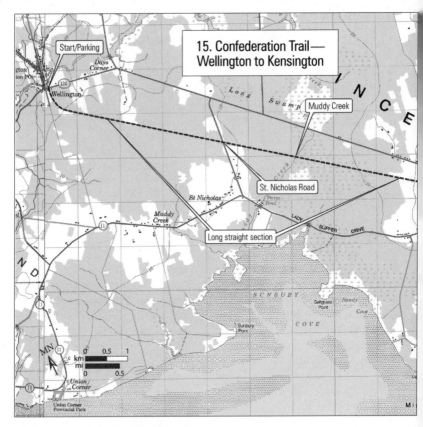

15. Confederation Trail—
Wellington to Kensington

fields on the right and thick forest to the left. You will pass the km 91 marker about 400 m/yd from the road. Once the turn ends, your route is arrow-straight, and dense forest lines both sides of the trail.

The path climbs slightly, and at about 1.4 km (0.9 mi), a power line crosses overhead, then turns to parallel the trail, on its right. About 200 m/ yd after the km 92 marker, the trail tops a small rise, and you are able to see that this straight section continues for a very long distance. (In fact, it may be the longest on PEI, nearly 10 km [6.25 mi] in length.)

Forest broken only by the occasional wet area lines the trail all the way to the crossing of St. Nicholas Road, 4.6 km (2.9 mi) from Wellington.

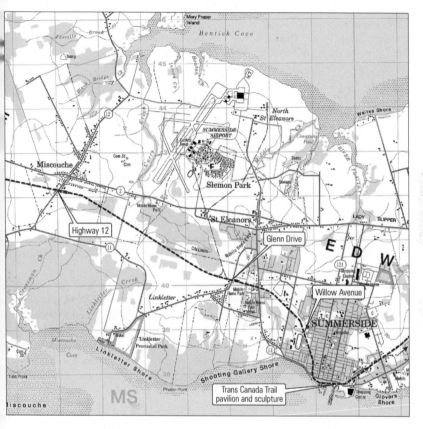

Though a somewhat monotonous stretch, I found it excellent for bird-watching, sighting a small hawk, and at least eight species of warblers in the thick vegetation.

At the road crossing, there is a trailhead parking area, though no picnic table. Once across the road, you gain an extended view of the upcoming trail, which is straight and des-

cends to a low spot before climbing again. It seems like a very long way.

I found this next section to be the most mentally challenging of the entire Confederation Trail. It seemed to require a long time to cross the visible area, which is almost entirely wooded and provides few views to either side. About 1.6 km (1 mi) from the road, the trail reaches the Miscouche

Marshes, the low point being a small concrete bridge over Muddy Creek, which drains the marshes to Sunbury Cove, far to the right (not visible).

About 100 m/yd from the bridge, there is a sheltered table and two interpretive panels. From there the trail climbs gently to reach Highway 12, at Miscouche, 4 km (2.5 mi) later. Across the road is a broad grass-covered field, where there is a bench, garbage cans, tables, community signpost, and an interpretive panel. The community of Miscouche, and noisy Highway 2, is to the left, connected by a sidewalk.

For the next 4.6 km (2.9 mi), the trail is almost always bordered by cultivated fields. Curving gently right, the path crosses Kinsman Road 1.7 km (1.1 mi) from Miscouche. The power line, which moved away from the trail shortly after reaching Miscouche, reconnects here, although it leaves again just before the path moves into a thickly wooded area. This is only a small patch of forest though, and the trail soon emerges to arrive at a junction with a spur line of the railway (which is not being used as a trail) just before reaching Glenn Drive, 14.7 km (9.2 mi) from Wellington.

You are now in the outskirts of Summerside, but it is a further 2 km (1.25 mi) before the trail enters the urban area. En route, it crosses South Drive and Greenwood Drive,

and it is after the second of these that the urban area, in particular the Summerside Raceway, becomes visible.

When the trail reaches the gates at Willow Avenue, where there is a bench, it changes completely into an urban route. Attempting to describe it precisely is difficult, because it crosses streets at odd angles, and passes between houses so closely that you can probably wave to residents at their tables. However, it continues to follow the route of the railroad, so it proceeds through the residential area until it reaches Water Street, 1 km (0.6 mi) from Willow Street.

The trail crosses Water Street, curving left to run along the edge of Summerside Harbour and to move into the commercial centre of the city. Some 150 m/yd later it crosses Queen Street, and arrives at the library, the sculpture, and the Trans Canada Trail Pavilion, 400 m/yd later.

You are in the centre of the city; any services you require, including those of a bike shop, are nearby. From here, the route heads out of the city centre, commercial properties gradually being replaced by residential, and, 1.5 km (0.9 mi) from the library, the first cultivated fields. There are many street crossings, and the trail will probably be busy with local walkers and cyclists.

About 800 m/yd further, and the

Footwear

Proper footwear is essential for your comfort and safety. Footwear options are endless, so care is important in making your selection; there is no "right" choice for everyone. But I can give one bit of advice: do not rely on the same footwear you use on roads and sidewalks for walking on trails.

Your feet require some time to become accustomed to new shoes, no matter how many kilometres/miles you have hiked. Spend several days walking around your neighbourhood before you wear new footwear on a long hike. Better to develop blisters close to home than in the backcountry.

trail reaches a junction with the Rotary Friendship Park, which connects on the left, where there is a large pavilion sheltering several benches. After that, it is a 2.1 km (1.3 mi) pleasant roll mostly through productive agricultural lands to the tricky road crossing of Highway 1A at Travellers Rest, where there is a trailhead parking area.

There are no facilities at the Travellers Rest trailhead, but there is a bench in 200 m/yd, and a sheltered table with two interpretive panels 400 m/yd further. The path continues straight for more than 3 km (1.9 mi), crossing Highway 120 at the km 116

(72 mi) marker, before turning left and reaching Highway 2, 3.7 km (2.3 mi) from Travellers Rest.

The next 1 km (0.6 mi), to Highway 106, is more wooded. After that, however, for the next 700 m/yd the trail passes between several large industrial facilities: biofuel on one side, French fries on the other. Back into the forest, briefly, there is a small bridge at km 119. The Old Station Road is crossed 400 m/yd later, and 700 m/yd further, at the Old Summerside Road, the trail has been moved slightly to the right in order to pass around a Cavendish Farms agricultural operation.

Your path is now directly alongside busy Highway 2, and for the next 1.6 km (1 mi), the two routes accompany each other toward Kensington. They only begin to diverge after the

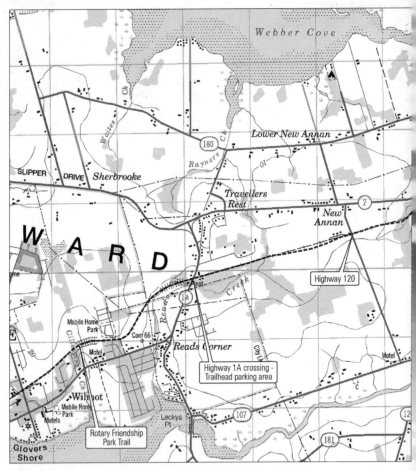

trail crosses Sunset Drive. It then moves behind some businesses and residences, and next to the Royal Canadian Legion Park. About 650 m/yd beyond Sunset Drive, you arrive at a large train engine, displayed behind a fence. Just past it, there is a collection of businesses, including a pub!

You have completed this route. When ready, retrace the path back to Wellington.

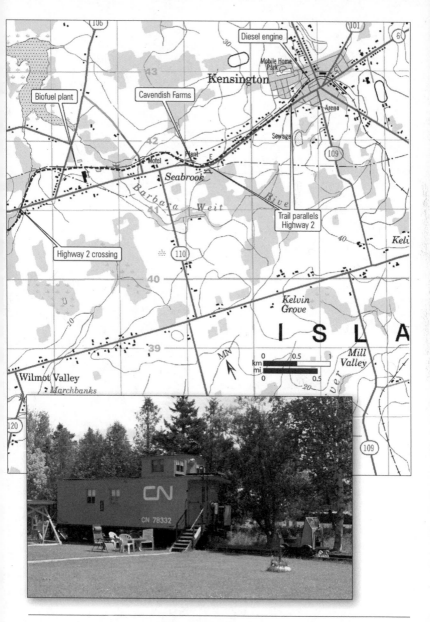

Diesel engine

Mobile Home Park

Kensington

Cavendish Farms

Biofuel plant

Arena

Sewage

Motel

Plant

E

Seabrook

Barbara Weit

River

Trail parallels
Highway 2

Highway 2 crossing

110

Keli

40

Kelvin
Grove

I S L A

Mill
Valley

MN

km

mi

Wilmot Valley

Marchbanks

20

109

CN

CN 78332

Purple Aster

As summer gives way to fall, the profusion of flowering plants disappears with the arrival of cold weather. One noticeable exception is the purple aster, which blooms from August to October. Looking like a small, coloured daisy, the purple aster grows almost 1 m (3 ft) high and can often be found in open woods where there are dry soils. The edges of former rail lines converted to trails make an excellent habitat for them.

There are two species of the purple aster, the late and the smooth, both native to North America. They are distinguished by their stem (if you really have to check.)

16. Confederation Trail —
Wood Islands to Murray Harbour

◄--- ► 46 km (28.75 mi) rtn
🕐: 3+hrs (biking)
🚴: 3-B
Type of Trail: crushed stone
Uses: walking, biking, snowmobiling

⚠: road crossings
🗋: adequate throughout
Facilities: benches, garbage cans, interpretive panels, picnic tables, washrooms, water

Gov't Topo Map: 11E15 (Pictou Island), 11L02 (Montague)

Trailhead GPS: N 45° 57.955' W 62° 44.935'

Access: From the junction of Grafton and Water Streets in Charlottetown, cross the Hillsborough Bridge, and drive 58.8 km (36.75 mi) on Highway 1 to the community of Wood Islands. Turn left onto Highway 4/Shore Road. The parking area is on the left in 200 m/yd in the Plough the Waves Centre.

Introduction: This is a short, but enjoyable, daytrip along two of the branch trails. The section between Wood Islands and Wood Islands Junction is particularly interesting because it is one of the few places on the entire Confederation Trail that does not follow a former railway line. As a result, it has distinct hills, and a few turns that can almost be described as "tight."

When the Murray Harbour branch of the railroad was built in 1904, there was no ferry service in Wood Islands; this did not begin until 1941. But when the Confederation Trail was developed, local residents demanded that it be linked so that off-province cyclists can be on the trail as soon as they arrive on PEI.

Route Description: From the parking lot, head to the Visitor Information Centre; the trail begins at a pavilion to its left, in front of a replica train station that is now a café. The wide, crushed-stone-surfaced track heads past another replica building to an elaborate provincial gateway, where there are three interpretive panels and a sign that states that Murray Harbour is 22.4 km (14 mi) away.

The first set of metal gates—these are usually found at every road crossing—is reached about 100 m/yd from the gateway. Just beyond it is the km

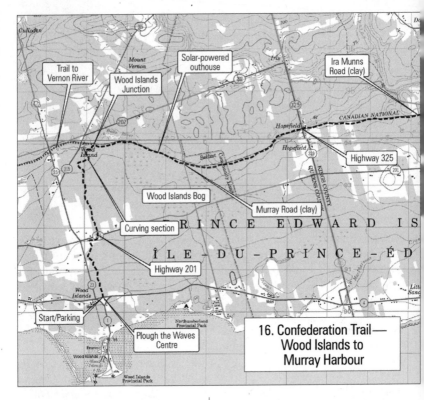

Trail to Vernon River

Wood Islands Junction

Solar-powered outhouse

Ira Munns Road (clay)

Highway 325

Wood Islands Bog

Murray Road (clay)

Curving section

Highway 201

Start/Parking

Plough the Waves Centre

16. Confederation Trail— Wood Islands to Murray Harbour

4 marker, and a distance post stating that Vancouver is 6,000 km (3,750 mi) distant!

The path now moves through an area of thick forest, winding its way to the next information board about 800 m/yd from the gate. (Only 5,999.2 km left to Vancouver!) And in another 100 m/yd, there is the first sheltered picnic table, to the left beside a small pond, flanked by three more panels.

About 500 m/yd from the shelter, the trail reaches a cultivated field, and makes a 90° right turn, followed 200 m/yd later by a 90° left turn. About 1.8 km from the Wood Islands Visitor Centre, the trail reaches Highway 201. Here you must turn right, and follow the road for 100 m/yd; the off-road pathway resumes across the road on your left.

There is a small hill to climb, reaching the km 2 marker 400 m/yd

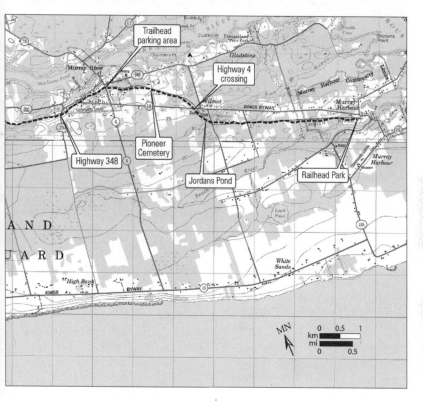

from Highway 201. A long straight section follows, with the path moving into an area of older trees, especially some towering white pine and hemlock. A few more surprisingly sharp turns remain before the pathway descends to connect with the Murray River Branch and Wood Islands Junction. I measured the distance from the Visitor Centre as 4.35 km (2.7 mi).

The junction is about 100 m/yd from the km 37 marker; however, it should be notated that this numbering system will change once the trail is completed to Stratford. There is a directional arrow that points right toward Murray Harbour, and it states the distance as 18.5 km (11.5 mi),

The terrain is quite soggy around the trail, with the Belle River on the left. It feels quite isolated, with no fields or houses in sight for some distance. About 1.8 km (1.1 mi) from

Map

What is the name of that river? How high is that hill? How much further to the next road crossing? Hiking without a map is like walking with your eyes closed: you have no idea what surrounds you. With a topographical map, you have answers to all those questions, an indispensable guide to your surroundings — and maybe your most important safety tool.

the junction, there are some sheltered tables accompanied by a collection of five interpretive panels. On the opposite side of the path sits a solar-powered outhouse.

The trail crosses the clay-surfaced Murray Road 600 m/yd later, curving around a blueberry-covered hill. (This is a commercial property, so no sampling, please.) From there it continues in thick forest, emerging only at Highway 325, 3.2 km (2 mi) from Murray Road. These are practically the first visible houses since Wood Islands.

The trail returns into forest, but now there are occasional glimpses of cultivated fields, particularly of blueberries. In fact, the next interpretive panel, beside a table 1.3 km (0.8 mi) from Highway 325, is titled "Blueberry Barrens." But forest dominates, initially spruce but with stretches of hardwoods and even tall white pine. About 1.6 km (1 mi) from the panel, clay-surfaced Ira Munns Road, which has gates, is crossed.

The remote section ends after the trail crosses Highway 348, 2 km (1.25 mi) from Ira Munns Road. (The last few hundred metres/yards before that are extremely attractive: tall aspen and/or yellow birch.) Suddenly there are houses everywhere, and for the next 1.25 km (0.8 mi), you will be crossing numerous streets and driveways, practically in people's yards.

There is an interpretive panel near the library, another just before cross-

Great Horned Owl

Though rarely seen, the great horned owl is one of Canada's most common large birds of prey. Easily distinguished because of its ear tufts — or "horns" — and large size, this nighttime hunter is more often heard, its unmistakeable whoo-hoo-ho-o-o penetrating the silence of the evening.

Great horned owls do not migrate, and usually remain fairly close to where they were born, particularly if food is abundant. They will sometimes hunt during daytime when it is cloudy and dark, especially underneath high thick forest cover, such as is found in the Camp Tamawaby Woodlot (p. 135). Listen carefully, especially when the young fledge, usually in early June.

ing Highway 4, and another after the crossing, near the gazebo, benches, picnic table, and community trailhead sign: Murray River. There is also a sign stating that Murray Harbour is 7 km (4.4 mi) further.

The trail re-enters the forest, mostly hardwoods, crossing a clay-surfaced road 1.2 km (0.75 mi) from Murray River. On the right is the Pioneer Cemetery, a tranquil, interesting spot. The trail crosses Highway 18, 1.2 km (0.75 mi) after that, where there is an interpretive panel about a train-bus collision. From there, it drops down to the high, steep-sided embankment spanning Jordans Pond, where there are two more information boards.

After this, the trail curves left, climbing, reaching the Toronto Road just 150 m/yd from Jordans Pond. From here, it is an almost straight ride the remaining 3.6 km (2.25 mi) to Murray Harbour. There are two more roads to cross, but nothing to hinder you (except for the "Spring Flowers" panel, 600 m/yd from Murray Harbour) until you arrive at the trailhead parking area, on Station Lane, where there are benches, more information panels, and Railhead Park, where there are many more information panels and the Harbour View Look Out.

End of the line; retrace your path to return to Wood Islands.

22. North Cape/Black Marsh Nature Trail

PRINCE COUNTY

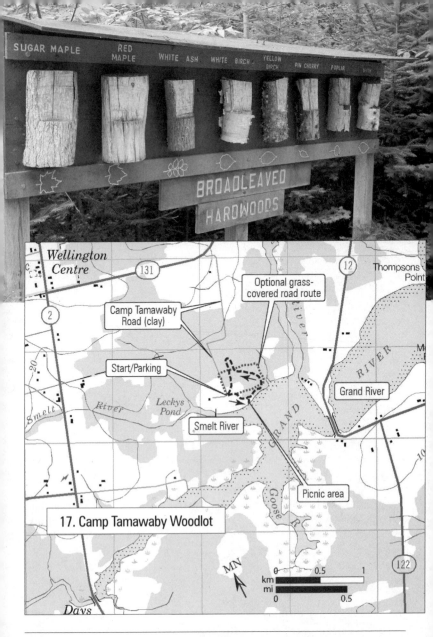

SUGAR MAPLE   RED MAPLE   WHITE ASH   WHITE BIRCH   YELLOW BIRCH   PIN CHERRY   POPLAR

BROADLEAVED HARDWOODS

Wellington Centre

131

12

Thompsons Point

2

Optional grass-covered road route

Camp Tamawaby Road (clay)

Start/Parking

Smelt River

RIVER

Grand River

M

Leckys Pond

GRAND

Picnic area

Goose R.

17. Camp Tamawaby Woodlot

MN

km   0   0.5   1
mi   0   0.5

122

Days

17. Camp Tamawaby Woodlot

◄---► 1.9 km (1.2 mi) rtn
🕐: 0.5+hrs
👫: 1
Type of Trail: compacted earth,
    natural surface
Uses: walking, snowshoeing, cross-country
    skiing

⚠: none
🔋: adequate throughout
Facilities: benches, interpretive panels,
    picnic table
Gov't Topo Map: 11L05 (Summerside)

Trailhead GPS: N 46° 28.624′ W 63° 57.593′

Access: From the junction of Granville Street and Highway 2 in Summerside, follow Highway 2 west for 18.5 km (11.6 mi). Turn right onto Highway 125 and continue for 1.7 km (1.1 mi), turning right onto Camp Tamawaby Road. Drive to the parking lot at the end of the road, 600 m/yd.

Introduction: The Camp Tamawaby Demonstration Woodlot is a gentle walk ideal for novices and families with young children. Most of the paths are grass or wood-chip covered and are wide enough for two to walk side by side. This path is well signed, has no hills and (almost) no wet spots, and there are benches and rest areas. The many interpretive panels provide details about the forests through which the trail passes.

If an additional walk is desired — or an optional route is preferred — stroll along the wood road, starting from the parking area. This loops around the woodlot to return to the Camp Tamawaby Road. Level and grass-covered, but without signage, the complete loop is 1.5 km (0.9 mi).

Route Description: From the large parking area, a sign indicates that the trail follows the wide, grassy track to the right. This area is entirely forested, and the former roadbed is carpeted with lush clover. After only 50 m/yd you reach a prominent sign, including a map and a brochure stand (which was empty when I visited). The trail turns right, off the road and onto a footpath.

From here, the path continues on a grassy surface — with occasional wood chips — through low, thick vegetation. The entire area is essentially level, and the path is wide enough for two to walk side by side. After only a few steps, you reach post #1. However, if there are no brochures, you will need to speculate on what is being profiled. Shortly after that, a sign indicates "balsam fir."

About 60 m/yd from the junction, a sturdy, railed bridge crosses a tiny rivulet. The trail meanders through the thick vegetation, limiting views to a few metres/yards on either side. Passing several more interpretive signs, about 250 m/yd from the bridge there is a junction, with a rest area to the right. Follow this, and in 75 m/yd you reach the shore of the Ellis River, where there is also a picnic table.

The main trail continues little more than 50 m/yd before reaching, and passing through, a stand of tall Norway spruce (so the sign says). For the first time in the walk there is shade, and with no low vegetation, there is often a pleasant breeze. However, after only a few seconds the trail returns to the lower, denser woods, where it remains for another 200 m/yd, at which point the footpath returns to the grassy road.

Crossing a small bridge, turn left. After barely 10 m/yd you turn right, and back onto a footpath. Within 75 m/yd, the trail reaches another stand of towering pine. A liberal sprinkling of wood chips defines the pathway through this section.

About 75 m/yd further, there is a display showing pieces of eight different conifers, permitting you to view the differences in bark and wood grain. Less than 50 m/yd later, there is a similar display for hardwoods—

or "broadleaved" trees, as they are labelled.

Winding and curving through the forest, the trail alternates between areas of thick brush and tall pines, and more interpretive stations, reaching a wood road 200 m/yd later. Once again, there are solid bridges crossing the ditches on both sides of the road. On the far side, the wood chips disappear and the path narrows somewhat. Pink flagging tape helps mark the way as the route wanders beneath more tall pine. However, the lower vegetation has not been cleared, giving this section the most natural appearance of the entire trail.

The path soon curves left, reaching a secluded bench about 150 m/yd from the road. Continuing to curve, the trail returns to recross the road at a spot less than 20 m/yd from the previous crossing. Back on wood chips, this area is once again sheltered beneath tall pines.

With only a few hundred metres/yards remaining, the trail passes mainly through open areas cleared beneath the pine. Less than 100 m/yd before reaching the trail's end, there is another picnic table, this one adjacent to a carved and painted rendition of Smokey the Bear. It provides a pleasant site to enjoy a snack before completing your stroll.

17. Camp Tamawaby Woodlot

19. Jacques Cartier Provincial Park

19. Jacques Cartier Provincial Park

20. John Hogg Kensington Public Forest

21. Lennox Island—
The Path of Our Forefathers

Lady's Slipper

In late May and early June, in shaded deciduous or pine woodlands, the forest floor can become a carpet of pale, pink blossoms, often growing in large bunches. Named for its distinctive shape, the lady's slipper – also known as the moccasin flower – was adopted as PEI's provincial flower in 1947.

Though seemingly plentiful when blossoming, these delicate orchids require several years to flower and will die quickly if picked. Lady's slippers also cannot be transplanted, as they will rarely survive a change of habitat. Take pictures, and leave them undisturbed.

Blueberries

When people think of agriculture on PEI, their first thought is usually of potatoes. However, in recent years the province has become a major producer of wild low bush blueberries, which are found only in eastern North America. PEI is an attractive growing location because its fields are relatively level and rock-free.

The industry has grown significantly, and today blueberries are considered a major crop. In 2013, there were more than 5,000 ha (12,500 ac) under cultivation, producing more than 4.5 million kg (10 million lb) of berries.

Blue Jay

One of the most colourful — and noisy — birds in the forest is the blue jay, which is slightly larger than a robin; it is also one of the relatively few species that does not migrate. There are few contrasts greater than the jay's startlingly brilliant cobalt feathers among the greys and browns of a winter forest. In fact, the blue jay's feathers are not actually blue, but only appear so because of a peculiar distortion of sunlight.

The blue jay was declared the provincial bird of Prince Edward Island in 1977.

23. Rotary Friendship Trail

24. Summerside Baywalk

25. Trout River

West Point Lighthouse
Built in 1875, the West Point Lighthouse is the tallest in PEI —
20.6m (67 ft 8 in) — and was operated for eighty-eight years with only two keepers, until it was automated in 1963. Distinguished now by its broad, black horizontal stripes, these were originally coloured red, until 1915. During World War II, the light was kept lit in winter to assist student aviators.

In 1984, the lighthouse was converted to an inn and museum, both of which continue to operate.

26. West Point Beach

Red elderberry

20. John Hogg Kensington Public Forest

◀ --- ▶ 4.5 km (2.8 mi) rtn

⏱: 1+hrs

👣: 1

Type of Trail: crushed stone, natural surface

Uses: walking, biking*, snowshoeing, cross-country skiing*, snowmobiling*

⚠: none

🔋: adequate throughout

Facilities: benches, interpretive panels

Gov't Topo Map: 11L05 (Summerside)

Trailhead GPS: N 46° 24.945' W 63° 37.015'

Access: From the junction of Granville Street and Highway 2 in Summerside, follow Highway 2 east for 3.5 km (2.2 mi). Turn right onto Highway 1A and continue for 3.2 km (2 mi), turning left onto Highway 107/Blue Shank Road. Drive 9.9 km (6.2 mi). The parking lot is on the left, just before Confederation Trail crosses the road.

Introduction: The compact 15 hectare (37 acre) John Hogg Kensington Public Forest boasts a mature Acadian forest, fields, and hedgerows. The 2.4 km (1.5 mi) allow the amateur botanist to discover the more than ninety species of plants that dwell on its grounds.

What I most enjoyed was the family of barred owls that I heard hooting mournfully every time I walked through the forest. Under the thick canopy of the tall, mature maple and

oak, it was dark even at midday, and these birds always seemed active. I was never able to capture more than a fleeting glimpse, but I enjoyed the search tremendously.

In winter, the Confederation Trail is used by the snowmobile association. Alternative access to the woodlot must be used for snowshoeing.

Route Description: From the parking lot, walk onto the Confederation Trail and turn left, in the direction of Kensington. The crushed-stone surface is excellent, level and without roots, ruts, or potholes. In addition to the 3 m/yd pathway, there is a wide, grass-covered verge on both sides of the trail.

Initially the trail is straight, and climbing, gradually but distinctly. For the first few hundred metres/yards there are raised embankments on both sides, and the vegetation is

Food

Even for the shortest stroll, a snack can be a pleasant addition. Many people like to stop and picnic; I prefer to nibble as I walk, so I carry nuts, dried fruits, and hearty breads. Anything is better than nothing, but try to avoid chips, chocolate bars, and snack foods with a high glycemic index, especially on long-distance treks or in inclement weather.

thick. However, by the time you reach the bench, on your right about 550 m/ yd from the start, the path has begun to curve. Within another 150 m/ yd, the trees on the left thin out, revealing a large field. And when you reach the km 125 marker, 750 m/yd from the start, you are gaining views to the right over an extensive area of cultivation.

Continue along the Confederation Trail, passing another bench 400 m/ yd later. To your right a tall communications tower dominates the skyline, but directly ahead you will see the large sign that announces the entrance for the John Hogg Kensington Public Forest on the left. (Actually, the entrance is about 50 m/yd beyond this sign; don't try to force your way through the trees.)

You leave the Confederation Trail, and its crushed-stone surface, about 1.3 km (0.8 mi) from the trailhead. The Public Forest's trail is natural surface, which initially means a lush, grassy carpet. At the entrance there is a very large sign, which includes

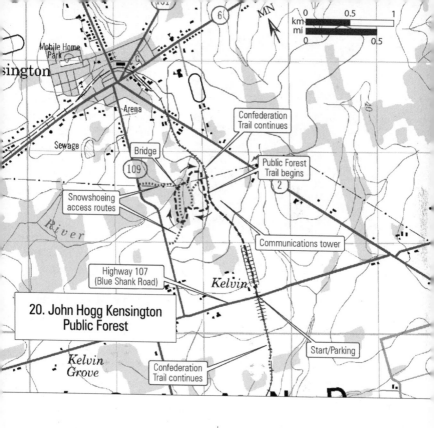

20. John Hogg Kensington Public Forest

Map labels:
- Mobile Home Park
- sington
- Arena
- Sewage
- Bridge
- 109
- Confederation Trail continues
- Public Forest Trail begins
- Snowshoeing access routes
- River
- Communications tower
- Highway 107 (Blue Shank Road)
- Kelvin
- Start/Parking
- Kelvin Grove
- Confederation Trail continues

a map of the entire trail system. This has two loops, one that stays entirely in a field, another that traverses forested land. Your current location is prominently marked.

Turn left, and follow the meandering path mown through the tall grasses, which are often luxuriant with wildflowers. After about 100 m/yd, the track curves right and works its way down a gentle slope to a junction, at the edge of the treeline, 260 m/yd from the sign.

Turn left, plunging into the forest. This footpath is much narrower, and in the summer ferns frequently obscure the treadway. Fortunately, the route is well signed with bright blue markers on trees. These are placed close enough that you should always be able to see the next one ahead of you.

Under a high hardwood canopy, the trail continues to wind its way through the forest. There are occasional tree roots to avoid, but no rocks. You might be able to see a field through the vegetation to the left for the next 200 m/yd, and you will also pass a rustic bench.

After 300 m/yd walking inside the forest, you reach the junction with the Wood Road, which is signed with red markers. Keep straight on the blue path, which soon begins to curve to the right. For the next 450 m/yd, until you reach the bridge, the trail wanders through dense forest. There is fairly good visibility because most trees are mature and tall, and there is a thick leafy canopy overhead. You might also occasionally notice the red trail, on the right, as the two routes come quite close several times.

At the bridge, turn right. For a few steps, you are on the red trail, but you will soon sight blue markers to your left: be sure to follow them. The remaining 260 m/yd of forested walk are through the thickest vegetation of the route, at times practically enshrouding the trail. At times the path is little more than a tight passageway through the brush.

You emerge suddenly, popping out into the field. At the next junction, back now on the grassy surface of the field pathway, turn left. The trail works around the perimeter of the field, turning right to parallel an old barbed-wire fence, then right again at the top of the gentle hill. To your left, not too distant, some of the buildings of Kensington are visible.

About 320 m/yd from when you re-entered the field, you reach another junction. To the right, a wide swath through the grass heads back down the hill. Keep straight, and within 200 m/yd you return to the entrance sign at the junction with the Confederation Trail.

Turn right, and retrace the 1.3 km (0.8 mi) back to the trailhead on Blue Shank Road.

21. Lennox Island—
The Path of Our Forefathers

◀ - - - ▶ 10 km (6.25 mi) rtn

🕐 : 3+hrs

🏃 : 2

Type of Trail: compacted earth, crushed stone, natural surface

Uses: walking, snowshoeing

⚠ : road crossings, motorized vehicles

🗓 : adequate throughout

Facilities: benches, interpretive panels

Gov't Topo Map: 11L12 (Malpeque)

Trailhead GPS: N 46° 36.208′ W 63° 51.257′

Access: From the junction of Granville Street and Highway 2 in Summerside, follow Highway 2 west for 34.8 km (21.75 mi). Turn right onto Highway 134 and continue for 5.8 km (3.6 mi), turning right onto Highway 12. In 1.3 km (0.8 mi), turn left onto Highway 163/East Bideford Road. Continue for 7.7 km (4.8 mi), turning left onto Eagle Feather Drive. The parking area/trailhead is on the left in 290 m/yd.

Introduction: There are few formal hiking paths on First Nations lands in Atlantic Canada, making the Path of Our Forefathers almost unique. This is also a very pleasant hike, passing through gorgeous stands of both hardwoods and softwoods, traversing several blueberry fields, and providing excellent views of the Malpeque Sand Hills on the islands that shelter Malpeque Bay.

Route Description: From the parking area, a wide crushed-stone path meanders through thick forest, at first mostly hardwoods, but soon changing to predominantly spruce. Several informal paths connect, including some used by ATVs. After 425 m/yd, you emerge into a field of cultivated blueberries; resist the temptation to sample!

Only about 30 m/yd into the field, you reach an unsigned junction. Turn left, following the wide track across the field almost 300 m/yd before the trail heads back into forest, where crushed stone resumes on the treadway. This is an attractive section, dominated by high hardwoods that spread a shady canopy of leaves overhead. You might notice buildings to the left; the trail here is little more than 100 m/yd from East Bideford Road.

At the next junction, about 400 m/yd from the field, turn right. You should find a trail marker here. Initially this looks like a former road, probably because it is arrow straight. After 200 m/yd, the path curves gradually left, and within 150 m/yd reaches the water's edge: Malpeque Bay, near the road and bridge connecting Lennox Island. At low tide, it is possible to walk along the beach, should you wish.

The trail is now parallel to the coastline, but with a buffer of trees between path and water. After 200 m/yd, there is a sharp right turn inland, but only to cross a swampy area on a sturdy bridge with railings. About 150 m/yd after the bridge, you reach a junction, where there is a bench. Keep left, crossing another bridge, then following a boardwalk; the ground here is quite wet.

Once back on dry ground, the crushed stone is replaced by larger gravel, or even sandy pebbles. It also narrows, as the vegetation on both sides crowds toward the centre. About 200 m/yd from the junction the path has worked its way back to the water's edge, and in a further 125 m/yd, there is a structure on the left and beach access. Within sight on the trail ahead is another bridge.

Less than 75 m/yd after this bridge there is another junction; keep left again and cross two more bridges in the next 50 m/yd. Beyond here, the trail surface is more natural, but also

wider. The forest is also very open and attractive, returning to high hardwoods and even stands of pine. You will pass one bench, less than 150 m/yd from the junction, then 250 m/yd later reach a crossing of the Oapus Trail, a clay-surfaced road.

There are trail markers on both sides of the road, ensuring you remain on the correct route. The path initially turns right, paralleling the road, but within 100 m/yd turns left away from it. After another 150 m/yd, you reach another clay road; turn 90° left, and follow what appears to be another straight-line former road section.

For nearly 500 m/yd you continue straight on the crushed-stone surface. There the trail curves left, and continues through the forest until it reaches another blueberry field 400 m/yd later. Continue through the middle of this field; there are no markers, and the path is considerably less distinct. However, head toward the opposite treeline, which you will reach in about 300 m/yd, just to the right of another clay road.

Enter the forest; within 75 m/yd the trail will cross the clay road, where you return to another well-surfaced former road. For the next 800 m/yd, your route proceeds through dense forest, usually with overhead shade, but sometimes not. The trail is wide and dry, and usually fairly straight. However, about 100 m/yd

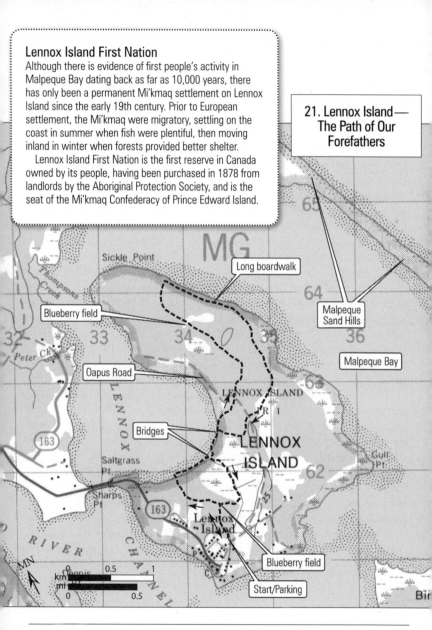

Lennox Island First Nation

Although there is evidence of first people's activity in Malpeque Bay dating back as far as 10,000 years, there has only been a permanent Mi'kmaq settlement on Lennox Island since the early 19th century. Prior to European settlement, the Mi'kmaq were migratory, settling on the coast in summer when fish were plentiful, then moving inland in winter when forests provided better shelter.

Lennox Island First Nation is the first reserve in Canada owned by its people, having been purchased in 1878 from landlords by the Aboriginal Protection Society, and is the seat of the Mi'kmaq Confederacy of Prince Edward Island.

21. Lennox Island— The Path of Our Forefathers

Sickle Point

Thompsons Creek

Long boardwalk

Blueberry field

Malpeque Sand Hills

Peter Ck

Malpeque Bay

Oapus Road

LENNOX ISLAND IR 1

Lennox

Bridges

LENNOX ISLAND

Saltgrass Pt.

Gull Pt.

Sharps Pt.

Lennox Island

Blueberry field

Start/Parking

RIVER

CHANNEL

km 0   0.5   1
mi 0   0.5

MN

after making a sharp right turn, you reach a junction with a side path; this conducts you the 50 m/yd to the shoreline, a very attractive site with a bench, offering excellent views of the Malpeque Sand Hills on Hog Island across the bay.

The trail continues paralleling the coastline, but winding and becoming grass surfaced. In 275 m/yd, you encounter the longest bridge/boardwalk of the hike, extending more than 100 m/yd. The ocean on the left is often close, affording good views of Malpeque Bay and the dunes on Hog Island. About 650 m/yd from the end of the boardwalk, the trail connects to the end of clay road, right at the waterline. There is a large clearing here, so if you had wished to walk along the shoreline for the last kilometre (0.6 mi), rather than the trail, you could reconnect at this spot.

Continue straight, through lush vegetation that largely hides any view of the ocean. About 300 m/yd later, there is a side trail, to the left, to another viewing station on the water's edge. Take advantage of it, because the main trail immediately turns sharply right and inland.

The track soon widens, and gradually returns to a crushed-stone surface. It also climbs perceptibly for the first time. Fortunately, there is a high, leafy overhead canopy for shade, and the climb is quite gentle. There are also several bird and bat boxes positioned on trees along this particular section.

After a woodland stroll of 800 m/yd, you reach and cross a clay road. On the opposite side, there is a sign indicating "Return." This winding, twisting pathway then traverses several types of forest, through low, boggy land, until crossing the Oapus Trail about 250 m/yd later. Continuing through forest, after another 450 m/yd it reaches a junction—one you have been to earlier in this hike.

Turn left and retrace your route to the next junction, 400 m/yd further. From here, you may continue straight and retrace the 1.9 km (1.2 mi) to the start. Or turn left, heading inland along what appears to be a service road. After 150 m/yd, you will see a beaver dam on your left, which the trail works around. From here, the path begins a long straight section, bordered by numerous pools and channels of water with low tree cover; there is no shade.

After 500 m/yd, the trail curves right, and 50 m/yd later you emerge at the corner of the very first blueberry field you encountered. From there it is 75 m/yd to the junction in the middle of the field, where you turn left and retrace the final 475 m/yd back to the trailhead and complete your walk.

22. North Cape/Black Marsh Nature Trail

◄---► 5 km (3.1 mi) rtn

⏱: 1+hrs

🏃: 1

Type of Trail: boardwalk, compacted earth, natural surface

Uses: walking, snowshoeing

⚠: cliffs, motorized vehicles

📱: adequate throughout

Facilities: benches, interpretive panels, washrooms, water

Gov't Topo Map: 21P01 (North Cape)

Trailhead GPS: N 47° 3.424' W 63° 59.752'

Access: From the junction of Central Street and Highway 2 in Summerside, follow Highway 2 west for 43.5 km (27.2 mi). Turn right onto Highway 12 and continue for 52.6 km (32.9 mi). The trailhead is to the left of North Cape Wind Energy Interpretive Centre.

Introduction: North Cape must have seemed like the logical place to establish one of the first wind farms in Atlantic Canada. At the very northern tip of PEI, home to a stunted spruce forest punished by the harsh climate, and with few residents because of the peat bog covering most of the area, it must have appeared ideal. So today there is a large number of these massive wind turbines towering above the low vegetation.

The entire western coastline of North Cape is vertical cliff, providing superb ocean views. And with more than twenty interpretive panels

spread along the trail, there is quite a bit to learn on this scenic, pleasant, and easy walk.

Route Description: From the parking lot, head toward the lighthouse. Just in front and to the left of this is a pavilion for the Black Marsh Nature Trail. This features a map of the route, and one of the twenty-five (or more) interpretive panels found along this path. Head to this, then turn left and follow the trail as it parallels the fence bordering the North Cape Wind Farm.

There are no trees on this part of the trail. To your left is a plethora of modern windmills and other wind-monitoring towers. On the right is the clay road, and just beyond that the cliff, which extends along this entire coastline. Within 300 m/yd, the trail is only a thin strip of grass sandwiched between road and fence, with metal barriers and rocks on the road side.

After another 300 m/yd alongside the road, the trail veers left. At panel #4, it splits into a coastal and a forest route. (There is a small map, indicating your current position, on every interpretive panel.) Keep left, on the forest section, which passes through a gate and becomes a grass-covered surface. Looming high above the low white spruce are several massive wind turbines.

After 350 m/yd travelling through the thick vegetation (which panel #5 tells you is not typical of PEI) you reach the base of one of the towers. A side trail connects to the road, but keep left, among the trees. This grassy path continues, curving gradually

right, crossing the road some 250 m/yd from the tower.

Across the road, you reach the coastal cliffs for the first time, where panel #8 overlooks the ocean next to a rail fence along the cliff-edge. This is quite a good lookoff, providing views of the cliffs and far into the Gulf of St. Lawrence. The trail continues left, along what appears to be an ATV track, with the rail fence, cliff, and ocean on our right.

After a further 350 m/yd, you reach an extensive boardwalk. Beyond here there are no trees nearby, only low vegetation and bog. In the distance, more wind towers speckle the landscape. In addition, in the distance,

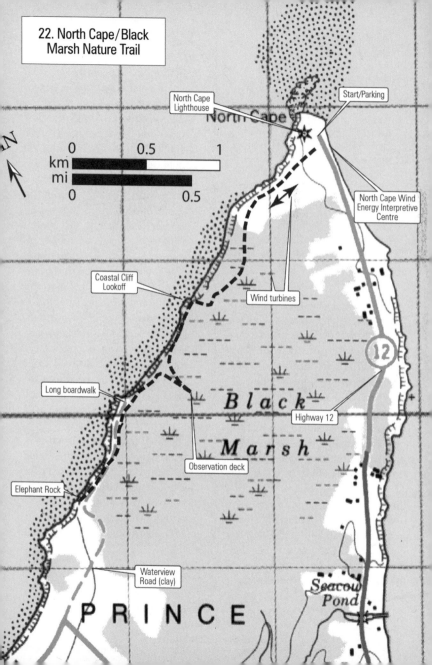

22. North Cape/Black
Marsh Nature Trail

North Cape
Lighthouse

Start/Parking

North Cape

North Cape Wind
Energy Interpretive
Centre

km
mi

0   0.5   1

0   0.5

N

Coastal Cliff
Lookoff

Wind turbines

Long boardwalk

B l a c k

Highway 12

Observation deck

M a r s h

Elephant Rock

Waterview
Road (clay)

Seacow
Pond

P R I N C E

Elephant Rock

It might not look like much today, but for more than twenty years that solitary rock standing separate from the coastline was a local tourist attraction. Wind and water had shaped and moulded the soft sandstones of North Cape into something resembling an elephant.

However, the same forces that created Elephant Rock soon destroyed it, its distinctive silhouette ground away by the relentless erosion of the harsh climate of North Cape. Today only photographs and the name, which has meaning only to the area's older residents, remain.

you can see a sea stack: Elephant Rock, as panel #9 explains.

Barely 50 m/yd later you reach a junction. Turn left, and follow the boardwalk to an observation deck erected above the bog—known as the Black Marsh—250 m/yd away. As there are no trees, you have an entirely unobstructed view of the bog. There are quite a few interpretive panels in this section, explaining the Black Marsh and the distinctive plants, birds, and animals that live there.

You retrace the boardwalk back to the main trail, although there is a junction 125 m/yd partway; keep left. From here the trail meanders through the thick grasses and skirts the peat bog. There are quite a few dead trees scattered among the grasses. About 350 m/yd along the main trail, there is an interpretive panel that explains their presence, along with a bench, should you wish to sit.

The boardwalk continues for another 400 m/yd, passing another bench, two picnic tables, and more panels. The trail ends overlooking Elephant Rock, where Waterview Road, which approaches from the opposite direction, also ends.

To return, retrace your route the 1.1 km (0.7 mi) back to panel #8. If you wish to take the coastal route, follow the clay road instead of returning through the forest route. Along the way there are some viewing platforms overlooking the ocean, and the final few interpretive panels. However, this is not a particularly scenic section, as it is set back from the cliff-edge and in woodland, so when it reconnects with the forest section about 500 m/yd later, you will probably be happy to do so.

The final 600 m/yd retraces the route alongside the wind farm's fence back toward the North Cape Wind Energy Interpretive Centre. You can add a few hundred metres/yards to the walk by exploring the headland near the lighthouse—a very scenic area.

23. Rotary Friendship Trail

◄---► 6 km (3.75 mi) rtn
🕐 : 1.5+ hrs
🏃 : 2

Type of Trail: crushed stone, compacted earth, natural surface

Uses: walking, biking, snowshoeing, cross-country skiing

⚠ : none
🗑 : adequate throughout

Facilities: benches, garbage cans, interpretive panels, picnic tables

Gov't Topo Map: 11L05 (Summerside)

Trailhead GPS: N 46° 24.935' W 63° 46.190'

Access: From the junction of Granville Street and Highway 2 in Summerside, follow Granville Street south for 900 m/yd. Turn left onto Walker Avenue and continue 550 m/yd, turning left onto Macewen Road. After 140 m/yd, look for a gravel road on the right; the civic address is #599 Macewen Road. The trailhead is at the end of a gravel lane, some 250 m/yd further along.

Introduction: In an area so extensively cultivated as the land near Summerside, woodland walks are rare. Fortunately, the Rotary Friendship Park is a modest, but welcome, 26 hectare (64 acre) wooded haven. The park features a maze of broad tracks, narrow footpaths, and informal trails utilizing almost every inch of its small area. It is easy to get confused on its many interconnected pathways, but with houses or fields only a few metres/yards away in every direction, you cannot be lost for long.

The Rotary Friendship Park is open from 0700 hours until 2200 hours daily.

Route Description: From the parking area, a broad, gravelled track—wide enough for a vehicle—heads into a surprisingly remote-feeling woodlot. Near the start the trees appear fairly young, so they are low and dense, and hide the nearby buildings of the surrounding community.

After less than 200 m/yd, the trail makes a 90° right turn to avoid a field. A fence lines the route on the left. Little more than 100 m/yd later you reach a junction, where there is also a large open area filled with benches, tables, plaques, and flags. In the ground, the Rotary Club symbol has been fashioned using bricks.

This is a great spot to sit and enjoy

a snack, but perhaps on the return, after you have completed your walk. Keep left at this junction, moving past the open area. The field is still on your left, young trees to the right. And rare for this part of PEI, the trail even climbs a little, giving better views into the cultivated field. About 60 m/yd later there is another cleared area with picnic tables. Past this, on the right there is a scabrous-looking pond. (Much of the park was once an industrial area, and some of the scars remain.)

Another gentle climb, and 100 m/yd further the trail turns right again at a 90° angle. A cultivated field and fence are still on the left. The trail resembles a country lane, with a crushed-stone surface and centre strip of grass. There is no overhead shade here, however. After a further 150 m/yd, you reach a T-junction (although there is an informal footpath directly ahead). Turn 90° left.

This takes you into an area where the trees are older, taller, and provide more shade. After 100 m/yd, the trail curves right and delivers you to another junction—let's call it junction "L"—50 m/yd later. Keep left again, and left at the next junction, which you reach almost immediately. The treadway is now almost completely grass-covered, and the trees bordering it almost all softwoods. The larch, to the left, are quite tall and healthy.

Within about 100 m/yd, you should pass a sign, on the right, which says this is the Wyatt Wildflower Meadow. You will notice paths mowed into the tall grasses between trees. Explore if you wish; the trail you are on skirts the perimeter.

The main trail turns right 250 m/yd from the last junction, and continues another 150 m/yd to the next junction, where there is a bench. To the right, the broad, grassy path continues. Instead, keep straight, and head onto a narrow footpath into the thick forest. This is a pleasant diversion, barely 150 m/yd in length, where your path roves through a small stand of mature trees. Look for the tree with a bearded face carved into it.

All too soon, this footpath reconnects to the broad grassy track, at what appears to be a tree nursery. There are many small spruces, in rows, and numerous patches of flowers. After 100 m/yd in the open, you reach another junction. Keep straight, on the footpath that heads back among the trees.

I enjoyed this section best of the entire hike. The single-width, natural-surface footpath meanders among tall hardwoods, with a thick carpet of ferns lining the trail. The route curves back and forth, making the most of the relatively small stand of trees, which is bordered by cultivated fields on three sides. A canopy of leaves

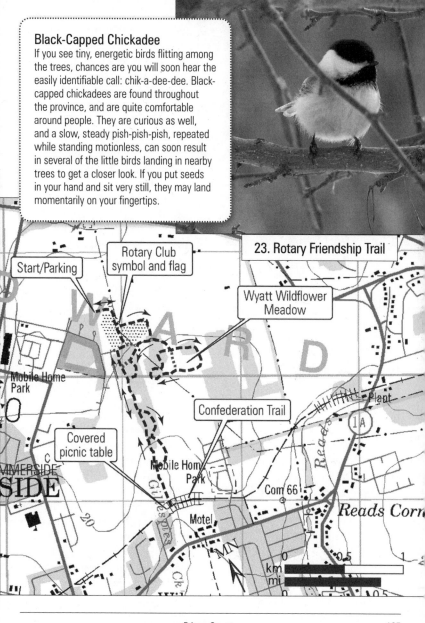

Black-Capped Chickadee

If you see tiny, energetic birds flitting among the trees, chances are you will soon hear the easily identifiable call: chik-a-dee-dee. Black-capped chickadees are found throughout the province, and are quite comfortable around people. They are curious as well, and a slow, steady pish-pish-pish, repeated while standing motionless, can soon result in several of the little birds landing in nearby trees to get a closer look. If you put seeds in your hand and sit very still, they may land momentarily on your fingertips.

23. Rotary Friendship Trail

Start/Parking

Rotary Club symbol and flag

Wyatt Wildflower Meadow

Mobile Home Park

Confederation Trail

Covered picnic table

Mobile Home Park

RIVERSIDE
SIDE

Com 66

Motel

Reads Corr

Reads

Plant

1 A

km
mi

providing shade high overhead, tinting everything with green. After only 500 m/yd, this footpath ends, reconnecting with the wider, more open track at junction "L," completing this section of the park.

Retrace the 150 m/yd back to the T-junction, continuing straight. After about 150 m/yd it curves left, then 25 m/yd later you should sight another footpath—one with a badly damaged and illegible signpost—on your left. Follow this, keeping left at each of the next two junctions with other footpaths. In 250 m/yd, this will reconnect to a wide, crushed-stone-surfaced track.

Turn left, and follow this broad, nearly straight route for the next 400 m/yd to the next junction with a footpath, which is on your left. Along the way, you will be shaded by some quite tall trees, and to your right you should be able to see some of the houses on Colin Avenue in Summerside.

When you reach the footpath, just where a large cultivated field begins on the right, turn left and follow it. You enjoy another 500 m/yd on natural surface, passing through thicker forest, with more spruce toward the end. Watch for bird feeders in the final 150 m/yd. This section is shaped like the letter "B," in two small loops that reconnect to the main trail in the middle.

If you do the full "B," when you rejoin the main trail, turn left. Head straight for 500 m/yd, cultivated fields bordering both flanks of the path. There, the Friendship Trail ends at and connects with the Confederation Trail. There is an excellent covered picnic table here, and should you wish to extend your walk into the community of Summerside, turn right.

At this point, you have walked nearly 3.9 km (2.4 mi). The return to the trailhead is much shorter. Return along the straight laneway, ignoring the footpaths—unless you wish to walk them again. After 1.4 km (0.9 mi), you reach a T-junction. Turn right; in 40 m/yd you reach another junction, where there is a bench. Turn left, and follow this as it passes beneath a power line, curves left, and returns to the junction with the Rotary symbol, 175 m/yd further. Keep straight, and retrace the 300 m/yd back to the trailhead.

24. Summerside Baywalk

◄ - - - ► 13 km (8.1 mi) rtn
🕐 : 3+hrs
🏃 : 3

Type of Trail: asphalt, boardwalk, crushed
 stone

Uses: walking, biking, inline skating*,
 snowshoeing*, cross-country skiing*

⚠ : road crossings
📱 : adequate throughout

Facilities: benches, garbage cans,
 interpretive panels, picnic tables,
 playground, washrooms

Gov't Topo Map: 11L05 (Summerside)

Trailhead GPS: N 46° 23.450' W 63° 46.715'

Access: From the junction of Granville Street and Highway 2 in Summerside, follow Granville Street and continue for 3.7 km (2.3 mi). Turn left onto Water Street (Highway 11) and drive 300 m/yd, turning left to stay on Water Street. After 500 m/yd, turn right into the trail parking area.

Introduction: There are few long coastal walking routes available in PEI, except on beaches. That alone makes the Summerside Baywalk exceptional. However, it is also a wonderfully scenic and varied trail, passing through the town's urban core, alongside the beach, across parkland, and within forested terrain.

It is also arguably one of the best-constructed off-road facilities in the province, paved over much of its route and with numerous facilities and interpretive panels throughout its length. As a result, it is almost always busy, with walkers and cyclists active everywhere along the path.

Route Description: Tucked between a Wendy's and a KFC on a busy commercial street, the trailhead can easily be missed. Yet there is a parking lot and a large gazebo with quite a bit of background information, including a map. You do not begin on the coastline, but you can see the water from the trailhead. Follow the boardwalk in that direction, as it skirts a wetland, reaching the shore of Summerside Harbour in 250 m/yd, where there is a multi-level observation platform. (There is even ground-level lighting for the boardwalk!)

You are in a lovely spot, a wonderful place to view the harbour, even if you did not walk another step. However, you have just begun, so read all the information panels, and continue along the boardwalk.

Barely 100 m/yd further, you cross a bridge that spans the drainage from the wetland. The trail passes behind the buildings lining bustling Water Street, reaching a massive steel bridge 200 m/yd later.

This directs you left, dodging the parking lot for a Foodland, and keeping your route on the shoreline. You have reached downtown Summerside, so there is little vegetation for the next section. In fact, for the next 400 m/yd the trail traces the edge of the waterfront, large buildings and parking lots on the right. However, there is still a dedicated boardwalk, benches, information panels, and even a shelter.

About 900 m/yd into the walk you reach the harbour, where the trail passes through the centre of the community. Your route heads right, passing next to the yacht club, then left behind the Centre for Performing Arts. About 200 m/yd later, the trail splits; keep left, along the water's edge. Your path actually passes behind a waterfront shopping area, Spinnaker Landing, turns right, and reaches Harbour Drive.

The route twists and turns, but remains close to the water, and there are numerous benches throughout this section. At Harbour Street, turn left, and follow the boardwalk as it works along the Summerside Marine Terminal jetty and passes several businesses. You reach Harbour Drive again at 1.7 km (1.1 mi).

The trail turns left, and runs parallel to the sidewalk until they converge 100 m/yd later. Continue on the sidewalk around a building; the boardwalk resumes, and you cross Queen Street at 1.9 km (1.2 mi). Turn right; in 50 m/yd you reach the Confederation Trail, where you turn left. This curves around to reach Water Street 150 m/yd later. (Confused yet? Hint: stay close to the ocean.)

Turn left, leaving the Confederation Trail. For the next 50 m/yd, there is a painted pathway paralleling Water Street. This turns left just before reaching a business, and connects with the Boardwalk at 2.2 km (1.4 km). The confusing section is over!

From here, the trail works behind several businesses, including one very popular restaurant, and reaches another official trailhead pavilion about 100 m/yd later. This is a gorgeous location, with Summerside Beach stretching ahead. The trail follows the shoreline alongside the beach for the next 600 m/yd. This is usually the busiest section of the trail, with Water Street close on your right, and many houses nearby. There is even a separate asphalt bike track paralleling the boardwalk.

The shoreline, and trail, curve left, away from the road. To the right

the bridge show that ATVs do travel this route.

About 50 m/yd past the bridge, there is another bench/garbage can combination. There is also a 1 km (0.6 mi) marker. I measured this point to be about 100 m/yd further, more if you went to the embank-. ment near the trailhead. Here you are a little higher than the brook, which remains on your left, and you are on an entirely dirt surface.

The path now moves away brief-ly from the stream, through thicker forest. About 200 m/yd later, power lines pass overhead, and after this the trail returns toward the water. After another 150 m/yd, you reach a junction, where there is also a bench/ garbage can and a shelter. The track that comes from the right and crosses the Trout River is used by local land-owners; the trail continues straight.

In the next 200 m/yd, the river is somewhat obscured by alder thick-ets, but just after post #11, the forest changes to older-growth beech and birch and the trail passes immediately beside the river, which is clear of ob-structing vegetation: a lovely spot.

About 350 m/yd further, you reach the 2 km (1.25 mi) marker, just before the trail crosses a small creek, at post #13. After post #14, 250 m/yd later, there are no further indications that you are still on a managed trail until you reach the 3 km (1.9 mi) marker.

White Spruce

Whenever the trail passes abandoned farms, the tree most likely recolonizing the fields is the white spruce. This bushy conifer frequently grows in pure, dense stands, particularly on well-drained, but moist, soil. However, they are often mixed with red spruce, balsam fir, and white birch. White spruce can grow up to 21 m/yd in height, and usually live for 250-300 years.

Wood from the white spruce is used to make wood pulp and lumber. They are also grown as Christmas trees, though balsam fir is usually preferred.

During this 750 m/yd section, there are no longer any bird boxes, or num-bered posts. You still have views of the river, and you will notice that the opposite bank is both higher and, oc-casionally, steep sided.

It possible to continue easily an-other 400 m/yd beyond the 3 km (1.9 mi) marker. There are no further signs, and the treadway becomes pro-gressively rougher, with occasional wet spots, but the river remains close by on the left, and it is a tranquil wooded area. But suddenly, the track becomes overgrown and impassable. No sign is required to tell you it is time to retrace your route back to the trailhead.

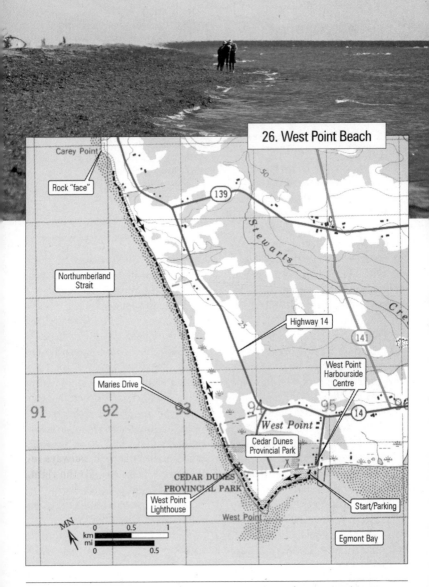

26. West Point Beach

Carey Point
Rock "face"

139

Stewarts

Northumberland
Strait

Highway 14

141

Maries Drive

West Point
Harbourside
Centre

91   92   93   94   95   14

West Point

Cedar Dunes
Provincial Park

CEDAR DUNES
PROVINCIAL PARK

West Point
Lighthouse

West Point

Start/Parking

MN

0   0.5   1
km
mi
0   0.5

Egmont Bay

26. West Point Beach

◀ - - - ▶ 9.5 km (6 mi) rtn

⏱ : 2.5 + hrs

🚶 : 2

Type of Trail: natural surface

Uses: walking, ATVing*

⚠ : wind and waves, motorized vehicles

📱 : adequate throughout

Facilities: garbage cans, interpretive panels, picnic tables, washrooms

Gov't Topo Map: 21I09 (O'Leary)

Trailhead GPS:N 46° 37.195′ W 64° 22.390′

Access: From the junction of Granville Street and Highway 2 in Summerside, follow Highway 2 west for 52.8 km (33 mi). Turn left onto Highway 14 and continue for 21.5 km (13.4 mi), turning left onto Harbour Road. Drive 700 m/yd to Cedar Dunes Park Road. Turn right, then park beside the West Point Harbourside Centre, to your left.

Introduction: One of PEI's finest features must be its amazing beaches. Many extend for considerable distances, permitting longer hikes than are usually available in its woodlands. West Point Beach is a particularly fine example, and it also boasts the highest lighthouse on the island as a beacon.

The West Point Lighthouse has a further distinction: it is Canada's only functioning lighthouse that is also an inn. It is also home to a museum and a restaurant, so it is well worth a visit. In addition, should you wish

to vary your walk, a short nature trail from the lighthouse circles a small wetland, and you can access Cedar Dunes Provincial Park's boardwalk.

Route Description: From the Harbourside Centre's parking area there is a clearly defined track through the beach grasses heading toward the ocean. Follow that, through the sand, for 150 m/yd until you reach the beach. On your left is the breakwater protecting West Point Harbour, which is often bustling with activity. In front, you'll see the magical blue waters of Egmont Bay.

There is no shade on a beach. On most days, a brisk breeze provides some relief, but a hat is always required on this walk. To the right, rising above the distant trees, are the tops of massive wind turbines

Turn right, and follow the coastline along the gleaming sand. To your right, there is a broad area of tall grasses covering the low dunes, with buildings set far back from the waterline. In summer, families head to the beach, outside the provincial park boundaries, and build fires that burn long after dark.

It is a pleasant 600 m/yd to the sandy tip of West Point, where you must turn 90° to the right. Just before reaching that point, you enter Cedar Dunes Provincial Park, where a sign warns of dangerous currents. Watch for terns skimming the shallow waters and diving for their dinners.

As you turn, you can see the black-and-white-striped lighthouse peaking over the sand dunes and the park's supervised beach. This section of beach is often covered in seaweed; you will probably need to walk closer to the dunes. It is about 450 m/yd to reach the lighthouse, and as you approach there are several boardwalks which access the beach. Take a few minutes to explore the area around the lighthouse; there are interpretive panels, and a boardwalk, along the inland side of the dunes, for the complete length of the park, about 750 m/yd.

Once past the lighthouse, about 1.3 km (0.8 mi) into your walk, you move into a more remote area. The low ground disappears, its beach grasses replaced by thick tangles of spruce. For the next 550 m/yd this dense tree cover continues, almost unbroken, until you reach a cluster of cottages and trailers. There is vehicle access to the beach here, and a street sign indicates that this is Maries Drive. Beyond, the windmills—more than a dozen are visible —loom much larger.

A fringe of beach grasses and dunes resumes to the right. The cottages end in 300 m/yd, leaving you once again with a deserted beach stretching away in the distance. However, there are often a few other walkers in sight, and tracks in the sand indicate that ATVs might also keep you company at some point.

You can actually see the end of the walk in the distance, where coastal cliffs begin rising about the beach, and there are quite a few houses. But that is far ahead, and until then you have sand, sun (hopefully), wind, and waves to enjoy.

To the left is open ocean, the Northumberland Strait. It is usually dotted with small boats, and you might detect the smudge on the horizon that is New Brunswick.

After a further 600 m/yd of sandy sauntering, you draw level with the first on the windmills. The dunes are gradually rising higher, hiding any view of the land behind them, although there is another trailer visible here.

About 500 m/yd later, you reach the next cluster of cottages, where there is again vehicle access to the sand. The beach has been narrowing as the seawall has been getting higher, but there is still ample space to amble. Past these cottages, the dunes, now dotted with spruce, are 3-5 m/yd high, and are becoming steeper.

It is 700 m/yd to the next house and less than 100 m/yd beyond that a major vehicle access. You have walked about 4 km (2.5 mi), and there is little room remaining. The dunes have become cliffs, with staircases required to provide access from the cottages. The beach continues to narrow, but it is possible to continue a little further.

Actually, another 700 m/yd remains before the beach completely runs out and you are faced with a cliff face. This is worth exploring, and wind and water sometimes carve the soft, exposed rocks into interesting shapes. When I was there, I saw a face that reminded me of New Hampshire's famous, now lost, "Old Man of the Mountain." But be cautious: at high tide there is very little beach space, and no shelter from waves.

I recommend that you walk until you run out of room, then turn around and walk back. This is a beautiful spot to spend a few hours strolling beside the ocean.

31. McKenna Scenic Heritage Road

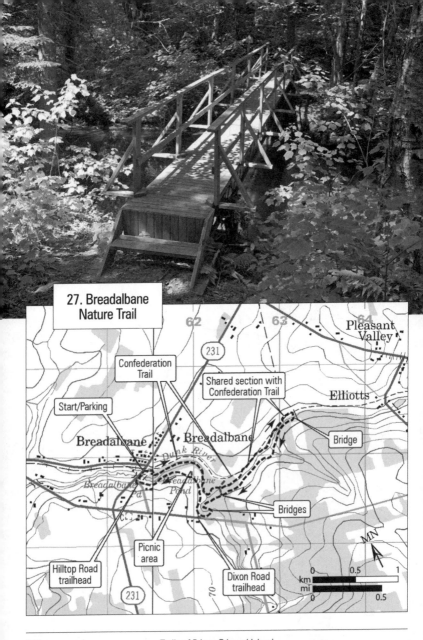

27. Breadalbane Nature Trail

Confederation Trail

Start/Parking

Shared section with Confederation Trail

Breadalbane

Dunk River

Breadalbane Pond

Breadalbane

Pleasant Valley

Elliotts

Bridge

Bridges

Picnic area

Hilltop Road trailhead

Dixon Road trailhead

27. Breadalbane Nature Trail

◀---▶ 7 km (4.4 mi) rtn

⏱: 2+hrs

🥾: 2

Type of Trail: crushed stone, natural surface

Uses: walking, biking*, snowshoeing, snowmobiling*

⚠: road crossings, cow parsnip

🚻: adequate throughout

Facilities: benches, interpretive panels, picnic tables

Gov't Topo Map: 11L06 (North Rustico)

Trailhead GPS: N 46° 21.440' W 63° 30.070'

Access: From the junction of Granville Street and Highway 2 in Summerside, follow Highway 2 east for 25 km (15.6 mi). Turn right onto Highway 231/Inkerman Road and continue for 2.3 km (1.4 mi). Turn right onto Holmes Road and park near the gazebo.

Introduction: Rated by the Island Trails as one of PEI's major woodland trails, the Breadalbane Nature Trail is a very enjoyable walk along the banks of the Dunk River. This path makes maximum and adroit use of the small fragment of natural land that remains in this agricultural area.

The entire route, with the exception of the portion that it shares with the Confederation Trail, has been built on private land. Please keep to the path.

Both cow parsnip and giant hogsweed, very similar in appearance, grow extensively along the river's edge. The invasive giant hogsweed can cause skin irritation, blistering, and burning, similar to poison ivy. It is particularly prevalent in June and July, so I recommend hiking this trail during other months.

Route Description: There is a lovely park in Breadalbane, situated between Holmes Road and the Confederation Trail, with tables, benches, and a playground. Walk across it and begin your hike where the Confederation Trail crosses Inkerman Road.

Follow the Confederation Trail over the Highway, and along the broad, crushed-stone pathway for 200 m/yd. At this point, you will see a small wooden bridge on the right and a footpath leading into the forest. There is also a trailhead sign, which features a map, but it is facing away from the Confederation Trail, so you need to cross the little bridge to view it. There is also a large warning sign about cow parsnip.

Once on the footpath, you will see an untended field to the right, with a house at the far end. The footpath continues straight only 25 m/yd, then turns left, onto what appears to be an old wood road. To your right and below is the shallow, slow-moving Dunk River; to the left, and slightly above, sits the Confederation Trail.

For the next 500 m/yd, the trail continues to navigate through the narrow band of trees between the river and the Confederation Trail, gradually curving to the right. The path stays under thick tree cover, providing welcome shade. The ground is slightly uneven, so the trail undulates modestly. Occasionally, especially in areas predominantly spruce, roots intrude into the treadway. There are even a few wet patches near little gullies, or where the path strays closest to the river.

Your route moves away from the Confederation Trail, following instead the meandering river. The woods through which you travel vary, mostly spruce, but occasionally hardwoods. After another 400 m/yd, just after passing through a small open area, there is a bench, on the left. However, the river here is hidden behind a low, dense layer of vegetation. You will hear it, but probably not see it.

The path curves left, working along the flank of a small hill. About 200 m/yd past the bench, you reach a junction signed only by flagging tape. Keep straight, because in less than 50 m/yd you reach a major bridge where there is another map, which marks your present location. You have walked about 1.5 km (0.9 mi) so far.

Continue straight, keeping the river on your right and slightly higher ground on the left. Occasional pieces of flagging tape mark your route. After about 250 m/yd close to the water, the trail climbs away a little, and passes through an area of white spruce, then red pine, where it might be difficult to distinguish the path in the carpet of needles.

Watch for a bench about 75 m/yd later, in a pleasant space among the pines. The trail continues working its way along and gradually up the gentle hillside, and 600 m/yd from the bridge it rejoins the Confederation Trail, where there is another map.

Turn right; for the next 350 m/yd the two trails share the same path. You will see why just before the km 142 marker, when you can see a pond to your right and immediately below the former railroad's embankment.

When you reach a sheltered picnic table, the nature trail returns to the forest on the right. It briefly drops down the slope to reach the water, then curves left and resumes following the river. You can enjoy another 500 m/yd on this gently undulating footpath before it returns to reconnect to the Confederation Trail.

Keep right; in less than 100 m/yd a road crosses the Confederation Trail. Markers direct you right, downhill and across a vehicle bridge over the small river. Almost immediately, the trail heads right, off this road, and back into the forest.

The river is still to the right, but now you are heading downstream. This is more of a mixed forest, although there are some very tall spruce scattered around. For the next 1.6 km (1 mi), the path meanders upstream, though often out of sight of the river, until it reaches a junction and the footbridge you encountered at 1.5 km (0.9 mi). At this point, you have travelled about 4.75 km (3 mi).

Continue straight; the trail is wide, level, and easy to follow. There is a rare spot to access the water, about 350 m/yd beyond the junction. And 100 m/yd after that, the trail turns sharply right, and crosses a Dunk River tributary on an elaborate bridge, with a staircase on the opposite bank.

From here, it is a short distance, less than 200 m/yd, but crossing two small bridges, to the Dixon Road trailhead, visible to your left at a junction on the main trail. Keep straight, unless you want to read the trailhead sign, and continue along the footpath as it tracks through very thick brush alongside a small creek. After 300 m/yd there is an unmarked junction; keep left.

As the trail continues, it finally moves out of the dense brush and into more open woodland. In addition, the riverbank becomes steeper as you rejoin the Dunk River. The trail alternates from being next to the river, and in thicker vegetation, to climbing the steepening bank, and in open woodland.

About 1.3 km (0.8 mi) from the Dixon Road Trailhead, there is a picnic area, with two tables, in a grassy area next to the river. This is a tranquil spot, to the right off the main trail. From here, the path climbs, and with the village in sight, the bank has become almost a cliff.

There is one more side path, almost at the end, where the track descends to the river beside a concrete structure. This may be used more by the community's youth. From there, less than 50 m/yd remains to the Hilltop Road trailhead, where the footpath ends.

Turn right, and walk along the Inkerman Road for 150 m/yd back to the park alongside the Confederation Trail.

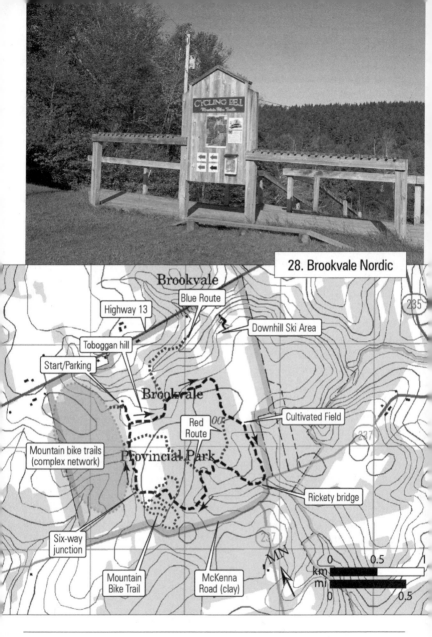

28. Brookvale Nordic

Brookvale

Highway 13

Blue Route

Downhill Ski Area

Toboggan hill

Start/Parking

Brookvale

Red Route

Cultivated Field

Mountain bike trails (complex network)

Provincial Park

Rickety bridge

Six-way junction

Mountain Bike Trail

McKenna Road (clay)

MN

km

mi

0   0.5   1

0   0.5

28. Brookvale Nordic

◀---▶ 6.5 km (4.1 mi) rtn

🕐: 1.5+hrs

👥: 2

Type of Trail: natural surface

Uses: walking, biking, cross-country skiing

⚠: none

📱: poor reception in some low areas

Facilities: benches, garbage cans, outhouses

Gov't Topo Map: 11L06 (North Rustico)

Trailhead GPS: N 46° 16.370' W 63° 25.410'

Access: From the junction of Highway 1 and Highway 2/Malpeque Road in Charlottetown, follow Highway 1 west for 4.7 km (2.9 mi). Turn right onto Highway 248, then left in 250 m/yd onto Highway 235/Kingston Road. Continue for 16.7 km (10.4 mi). Turn left onto Highway 13, and drive for 3.1 km (1.9 mi). Turn left, at #1800, onto a gravel road. Follow it for 800 m/yd to a parking lot beside the Nordic Centre. The trailhead is between the two main buildings.

Introduction: The Brookvale area is home to some of the most popular outdoor facilities on PEI. In the winter, the Brookvale Winter Activity Park offers downhill skiing, snowshoeing, and more than 24 km (15 mi) of cross-country (nordic) ski trails. When there is no snow, mountain bikers can traverse more than 40 km (25 mi) of single track.

Brookvale is criss-crossed by a complex, interconnected network of pathways, especially in the area used most often by mountain bikers. I have selected to profile a (hopefully) easy-to-follow loop that essentially follows the Red Route of the cross-country ski trails. This should serve as an introduction to the property, after which you can more confidently explore—and probably get confused among—the many other pathway options available.

Route Description: From the parking area, climb up to the Nordic Lodge and past the waxing hut, where you will find, on your right, a map of the trail network. From here, follow the Yellow Recreational Trail, which heads due south from the map along a broad, grassy track. To your left is the toboggan hill, while the forest is on your right.

In about 250 m/yd you reach the first junction, where there are many signs. Turn left, keeping on the Yellow route. You have two choices of path: one that leads behind the fringe of trees atop the toboggan hill or one that leads slightly to the right up a hill on a track mown through a grassy field. Both reconnect at the next junction—and there will be very many junctions on this trail—300 m/yd later, but the one on the toboggan hill offers the best view.

The sign at the next junction directs you straight, where you enter an area previously clear-cut area, now regenerating in trees. This meanders slightly downhill, and enters the forest in 175 m/yd. Keep straight, ignoring the side paths on the right. In 75 m/yd, you reach the third junction, with the Blue Route, where you turn right, and the trail begins to climb.

This is a lovely section of gorgeous hardwoods, although there are some spruce and even pine mixed in. Too soon—in 275 m/yd—the trail emerges into another regenerating area of smaller trees, and there is a trail heading right uphill. Continue straight here, and again 175 m/yd later when a groomer access road crosses. At this point, the path returns into older forest, which is now mostly conifers.

After another 150 m/yd, the trail turns sharply right, and other narrow tracks join on the left. Your climb also resumes, though not steeply. The forest hugs the path closely here, and

has a more remote feel than earlier in the walk. About 300 m/yd after the right turn, look to the left; you should be able to see a house, entirely off the grid, tucked among the trees.

The next junction is reached 150 m/yd later; keep straight. But turn left at the next intersection, only 75 m/yd further: keep on the Yellow route. Now you have an overhead canopy, as the trail is narrower. It is also no longer climbing. Your path crosses a grass-covered road, marked "Private Property," 100 m/yd later, and reaches a cultivated field 100 m/yd after that.

Turn right, and walk along the edge of the field; the trail re-enters the forest after 100 m/yd. Now in mostly hardwoods, the path begins to descend, the land higher on your left and lower to the right. This is an attractive section, and the trail meanders downhill for nearly 400 m/yd before making a sharp turn right. It also narrows considerably, and after passing between two tall maples, crosses an unrailed, rickety bridge.

Now the trail begins to climb, and for the first time, the treadway is soggy and soft. There are also distinct, and deep, ATV furrows. There is another sharp right turn in 150 m/yd, and the climb continues. Keep straight 75 m/yd later, when a wood road crosses. After this, the trail widens, and becomes drier. With the forest a mixture of hard and softwoods, you again are passing through another attractive section.

At the next junction, 300 m/ yd later, you reconnect with the Red route. Turn left, and left again less than 50 m/yd later. This is very wide—it is wide enough for five—and heading downhill again. It soon curves right and reaches the next junction after 250 m/yd.

The wide track, the Red route, heads right. Your path, the Yellow, heads left and is much narrower, lined by ferns. It descends to another simple bridge, 250 m/yd later, then climbs back, on the soggiest section yet, for the next 150 m/yd. But then the ground dries, the trail stabilizes, and the ruts disappear.

By the time an unsigned ATV trail connects on the left, about 150 m/yd further, you are walking through an attractive stand of hardwoods. You reach the crest of the hill 100 m/yd later, and the next junction 400 m/yd after that.

Keep left, as the very wide trail makes a long, gentle turn to the left. To your right you can see that you are near the edge of the forest. The next junction is in 200 m/yd; keep straight. Then turn left at the next intersection, just 25 m/yd later. On your right there is only a fringe of spruce separating the trail from a large field.

After a further 100 m/yd you reach

Destination Trails

Although there are many pleasant walking paths and scenic heritage roads in PEI, the province does not contain any true wilderness. However, there are a number of woodland areas where it is possible to access some of its more remote terrain. Island Trails, a volunteer, not-for-profit organization, has developed seven trail networks in places they consider to be worthwhile day-trip destinations. Their trailheads are signed similarly, and all are well marked with maps posted at all junctions.

Six of these trails are listed in this guide: Breadalbane Nature Trail, Boughton River, Dromore Woodland Trail, Gairloch Road, North Cape, and Winter River. The seventh, Forest Hill, was closed in 2014 for extensive maintenance work.

a major junction, where there are six directions to choose from. Make a 90° turn right, and follow the "medium" path back to the trailhead. This wide, grassy track follows a spruce-lined lane, with fields on the right and forest on the left. It is essentially straight, though with a few curves.

After walking 700 m/yd, you reach an intersection with a number of other routes: continue straight; you should be able to see the lodge. After a further 175 m/yd you reach the very first junction. Continue straight the remaining 250 m/yd to the trailhead.

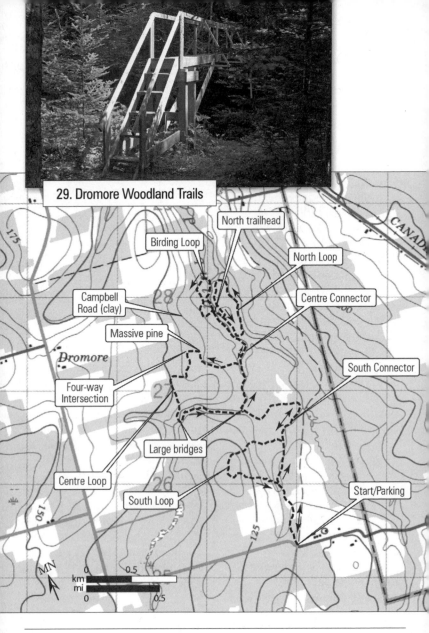

29. Dromore Woodland Trails

North trailhead

Birding Loop

North Loop

Campbell Road (clay)

Centre Connector

Massive pine

Dromore

Four-way Intersection

South Connector

Centre Loop

Large bridges

South Loop

Start/Parking

MN

km
mi

0   0.5

0   0.5

29. Dromore Woodland Trails

◄---► 16 km (10 mi) rtn

⏱: 4+hrs

🚶: 4 (distance)

Type of Trail: natural surface

Uses: walking, snowshoeing, cross-country skiing

⚠: none

👞: adequate mostly, but poor in gullies along the Pisquid River

Facilities: garbage can

Gov't Topo Map: 11L07 (Mount Stewart)

Trailhead GPS: N 46° 17.030' W 62° 49.080'

Access: From the Intersection of Highway 1 and Grafton Street in Charlottetown, cross the Hillsborough Bridge, following Highway 1 east for 12.5 km (7.8 mi). Turn left onto Highway 5, continuing for 11.75 km (7.3 mi). Turn left onto Highway 216/ Avondale Road. Drive 4.6 km (2.9 mi). At the intersection, the trailhead is directly ahead.

Introduction: One of the longest forest footpaths available on PEI, the Dromore Woodland Trails are situated in one of the largest wilderness areas in the province. These paths are also the island's section of the International Appalachian Trail, a network with links in Maine, Québec, and all the Atlantic provinces.

The numerous bridges on this trail are all in excellent shape, and most junctions have maps of the route and mark your position. Signage is usually quite good, so you should be able to hike this with confidence. But bring your mosquito repellent!

Route Description: There is a large signpost, featuring a map, at the trailhead, so you can see that this is a complicated, interconnected trail network. However, from the start, there is only one path, a narrow footpath that immediately heads into the surrounding forest.

For the next 900+ m/yd, to the first junction, you should enjoy a pleasant woodland walk. The forest cloaks the pathway, providing shade and a green curtain to either side. Meanwhile, the trail meanders between the trees, crossing the occasional small structure over wet spots. It is mostly through softwoods, but there is one major area where the alders and raspberries nearly choke off the path.

When I walked this, only occasional orange flagging tape marked the route.

Fortunately, there is a small map conveniently positioned at the junction, showing your position. Continue straight; it is only 650 m/yd to the next junction, where you will find the next map. This time the path runs parallel to a small creek, so the ground is often spongy and wet.

Again, continue straight, leaving the South Loop and following the South Connector. This follows the creek another 200 m/yd, then turns left and crosses it over a railed bridge. It resumes following the brook, but this is now to your right. Expect lots of boggy sphagnum moss in the treadway. After 150 m/yd, the trail turns left again, leaving the brook.

At first you are among spruce, the trail a brown line craved through bright green moss. However, the vegetation changes, and as the trail curves continuously, you emerge into an open area 400 m/yd later. In summer, ferns almost hide the path. Except for a brief wooded—and very soggy—interlude, you continue in low vegetation until you cross a road 450 m/yd further.

After another 125 m/yd of low, dense hardwoods, you reach more mature forest. That is because you have arrived at the Pisquid River, where there is a steep slope down to the water. About 25 m/yd later you reach the junction with the Centre Loop; turn right. The path works along the slope, descending, with the aid of a rope, to an elaborate bridge crossing the river just 65 m/yd further.

Cross, and turn right. Your path now follows the river, quite close, as it bubbles its way toward the ocean. You have a pleasant 800 m/yd alongside the Pisquid before you reach the next junction. Again, there is a map marking your location. Keep right, and walk along on the Centre Connector.

Actually, the trail continues to follow the river, on the top of a low slope above the water. This forest is pleasant, taller trees providing good shade. However, the river is often obscured by thickets of alders. After 700 m/yd, the footpath moves onto a former wood road, so your route is much wider. And 100 m/yd further, you reach the North Trailhead, #429 Campbell Road.

Two loops begin from this spot. Keep right, follow the Campbell Road, crossing the river. As soon as you are across, turn right onto a footpath; this is the North Loop. The Pisquid River is still on the right, but now you are heading upstream. After some quite wet spots, this meanders along a slope facing the river, sometimes more than 5 m/yd above the water.

After nearly 600 m/yd, the path curves away from the river and re-

crosses the Campbell Road. It drops down a gentle slope to resume its track alongside a creek, but a different one. Your path works along the slope, higher ground to the left. Over the next 700 m/yd you follow the creek; then, shortly after crossing a bridge, the trail makes a sharp left turn and heads up toward the top of the hill.

From here, the path meanders along the hillside for another 200 m/yd, then turns nearly 180° left, almost back on itself, and drops back down the gentle slope. You return to the Pisquid River, which you follow to the Campbell Road, in 500 m/yd.

Turn right, and head back over the bridge. On your right, as soon as you

cross, is the entrance to the Birding Loop. I quite liked this portion of the trail. It is only 1.3 km (0.8 mi) long, but it follows the brook (at first), has a few nice bridges and then wanders up a hillside through some attractive woodland.

It returns to the Campbell Road about 200 m/yd from the North Trailhead sign, which is to the left. Once there, retrace the 800 m/yd Centre Connector back to the junction with the Centre Loop. Turn right here. This heads away from the river and into a mixed forest. For the next 600 m/yd it wanders through feature-less forest. The trail then enters an area of tall pine, where it turns sharply right. Less than 150 m/yd later you reach the foot of a massive pine.

The trail turns left, and in 225 m/yd it reaches an open four-way intersection. Fortunately, a large "Trail" sign with an arrow directs you left, back into the woods. You have another meandering 550 m/yd before you cross a grass-covered road, then a further 550 m/yd of wooded walk before you descend a significant ravine to reach the elaborate bridge that crosses the Pisquid River, 150 m/yd later.

The next section was my favourite of the system, as the trail follows the river, working up and down the steep-sided ravine bordering it. For the next 1.3 km (0.8 mi), until you reach the junction with the South Connector, the path often demands considerable effort as it climbs 10-15 m/yd up and down the slope.

At the junction, turn right and return the 1.4 km (0.9 mi) to the junction with the South Loop. Turn right again, crossing a small creek (on a miniature bridge). After passing through a stand of white spruce, the path reaches a small, attractive meadow 125 m/yd later. But then it returns beneath the trees, and remains there for the remainder of the walk. The trees gradually transition from softwoods to hardwoods, although you will pass one large white pine.

For the next 2 km (1.25 mi), the trail roams through the trees. You receive warning that you are near the end when you reach an area of thick alders and grasses. A small one-rail bridge conveys you across the small creek, and 75 m/yd later you reach the intersection. Keep right one last time, and retrace the initial 900 m/yd back to the trailhead.

30. Gairloch Road

◄---► 7.5 km (4.7 mi) rtn
🕐: 2+hrs
🏃: 2
Type of Trail: natural surface
Uses: walking, biking, snowshoeing

⚠: none
🔧: adequate throughout
Facilities: benches
Gov't Topo Map: 11L02 (Montague)

Trailhead GPS: N 46° 2.313' W 62° 49.305'

Access: From the intersection of Highway 1 and Grafton Street in Charlottetown, cross the Hillsborough Bridge, following Highway 1 east for 35 km (21.9 mi). Turn left onto Highway 5, continuing for 11.75 km (7.3 mi). Turn left onto Highway 207/Garfield Road and drive 7.9 km (4.9 mi). Turn left onto Highway 204/Gairloch Road and follow it for 1.4 km (0.9 mi). Park on the right, where the Confederation Trail crosses the road: #2205 Gairloch Road.

Introduction: This trail system is another of the Island Trails designated "Destination Trails." It is located in a mostly wooded area, and is probably as remote as it is possible to be in PEI. This trail system is essentially one large loop, although, because it is also intended for mountain biking, it curves and twists much more than the usual footpath.

Although the bridges are excellent,

and there are even a few benches, I would not recommend this trail for families with small children. Some comfort with navigation or map reading might also be helpful. However, I quite enjoyed the hilly, uneven terrain and winding route.

Route Description: From the parking area, walk about 25 m/yd along the Confederation Trail. A footpath descends into the woods to your left, and there is a small map posted there. This well-defined track gently drops through the young spruce, well marked by flagging tape, to a bridge 500 m/yd from the Confederation Trail. The frequent and sometimes tight turns provide warning of what much of this trail will be like.

Once across the very wide bridge you encounter a junction, the start of the loop, where there is another map. Turn left, heading clockwise, up the uneven hill. Somewhat surprisingly,

the treadway contains many tree roots, making it somewhat rough. Of course, the trees are almost entirely spruce and fir, and the track is often a brown path cut through the green mosses on either side. There are also, near the start, several informal paths that separate and reconnect frequently.

The trail climbs, moving into a plantation of red pine, then back into spruce. It twists its way for 550 m/yd until it crosses an old wood road, close to Gairloch Road, where there is another map indicating your position. Heading back into white spruce, the trail turns sharply right, and works its curving route distinctly downhill for 425 m/yd before veering sharply left, then right, and dropping—almost steeply—into a little gully.

It soon climbs out, reaching a tall pine, where there is a bench, less than 100 m/yd later. The path re-turns into the gully, climbing out 175 m/yd later on a short, steep slope. At the top, you connect to a former wood road, and the climb is much more gradual. About 200 m/yd after you begin this climb, you reach a spot where many of the surrounding trees are decorated with old buckets. You might first think, "Maple syrup!" but all the trees are spruce.

The path repeatedly drops into, and climbs out of, this gully. So you will have plenty of opportunity for hill work—unusual in PEI. After at least seven visits into this gully, you reach a significant bridge, and a bench, about 600 m/yd from the buckets. After this, the trail runs fairly straight until you reach a junction, where there is a map, and a bench, 225 m/yd further. Gairloch Road is to the left; turn right, continuing on the loop. You have walked nearly 3 km (1.9 mi).

The trail plunges back through and across the gully. After 250 m/yd, in sight of a house, the trail turns right almost 180° and climbs to connect with a forest road 200 m/yd later. There is a map here, and a bench, again beneath a tall pine, situated shortly before the road.

You now enjoy a long straight section, the trail bordered by young

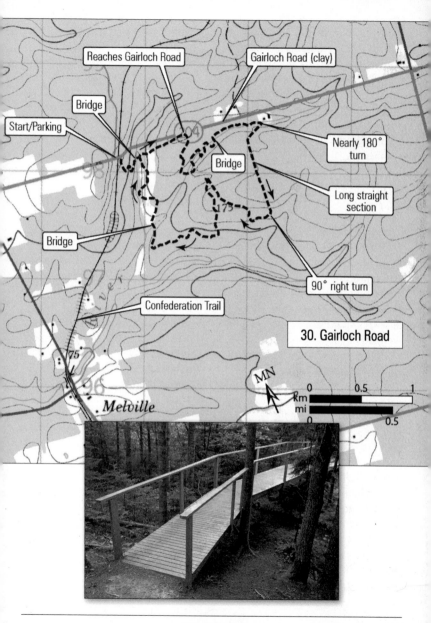

Reaches Gairloch Road

Gairloch Road (clay)

Bridge

Start/Parking

Nearly 180° turn

Bridge

Long straight section

Bridge

90° right turn

Confederation Trail

30. Gairloch Road

MN

0   0.5   1
km
mi
0   0.5

Melville

birch and other hardwoods, for nearly 600 m/yd. The road continues, but the map directs you sharply right, onto another, though less distinct, forest road. Watch carefully, because 160 m/yd later the trail leaves this road and turns right, into thick forest, on a narrow, uneven footpath. There is another map here.

This winding track is the roughest section yet, and you might wonder how mountain bikers could fit through this narrow passage. After 425 m/yd, this reaches the end of another wood road, an open area where there is a map. But your path heads into a beautiful red pine forest, where a further 275 m/yd of meandering is required before you reach the next checkpoint, a T-junction on another wood road.

Again, there is a map that indicates your position. Turn left, keeping straight for 350 m/yd, as the path gently descends. Watch for the map, on the right, which is the direction you turn. Although this shows as a wood road, it is so overgrown that it appears more like a footpath through the brush. But this, too, is fairly level and straight, though with a few turns, and continues thus for 525 m/yd.

When you reach a bench, though with no map, your route turns right and returns to being a rough footpath. Though the trees are young and densely packed, the trail is well marked with flagging tape. From here, the path descends to reach a bridge over the Flat River North, 300 m/yd later.

Once across, the trail climbs back up the hillside, through attractive young pine, connecting to another wood road in 200 m/yd. Follow the distinct track through the low vegetation for 125 m/yd; to your left is a map, and a well-defined path heading back into the forest.

The trail resumes its snaking course, working up and down the hilly terrain. To your left is lower ground, and you might occasionally hear or catch glimpses of the Flat River North there. After an additional 825 m/yd of woodland wandering, you reach the junction at the first bridge you crossed. Turn left, and retrace the 525 m/yd back to the trailhead.

31. McKenna Scenic Heritage Road

◄╍╍╍► 9.5 km (6 mi) rtn

🕐: 2.5+ hrs

👤: 2

Type of Trail: compacted earth

Uses: walking, biking, ATVing, horseback riding, snowshoeing, cross-country skiing, snowmobiling

⚠: vehicle traffic

🗪: adequate throughout

Facilities: none

Gov't Topo Map: 11L06 (North Rustico)

Trailhead GPS: N 46° 15.445′ W 63° 26.520′

Access: From the junction of Highway 1 and Highway 2/Malpeque Road in Charlottetown, follow Highway 1 west for 4.7 km (2.9 mi). Turn right onto Highway 248, then left in 250 m/yd onto Highway 235/Kingston Road. Continue for 16.7 km (10.4 mi). Turn left onto Highway 13, and drive for 5.1 km (3.2 mi). Turn left onto Highway 246/South Melville Road and drive for 1.5 km (0.9 mi). McKenna Road is on the left. Park near the intersection without obstructing traffic.

Introduction: Often cited as one of the best hikes in Prince Edward Island, this route is not even a trail, but officially still a road. It is named for Hugh McKenna, a property owner in the area, and was constructed in 1904. However, its designation as a scenic heritage road means that it is preserved very much as it was when its primary traffic was horse-drawn carts or local farm equipment.

Expect a pleasant stroll beneath a sheltering overhead canopy of towering hardwoods and softwoods, cooling breezes, and sunlight dappled on the road's surface by the surrounding leaves. The McKenna Road is particularly popular in the fall, when the magnificent colours of the many maples and other hardwoods fashion a festive forest decoration.

Route Description: The road does not look very promising at first: wide, without any tall trees bordering it, and surrounded by broad fields. For the first 400 m/yd, it descends more than 30 m/yd to cross the vegetation-choked DeSable River. On the opposite side of the bridge, the road forks; keep left.

Things soon look better as your path curves slightly left and begins

Sugar Maple

It might be fair to state that no deciduous tree is valued more than the sugar maple, which is found throughout PEI in every hardwood forest. Growing as high as 35 m/yd, and ornamented with its iconic pointed leaves, the sugar maple is one of the most colourful trees in the fall, and in the spring it is the major source of the sap required for making maple syrup.

Sugar maple is also used for furniture and other forest products. A long-lived tree, and common in mature forests, extensive sugar maple stands are found whenever soil conditions permit. It is also often found in the company of yellow birch, oak, beech, and red maple.

to climb. After another farm road branches to the left, about 500 m/yd from the start, the McKenna Road rapidly narrows, with the trees on either side becoming both taller and closer. Instead of ditches, there are embankments on both sides, the road becoming a sunken lane between them. No electrical wires, or poles, are

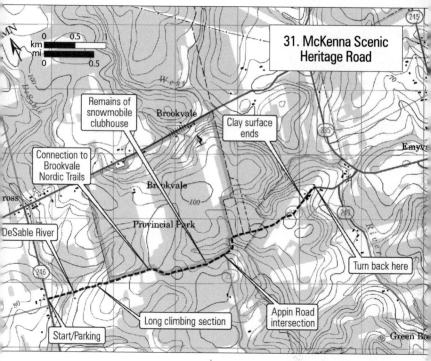

in sight. The clay surface of the road adds a distinctive PEI aspect.

There is no overhead canopy yet, but significant shade, which will be welcome as you begin to climb. For the next 650 m/yd, until the road nearly levels, the climb is quite pronounced. There are cultivated fields on both sides, with frequent access points along the way. However, these fields are private property, so do not venture into them.

By this point, the forest canopy has almost completely changed to hard-woods: maple, beech, and birch. The road continues straight for another 600 m/yd, still gradually climbing. As it does, the bordering embankments diminish in height, never quite disappearing, but less of an obstacle and more like trimming.

At 1.75 km (1.1 mi), the straight section ends at an intersection. To your right, the fields that have accompanied the entire walk finish, and there is vehicle access here. Left is another track, which leads, in about 50 m/yd, to Brookvale Nordic's trails.

McKenna Road curves to the right, and begins to gently descend. The climb from DeSable Brook, to this point, has been more than 50 m/yd.

It is another 1.25 km (0.8 mi) to the intersection with the Appin Road. En route, you are veiled by a lush overhead canopy. The road curves first right, then straightens again, undulating across the gently rolling terrain. At 2.65 km (1.7 mi), there are the remains of a cabin—the local snowmobile clubhouse—on the left; it burnt down in January 2015. And 50 m/yd before Appin Road, also on the left, there is a metal gate blocking an old, grassy road.

Although signs for restaurants direct you right, along the Appin Road, resist the temptation; they are further away than you wish to walk. McKenna Road soon curves left, and drops to cross a small brook. This is followed by the most aggressive climb of the walk, nearly 40 m/yd in only 350 m/yd. Near the top, a road sign directs ATV traffic left at a prominent intersection.

Keep straight. A gentle climb continues for another 150 m/yd before the road levels, followed by another 200 m/yd of undulations before the unmistakable descent. Overgrown side tracks are frequent, but should cause no confusion. The predominantly maple canopy, in fall, is a riot of colour.

You continue a forest stroll for 700 m/yd from the intersection before you notice a field, and fence, to the right. Within 200 m/yd, there are fields on both sides of McKenna Road, and you can see the first buildings ahead. After another 200 m/yd, you reach a driveway to a house on your left, and in another 100 m/yd the marvellous red-clay surface is replaced by asphalt.

But before you turn back, walk a little further, just past the large barns on your right. You will gain as scenic a pastoral view as Prince Edward Island can offer anywhere, of the various working farms bordering the West River, which flows below your vantage point (See picture on pp. 178-179).

You have walked 4.75 km (3 mi). Retrace your route to return.

32. Pigot's Trail

◄---► 5.3 km (3.3 mi) rtn

⏱: 1+hrs

👟: 1

Type of Trail: crushed stone, compacted earth, natural surface

Uses: walking, biking*, snowshoeing, cross-country skiing, snowmobiling*

⚠: road crossings, hunting

🎒: adequate throughout

Facilities: benches, garbage cans, interpretive panels, picnic tables, washrooms

Gov't Topo Map: 11L07 (Mount Stewart)

Trailhead GPS: N 46° 21.980' W 62° 52.225'

Access: From the junction of Highway 1 and Highway 2/Malpeque Road in Charlottetown, follow Highway 1 east for 3.3 km (2.1 mi). Turn left onto Highway 2, driving for 23.1 km (14.4 mi) to the community of Mount Stewart. Turn right onto Highway 22/Main Street. In 350 m/yd, the road crosses Confederation Trail. Turn right and park in the lot of the Hillsborough River Eco-Centre.

Introduction: This Mount Stewart Wildlife Management Area protects wetlands along the upper reaches of the Hillsborough River. Pigot's Trail visits the Allisary Creek Impoundment, which is a significant component of this conservation zone.

Expect to sight a wide variety of waterfowl, as well as the warblers and other small birds that inhabit dense thickets. Eagles regularly hunt along the Hillsborough River, and small aquatic mammals, such as beaver and muskrat, are also commonly observed.

The actual Pigot's Trail is fairly short, so I have added a little of the Confederation Trail to extend the walk, and started this walk from an easier trailhead that has many more amenities.

Route Description: The Hillsborough River Eco-Centre is situated at the junction of two branches of the Confederation Trail. Do not take the section facing the parking area. Instead, follow the one running behind the building, which crosses Main Street at its intersection with Smith Street. From here, it is a pleasant stroll through the middle of the community of Mount Stewart, on a mostly grass-covered track, passing

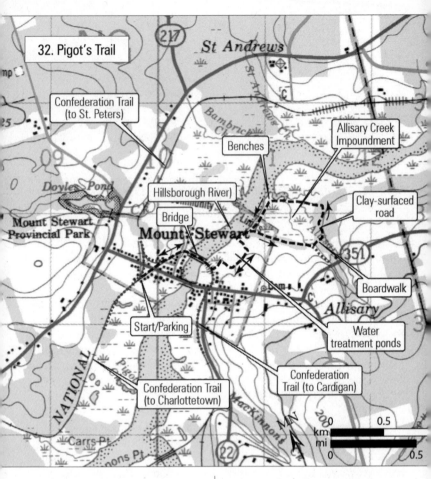

32. Pigot's Trail

Confederation Trail (to St. Peters)

Allisary Creek Impoundment

Benches

Clay-surfaced road

Hillsborough River)

Bridge

Doyles Pond

Mount Stewart Provincial Park

Mount Stewart

Boardwalk

Start/Parking

Water treatment ponds

Allisary

NATIONAL

Confederation Trail (to Charlottetown)

Confederation Trail (to Cardigan)

Carrs Pt

km

mi

0.5

0

0.5

quite close to many houses and crossing the occasional quiet street.

By the time you reach the long bridge crossing the Hillsborough River, you will have walked about 500 m/yd, and had the opportunity to read at least one interpretive panel.

Continue across, and after another 250 m/yd you will be quite close to a gravel road, on the left. Leave the Confederation Trail; you will see a sign directing you toward Pigot's Trail.

Follow the gravel road for about

100 m/yd. Directly ahead of you is a large water treatment pond, surrounded by a fence. Heading right, tracing a route around it, is a clay road; follow that. Hopefully, you wore a hat, because for the next 400 m/yd this road crosses a broad field that offers no shade.

As the road approaches the river, there are several tracks cut through the tall grass. Keep right, leaving the road, and follow the broad, grass-surfaced route to the treeline 25 m/yd away. Turn right, and continue along the grassy pathway, thick trees and river to the left, the field on your right.

For about 100 m/yd this is straight. Just before reaching the riverbank, it curves right. Only 25 m/yd further there is a junction, although I actually missed it when I walked this trail. So do what I did, and continue straight, once again with dense vegetation lining your left, a broad field, on your right, with a thin strip of trees in between. This field borders the trail for the next 500 m/yd, where you will find a "Trail" sign, just before the path enters a thicket.

You are in this grove barely 25 m/yd before the path re-emerges onto another field, where a boardwalk conveys you across a soggy area. The route continues along the bottom of this field, and in 100 m/yd you will reach another junction. Turn left, onto a narrow footpath heading closer to thick vegetation and the marsh, which is to the left.

Just before re-entering the woods, there is another, longer boardwalk, as the ground in this area is very wet. For the next 200 m/yd, the trail meanders among the thick spruce, with frequent puncheons (small boardwalks) traversing the worst wet spots.

The path enters onto a broad clay-surfaced road, where you turn left. As you walk along here, there will be infrequent glimpses of the marshland to the left. Follow this road 250 m/yd, to its end at a large clearing that appears to serve as a parking area. At the far end of this a smaller but still vehicle-passable track continues, curving left.

You have walked nearly 2.5 km (1.6 mi), and are about to begin the best part of this walk.

Ducks Unlimited

Ducks Unlimited Canada is a national not-for-profit, formed in 1938, that has worked to conserve, restore, and manage wetlands (bogs, fens, marshes, swamps, and shallow/open water). In its history, the organization has conserved 2.5 million ha (6.2 million ac) and completed over 9,000 habitat conservation projects.

In PEI, Ducks Unlimited has worked in cooperation with the provincial government, local conservation groups, and private landowners to restore and preserve more than 100 separate wetland areas, particularly in the eastern part of the province. The Allisary Creek wetland is one of the largest.

Once past a metal gate, the trail traverses an earthen embankment that impounds a large wetland and pool of open water. There is water and marsh on both sides of this fairly wide levee, but the treadway is dry and covered in grass. However, the trees growing on it are low and not very thick, so there is little shade.

This pool, the Allisary Creek Impoundment, is an important component of the Mount Stewart Wildlife Management Area, and is co-managed with Ducks Unlimited. Home to many species of waterfowl, it is a popular destination for birders.

The trail continues straight for 500 m/yd until it reaches the Hillsborough River, near the mouth of Allisary Creek, which is on your right. There is an open area in this corner, hosting two benches. The path turns 90° left, and continues along another embankment a further 350 m/yd, where it reconnects at the first junction—the one I missed earlier. You have walked about 3.9 km (2.4 mi).

From here, turn right, and retrace the 1.4 km (0.9 mi) back to the Hillsborough River Eco-Centre.

33. Port-la-Joye — Fort Amherst National Historic Site of Canada

◄---► 4.25 km (2.7 mi) rtn

🕐: 1+hrs

👣: 1

Type of Trail: crushed stone

Uses: walking, snowshoeing

⚠️: cliffs, road crossings

📱: adequate throughout

Facilities: benches, garbage cans, interpretive panels, outhouses, picnic tables

Gov't Topo Map: 11L03 (Charlottetown)

Trailhead GPS: N 46° 11.723' W 63° 8.139'

Access: From the junction of Highway 1 and Highway 2/Malpeque Road in Charlottetown, follow Highway 1 west for 8.5 km (5.3 mi). Turn right onto Highway 19 and continue for 16.8 km (10.5 mi). Turn left onto Blockhouse Road, and drive for 400 m/yd. Turn left onto Hache Gallant Drive and continue to the upper parking area 750 m/yd away.

Introduction: Port-la-Joye — Fort Amherst National Historic Site of Canada is the location of eighteenth-century forts built by both the French and the English. The remnants of the forts' earthworks are quite prominent, and sit atop a hill dominating the entrance to Charlottetown Harbour.

The trails have recently been upgraded, and are in excellent condition. Benches and picnic tables can be found everywhere, and there are many interpretive panels, particularly near the fort. This is a scenic location, and ideal for a family stroll.

Route Description: From the parking area, head toward the multipurpose centre. From there turn right, following the crushed-stone pathway — Survey Lane — across the road toward a small, white building. Wide, grassy fields surround you, punctuated by occasional large trees. Survey Lane passes the building, then gently descends a hillside. Ahead lie the blue waters of Hillsborough Bay.

About 350 m/yd from the start, the trail reaches the lower parking area. Off to the left you should see a sandstone sculpture; head to that. It is surrounded by interpretive panels, picnic tables, and flowers (in season). Keep left, along the Skmagan Trail, which heads toward the ocean. In

200 m/yd, you reach the water, where there is a small beach area. You will notice from this point there is a small cliff along this entire stretch of shore, posted with prominent warning signs.

You also connect with the Coastal Forest Path, which joins from the left. Keep straight, following Skmagan as it passes through a forested area, emerging 200 m/yd later at its intersection with Alliance Alley: trail #4. You are presented with another large field, and your first view of the city of Charlottetown, across Charlottetown Harbour.

Continue on this route, as it traces the curve of the coastline. You have a completely unobstructed, grand view of the water, and although the trail is set back more than 20 m/yd from the edge of the shoreline, there is no need to be closer. There are numerous benches along here, testament to the superb vista. After 150 m/yd, trail

#2 (DePensens Path) connects on the left, and 300 m/yd beyond that, trail #1. Continue another 100 m/yd to the small lighthouse. From here, you can see a footpath through the grass leading to a small sandy beach, should you want to dip your toes.

Return to trail #1, the Old Harbour Path, and walk uphill. In 150 m/yd, near the crest, you reach an interpretive panel. To your right are the earthworks of the fort. Your route continues in front of these earthworks, where there are tables, benches, and more interpretive panels. Trail #2 connects just before you reach a large monument, topped with a cross, to "The Grand Derangement," the deportation of the Acadians, 100 m/yd later.

From here, the path curves around the earthworks, and continues toward the upper parking area. You may wish to make a side trip into the middle of the fort's remains. Just before reaching the parking lot, you arrive at an intersection with Alliance Alley, on the left, and the Warren Farm Path. Dead ahead are two flags, one on either side of a large interpretive panel.

Turn right; your route leads away from the water, and into the lands that were farmed by the earliest inhabitants of Ile Royale. For the first 600 m/yd continue straight, ignoring the tempting options to your right

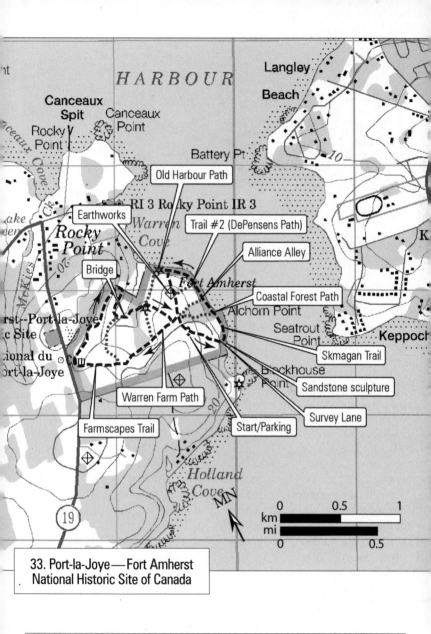

HARBOUR

Langley
Beach

Canceaux
Spit
Canceaux
Point

Rocky
Point

Battery Pt

Old Harbour Path

RI 3 Rocky Point IR 3

Earthworks

Warren
Cove

Trail #2 (DePensens Path)

Rocky
Point

Alliance Alley

Bridge

Fort Amherst

Coastal Forest Path

Alchorn Point

rst--Port-la-Joye
c Site

Seatrout
Point

Keppoch

Skmagan Trail

ional du
rt-la-Joye

Blockhouse
Point

Sandstone sculpture

Warren Farm Path

Survey Lane

Farmscapes Trail

Start/Parking

Holland
Cove

MN

| 0 | 0.5 | 1 |
km
mi
| 0 | | 0.5 |

33. Port-la-Joye—Fort Amherst
National Historic Site of Canada

19

at 50 m/yd and 250 m/yd. Enjoy the open fields, as the path descends into a small treed area, and another junction.

Keep straight, now on the Farmscapes Trail. For another 400 m/yd this climbs slightly, then turns sharply right, just before reaching Highway 19. For the next 750 m/yd, the path wanders along the hillside, along the edge of a forested area, with open fields on your right. Just when it looks as if you are going to reach some houses, the trail makes a long sweeping curve to the right, and drops to reach a junction, beside a creek, 200 m/yd later.

You cross the creek, on a very sturdy bridge, and enter a thick spruce forest. The trail, wide and in excellent condition, curls among the trees for a little more than 200 m/yd. It emerges at a four-way intersection. To your left is the lighthouse you first visited; to the right is another small light station. But keep straight, heading up the hill on your way back to the upper parking lot.

You climb up the hillside, the low mound of Fort Amherst's earthworks on the left. In 250 m/yd you connect with the Warren Farm Path in sight of the parking area. Turn left, and complete the final 75 m/yd.

27. Breadalbane Nature Trail

Eastern Larch

Also known as tamarack, Alaska larch, and American larch, the eastern larch is the most distinctive conifer; every fall, it sheds its needles, and in the spring it blossoms in tiny purple flowers.

Often the first species to grow in bogs and other wetlands, the larch is one of the dominant tree species of the northern boreal forest. The First Nations peoples used its roots to sew birchbark strips into their canoes, while the bark had medicinal uses. Some claim that the gummy sap, when chewed, is as sweet as maple sugar.

28. Brookvale Nordic

30. Gairloch Road

32. Pigot's Trail

MOUNT STEWART
WILDLIFE
MANAGEMENT
AREA

PIGOTS TRAIL →

Prince
Edward
Island

Village
of
Mount Stewart

Acadian Deportation

The story of the deportation of the Acadian population of Nova Scotia in 1755 is well known, thanks to the poetry of Henry Wadsworth Longfellow. Less familiar is the deportation of the French population of Île Saint-Jean — Prince Edward Island — that took place in 1758 following the English capture of the fortress of Louisbourg.

Of the 4,600 Acadian residents of the island, more than 3,000 were rounded up and shipped to France in the late fall. Storms sank three of these ships, while disease aboard the others claimed more lives. It is estimated that more than 1,600 people lost their lives during the crossing.

33. Port-la-Joye — Fort Amherst National Historic Site of Canada

Great blue heron

Potato blossoms

Ruffed Grouse

At risk of a heart attack? Then be careful while hiking on any wooded trail, because if you pass close to a ruffed grouse it is likely to remain very still until you are almost upon it, then explode into noisy flight through the brush.

However, in the spring, should you appear to threaten her brood of chicks, a mother grouse might charge toward you, puffing her feathers to double her normal size and hissing menacingly. Since we are talking about a small bird that looks like a wild chicken, your risk of injury is small (although it does look intimidating).

The ruffed grouse is not migratory, so it might be encountered at any time of year. It is relatively abundant and a popular game bird. In fact, one of its Latin names, *Bonasa*, means "good when roasted."

36. Winter River

Eastern Hemlock

The eastern hemlock prefers shade, cool and humid climates, and rainfalls exceeding 750 mm (29 in) a year. In these convivial conditions, the long-lived hemlock can reach heights exceeding 50 m (164 ft) in the Appalachians, although 30 m (100 ft) is more common in Canada.

Hemlocks can live up to 600 years, and during that time will create a pure stand that crowds out other species. In an old stand, often found on the north-facing slope of a steeper hillside, with a canopy high overhead, the ground beneath the towering trees supports no other life than mosses and lichens.

34. Strathgartney Provincial Park

◄---► 9 km (5.6 mi) rtn

⏱ : 2.5+hrs

🚶 : 4 (navigation)

Type of Trail: asphalt, natural surface

Uses: walking, biking*, horseback riding*, snowshoeing

⚠ : navigation

📷 : adequate throughout

Facilities: benches, garbage cans, outhouses, picnic tables

Gov't Topo Map: 11L03 (Charlottetown)

Trailhead GPS: N 46º 13.010' W 63º 20.115'

Access: From the junction of Highway 1 and Highway 2/Malpeque Road in Charlottetown, follow Highway 1 west for 18 km (11.25 mi). The park entrance is on the left. Park in the lot outside the gates.

Introduction: Strathgartney Provincial Park, opened in 1959 on 53 ha (131 ac) in the central hills of PEI, is respected for its scenic position along the deep, wooded ravines bordering the West River. Officially open from mid-June to mid-September, its trails are most popular in the fall, when its resplendent hardwoods sport their vivid colours.

Even if the park is open, I recommend starting from the gates at Highway 2. The grounds are so lovely, they should be enjoyed.

I have rated this route as being suitable for experienced people because of the challenges of successful-ly navigating the plethora of possible routes near the golf course.

Route Description: From the gates, follow the road to the far end of the asphalt, about 650 m/yd. You will pass picnic tables, benches, a playground, park buildings, and even a Frisbee golf course. To the left, across a field and lower than the road, you will see a white trellis at the forest edge. Walk toward this; as you approach you will see that it is labelled "Nature Trail."

The route becomes an uneven footpath as soon as you enter the forest, which is mostly tall hardwoods. A well-defined track crosses a bridge, and immediately climbs. Tree roots and a surprising number of rocks intrude into the treadway, but there is good shade and very little understory, so you can see a fair distance.

After about 200 m/yd uphill, along a fairly straight path, you reach the

crest, where shortly afterwards an adjacent tree is signed "Striped Maple". About 200 m/yd later, just when you probably first sight the West River, on the left and considerably lower, the trail curves right.

It descends to river level, reaching the water in 350 m/yd. During the descent, the path works down the steep slope, providing excellent views of the river valley. On this hillside, softwoods are more common. There are also several more numbered signposts, but a few appeared to be missing.

Within 50 m/yd of reaching water level—well, perhaps still 2 metres/yards above—you reach a junction with an interesting choice. Turning right returns you to Strathgartney Park Trailhead. But directly ahead is

the Goat Trail, which cautions about steep grades. How could anyone resist? Straight ahead, of course!

This route is now more challenging. It continues to follow the river, heading upstream. It is narrower, the ground is more rugged, and the vegetation surrounding the path is both denser and crowds the edges. But it is also quite tranquil. The river is very close, and there are several opportunities to access the water. No human habitation is visible on the far bank, nor are there any automobile noises, even though the Trans-Canada Highway is less than 2 km (1.25 mi) distant.

This is a lovely walk, scenic and serene. After 600 m/yd, the narrow path curves sharply right, still following the course of the river, and within 150 m/yd it begins to climb. This provides increasingly better views of the valley to your left, but becomes progressively steeper. About 400 m/yd after you began to climb, you are at least 30 m/yd above the river, and have had to scramble the last few metres/yards.

The trail moves out of sight of the water, climbing inland to reach the next junction 350 m/yd later. Turn left, heading toward the Equestrian Park and Bonshaw Bridge. At a higher elevation, we are back in a hardwood forest. Evidence of mountain bike use, such as jumps, will be encountered.

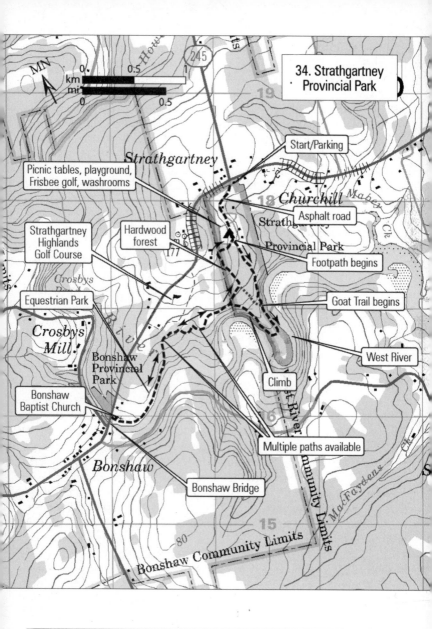

MN

0   0.5   1
km
mi
0   0.5

34. Strathgartney Provincial Park

Strathgartney

Start/Parking

Picnic tables, playground, Frisbee golf, washrooms

Churchill

Asphalt road

Strathgartney

Provincial Park

Strathgartney Highlands Golf Course

Hardwood forest

Footpath begins

Goat Trail begins

Crosbys

Equestrian Park

Crosbys Mill

Bonshaw Provincial Park

West River

Climb

Bonshaw Baptist Church

Multiple paths available

Bonshaw

Bonshaw Bridge

MacFaydens

15

80

Bonshaw Community Limits

After 250 m/yd, the path reaches the edge of the forest, turning left to work around the open ground. You might even notice a low, moss-covered stone wall among the trees. For the next 1 km (0.6 mi), the path will remain close to these fields on the right: the Strathgartney Highlands Golf Course. However, be careful, because mountain bikers have cut many interconnecting paths through this hilly terrain, and it will be easy to become confused. Watch for flagging tape to keep on the correct route, which leaves a wood road, to the left, at about 3.8 km (2.4 mi), and heads downhill toward the river.

The trail meanders across the hillside, through healthy woodland. About 250 m/yd after leaving the wood road, another track connects on the right, and 125 m/yd later the trail reaches water level. West River can be seen to the left.

Just 75 m/yd later, the trail comes out of the woods and crosses a large field. This is the Equestrian Park, and your route, while remaining close to the edge of the forest, crosses the grass and works around several horse jumps. To your right, uphill, are more of the park's facilities, including its buildings and parking area.

The footpath is clearly imprinted in the grass, and continues between jumps 12 and 13. It makes a brief detour to the left, into a wooded area where there are glimpses of the river, then returns to pass jumps 14 and some others.

Just past jump 15, about 650 m/yd after entering the Equestrian Park, the trail leaves the field and returns to forest, curving right. Traffic noises are very loud. After another 200 m/yd, the trail ends, in a parking area beside the Bonshaw Bridge. The river is just a few paces to the left. On the right is the Bonshaw Baptist Church.

You have walked 5 km (3.1 mi). Retrace your route the 2.5 km (1.6 mi) through the Equestrian Park, past the golf course, and back to the intersection reached when the trail climbed from the river. If you enjoyed the walk along the river, turn right, and retrace the remainder of your route back to the trailhead.

Otherwise, continue straight toward Strathgartney Park, along a different path. This path goes through a hardwood forest to reach another signed junction less than 50 m/yd later. Turn left—to the right the path goes downhill for 300 m/yd to the first junction—and head uphill.

This climb is through the most scenic forested portion of the entire walk. The entire hillside, with few exceptions, are hardwoods with no understory. Their layer of leaves suffuses everything with a green tinge. When I walked it, the gentle rustle of the leaves swaying in the breeze and

the sweet quaver of thrushes were the only sounds.

This might also be the longest climb on Prince Edward Island, particularly if you started from the river. It grinds uphill for more than 400 m/yd, passing posts 13, 14, and near the top, 15.

About 525 m/yd from the junction, you reach post 16, which indicates that the buildings you can see through the trees on the left are the Strathgartney Homestead. But the trail curves right, and begins to descend. After a further 150 m/yd walking through the appealing hardwoods,

the trail ends; there is even a sign that says so.

You emerge from the forest on the grassy field near the end of the asphalt. Head there, and retrace the final 650 m/yd back to the park entrance.

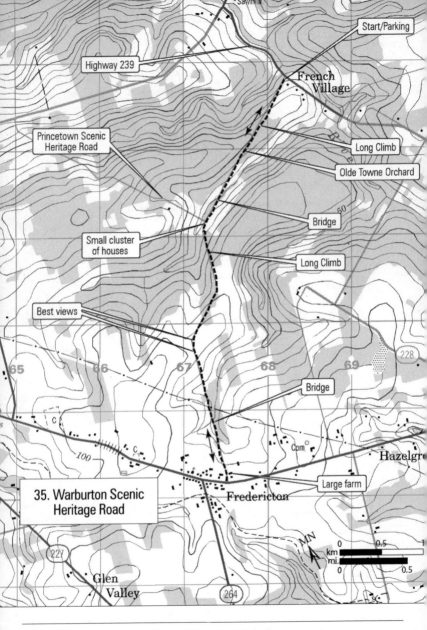

Start/Parking

French Village

Highway 239

Long Climb

Olde Towne Orchard

Princetown Scenic
Heritage Road

Bridge

Small cluster
of houses

Long Climb

Best views

228

65   66   67   68   69

Bridge

100

35. Warburton Scenic
Heritage Road

Com

Hazelgr

Large farm

Fredericton

MN

0   0.5   1
km
mi.
0   0.5

227

Glen
Valley

264

35. Warburton Scenic Heritage Road

◄---► 10.5 km (6.6 mi) rtn
⏱: 2.5+hrs
🚶: 2
Type of Trail: compacted earth
Uses: walking, biking, horseback riding,
  ATVing, snowshoeing, cross-country
  skiing, snowmobiling

⚠: vehicle traffic
🗑: adequate throughout
Facilities: none
Gov't Topo Map: 11L06 (North Rustico)

Trailhead GPS: N 46° 24.135' W 63° 24.805'

Access: From the junction of Highway 1 and Highway 2/Malpeque Road in Charlottetown, follow Highway 2 west for 20.7 km (12.9 mi). Turn right onto Highway 239, driving for 6.4 km (4 mi). Warburton Road is on the left. Park so as to not obstruct traffic.

Introduction: The Warburton Scenic Heritage Road was constructed in 1898, and does not appear to have changed since. With its clay surface, narrow width, and high, overhanging canopy of trees, you would not be surprised if you spotted a horse-drawn wagon approaching around a corner, rather than an ATV. The Princetown Road, which this crosses, dates to the 1770s and is one of PEI's earliest and most important carriageways.

At its highest point, there are panoramic views of the surrounding farmland. As with many of the scenic heritage roads, fall is the most popular time for walkers, when the adjacent hardwoods are a panoply of colour. However, I particularly enjoyed walking this route in the winter. It is unploughed, and bitingly windswept in some sections, but startlingly beautiful.

Cyclists may find the section near Fredericton Station too rutted to safely ride, especially on the steeper hillsides.

Route Description: The road immediately heads beneath a shelter of high hardwoods, which will shade much of this route. It also climbs, and does so for the first 550 m/yd. For most of this distance there is a field to the left, although it is separated by a row of trees. The road is also sunken below the level of the banks on either side, so the field is actually a little above it.

On the right is a solid wall of vegetation, although numerous paths and tracks lead off from the road into the trees.

When dry, the clay is as solid as rock. When wet, it turns in a thick, viscous gumbo. Spring hiking can be a challenge, but very good exercise.

About when the trail begins to level, there is a large house to the left, with a fence alongside your route and many "No Trespassing" signs. Forest lines both sides now, predominantly hardwoods, although many small softwoods cluster near the road edge.

At 875 m/yd from the start, you reach the crest of the hill. And the trail begins to descend right away, even more steeply than it climbed, although not greatly so. The ground on your right remains higher than the road, while that on the left falls away.

As you descend, the woods on the right appear to have been thinned, and there is a clearing to the right 350 m/yd below the crest. However, to the left there appears to be a field, and in another 100 m/yd the road reaches the Olde Towne Orchard, an apple grove. At harvest, cars frequent the section of the Warburton Road between here and Highway 239. They do not travel fast on the narrow clay surface, and the straight road ensures good visibility.

The Warburton Road continues, still descending, the apple grove visible to the left. About 200 m/yd later, there is a small house—a cabin, really, as there is no electricity—on the right, #310. There are now fields on both sides, though trees still border Warburton Road.

About 100 m/yd later the road reaches bottom, where it crosses a small creek, and where the road itself is often wet. The vegetation here is much thicker, with alders and low scrubs. The road also curves a little, to cross the creek.

Once across, the road does not remain level long, but starts to climb once again, though gently at first. More fields, and higher ground, are visible to the left, while the creek is close at hand to the right. As the road curves a little, conforming to the creek path, more houses come into view. About 350 m/yd from the creek crossing, you arrive at the intersection with the Princetown Scenic Heritage Road, though this is unsigned. There are several small houses and fields nearby.

You continue straight, the Warburton Road curving left and climbing. A long, straight uphill follows, the forest hugging closely on both sides, gorgeous hardwoods shrouding your route. This continues for the next 500 m/yd, until you reach another cultivated field, to the left.

There are a further 300 m/yd of straight road, still gradually climbing,

next to the same large field, before the next curve to the right. After this, the road settles into another straight section, the clay track looking like a tunnel through the bordering vegetation. After a further 400 m/yd, the trees give way to fields on both sides, the ground to the right considerably lower, providing increasingly far-reaching views. The remains of barbed-wire fences line both sides.

After a further 300 m/yd, the road emerges from its foliage cloak — the end of the tunnel — and you reach another turning point. It is a delightful vista. Rolling hills extend in every direction, all of those nearby cultivated. Every time I stood at this spot, I was able to observe a hawk or harrier cruising above the fields, searching for its dinner. However, despite the cultivation, no human structure is visible.

The road curves left, climbing just a little more. Within 125 m/yd you reach the highest point. From here, the farms buildings near Fredericton Station are visible on the far ridge, and the traffic sounds from busy Highway 2 are detectable. However, the view is even more extensive, as the slopes of the gully you are entering have been almost entirely cleared.

The road drops about 30 m/yd over the next 550 m/yd, until it crosses another creek and re-enters a forested area. The next 700 m/yd is quite attractive, as the road is once again lined by tall hardwoods, even though there are fields quite close to the right.

In the final 450 m/yd, the road leaves the trees and climbs to end at Highway 2. In the last 100 m/yd, the route pass alongside a large farming operation, several buildings on the left, with trucks and a variety of specialized equipment parked on the right. This could be quite interesting, but the sound of high-speed traffic is overpowering.

You have walked or biked about 5.25 km (3.3 mi). Turn around, and retrace your route back to Highway 239.

Hiking with Dogs
Conflicts between those with dogs and those without are among the most frequent on trails. Respect other hikers.
* Keep your dog on-leash when so regulated. When encountering walkers without dogs, bring yours under control — including putting it back on-leash until others pass.
* Master the "come back" call. Before you let your dog off-leash on a trail, ensure that it will return as soon as you call.
* Make sure that your dog's tags are securely attached, in case you become separated.
* Just as you need supplies for yourself, you will need some for your dog. Water and food are critical — there is no guarantee that you will find any on the trail — as is a small pet first aid kit, including flea and tick protection.
* Always pack out your dog's poop, unless regulations permit dog waste to be buried. (Check before you hike.)

36. Winter River

◄---► 6 km (3.75 mi) rtn
🕐 : 1.5+hrs
🚶 : 2

Type of Trail: compacted earth, natural surface

Uses: walking, biking*, ATVing*, snow-shoeing, cross-country skiing*, snowmobiling*

⚠ : vehicle traffic
📱 : adequate throughout

Facilities: benches, garbage cans

Gov't Topo Map: 11L06 (North Rustico)

Trailhead GPS: N 46° 21.225' W 63° 3.720'

Access: From the junction of Highway 1 and Highway 2/Malpeque Road in Charlottetown, follow Highway 1 east for 3.3 km (2.1 mi). Turn left onto Highway 2, driving for 6.7 km (4.2 mi). Turn left onto Highway 222/Suffolk Road for 2.9 km (1.8 mi), then turn right onto Highway 229. After 1.9 km (1.2 mi)), continue straight on East Suffolk Road Extension for 1 km (0.6 mi). Trailhead parking is on the left where the asphalt ends.

Introduction: The low ground of the Winter River Watershed provides the water supply to the city of Charlottetown. This trail visits the riparian zone and its adjoining woodlands in a stacked loop, permitting either a short or a medium-length hike. I have chosen to highlight the outer loop. Shorter walks can be obtained

by selecting any of the interior connectors.

I did not include the section managed by the Queens County Wildlife Federation, because when I walked it, the signage was very poor, and several times I was uncertain whether I was still on the path. Experienced walkers may wish to include it.

Route Description: From the parking area, the Winter River trail is marked with blue flagging tape; a slender, uneven footpath, wedged between rows of white spruce, meanders through thick vegetation. Fallen logs border each side, and many tree roots are available for you to trip over.

After 350 m/yd amidst impenetrable brush, the path reaches the clay-surfaced East Suffolk Road, where there is map. Continue straight/

heads back among the trees. Once across this road, the forest changes. Spruce, rather than alders, edge the trail, and the meandering footpath is drier. For the next while you should enjoy a pleasant woodland stroll. Your view is limited to a few metres/yards on either side, but there are many ferns, mosses, and wildflowers.

About 475 m/yd from the road, there is a rough-hewn bench, and a grove of hardwoods. Just 50 m/yd later, you reach the junction with the Purple Trail, where there is another map. Keep straight, on the Blue Trail, crossing a small boardwalk over a dry (in summer) creek bed.

Little more than 100 m/yd further, there is a much larger bridge, with railings, through a low area that looks harmlessly dry in the summer and fall. The trail actually finds a small hill to climb, and then proceeds to zigzag around and over this low rise. You will need to carefully watch the worn route in the spruce needle forest floor, because the path turns back on itself more than once. In fact, at one point I could see different sections of the trail both to my left and to my right. (It reminded me of the security line queue in an airport.)

After walking—I'll be honest, I lost track, but I think about 300 m/

left and follow the road for about 200 m/yd, turning onto the first road on the right. After you turn, there is a small pond on the left, and a boggy area on the right.

Watch carefully, because the map at the next junction, on the left in 100 m/yd, might be nearly hidden by thick vegetation. Turn right here, heading behind the small pond on a very narrow footpath. The ground is fairly damp, so alders are common. You reach a short boardwalk within 150 m/yd, and then several other places where pieces of wood have been placed to try to provide dry footing. I found the mosquitoes through here particularly aggressive.

The trail crosses another wood road less than 150 m/yd later. A large "Trail" sign indicates where the path

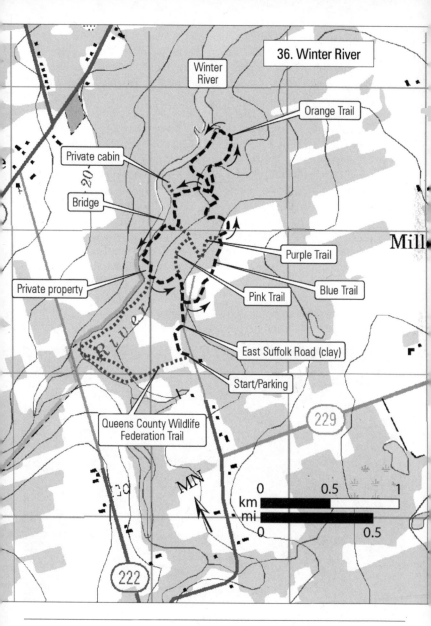

36. Winter River

Winter River

Orange Trail

Private cabin

Bridge

Purple Trail

Blue Trail

Private property

Pink Trail

East Suffolk Road (clay)

Start/Parking

Queens County Wildlife Federation Trail

Mill

River

20

229

222

MN

km
mi

0   0.5   1

0   0.5

yd—from the bridge, you reach the junction with the Orange Trail. Turn right, following the ridge line through the very thick spruce forest. It is dark through here, as the trees are so tightly packed. The trail drops off the ridge, then wanders along near the bottom of it. At 325 m/yd, at the base of two old, tall spruces, the path turns sharply right and climbs back up a hill. It resumes its meandering course through featureless forest, cresting the ridge about 200 m/yd later. The path drops downhill again, reaching the tiny Winter River Direct in 50 m/yd. The trail turns left, and follows the rivulet, with higher ground on both sides.

The trail soon heads back over the small hill on the left, and returns to the Winter River near the creek's outlet 225 m/yd further. From here, the trail parallels the wide waterway for the next 500 m/yd. This is a very pleasant section, with two well-placed benches overlooking the river and one railed bridge over a teensy-tiny creek. The path is slightly higher than water level, and the spruce forest is open enough to permit cooling breezes.

After making a 90° turn left, the trail climbs uphill, away from the river, and weaves a snaking course through dense forest back to the junction with the Blue trail in 450 m/yd.

Turn right, immediately heading back downhill. This much wider path reaches a map in 350 m/yd. Straight ahead is someone's cabin; turn left

Trails of Prince Edward Island

and you will reach a side path to the river 150 m/yd later. This will take you to another bench alongside the river, with a pleasing view. The trail runs roughly parallel to the river, but set back enough that you rarely have a good view.

Just 75 m/yd from the side trail, there is an elaborate bridge crossing another, larger creek. On the far side is the junction with the Pink Trail. Keep right, on the Blue Trail, which returns to the Winter River. For the next 800 m/yd, trail and river remain close. The terrain is somewhat hilly, and the trail climbs up and down.

There is one more large bridge, and another bench with a river view, before the trail makes a sharp left turn and heads distinctly away from the water.

The next junction is with the Queens County Wildlife Federation Trail. You keep straight, reaching the end of the East Suffolk Road 40 m/yd later. From here follow the road, with a few short wooded shortcuts, the 900 m/yd back to the trailhead.

44. Singing Sands Beach

White Pine

Lumber was once the most important resource of eastern Canada, and the queen of the forest was the majestic eastern white pine. Living up to 400 years and towering more than 50 m/yd, the white pine was highly desired for its use in ships' masts. This species was one of the predominant trees in PEI, but wholesale cutting and fires reduced it to only scattered patches and occasional surviving individual trees.

White pines prefer well-drained soil and cool, humid climates, but they can also grow in boggy areas and rocky highlands. They are one of three pine species native to the region, and can be distinguished by their bundle of five needles together. They retain their needles and green colour throughout the year.

tuous, soon turning right nearly 180°, then almost as far to the left. It continues its sinuous path for about 1 km (0.6 mi), until it reaches JF's Drop.

After a further 200 m/yd, the trail makes a curve left and, though still winding, becomes straighter. It is 1.5 km (0.9 mi) to the next junction, the other side of the Green Trail. Along the way, you will pass Hemlock Grove and Lowell's Bridge, an elaborate structure with railings.

Keep on the Blue Loop, following the distinct track through the varying stands of forest. For 300 m/yd, until the Old Road Culvert, the path undulates somewhat but is fairly straight. After that point, it begins another twisting section, corkscrewing over the landscape until it reaches the junction with the Red Loop, 900 m/yd later.

You have travelled about 8.5 km (5.3 mi) to this point. There is a map at the junction, but you turn right. The ground here is somewhat uneven, and the trail begins a series of wanderings up and down the low ridges.

A "4 km" marker is reached 300 m/yd from the junction, and the trail comes within sight of Highway 4 about 250 m/yd later. It curves away, entering another series of turns. After 125 m/yd it reaches the Old Foundation, and 225 m/yd beyond that it emerges from the forest into the large grassy area of the trailhead/parking area.

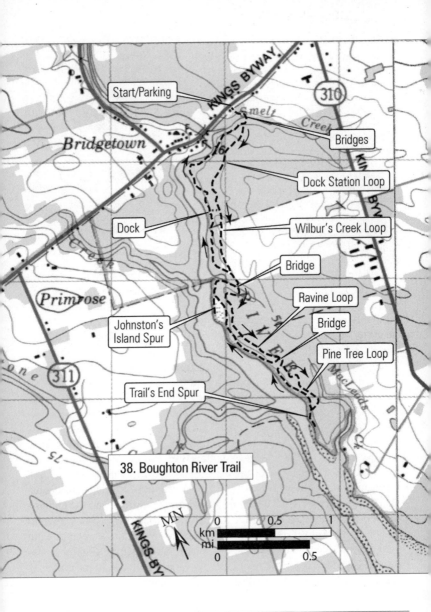

Start/Parking

KINGS BYWAY

Smelt Creek

310

Bridges

Bridgetown

Dock Station Loop

Dock

Wilbur's Creek Loop

Bridge

Ravine Loop

Primrose

Bridge

Johnston's
Island Spur

Pine Tree Loop

311

Trail's End Spur

MacLeods Cr.

38. Boughton River Trail

MN

| 0 | 0.5 | 1 |
km
mi
| 0 | | 0.5 |

KINGS BYWAY

38. Boughton River Trail

◄ - - - ► 9 km (5.6 mi) rtn
🕐 : 2+hrs
🏃 : 2
Type of Trail: natural surface
Uses: walking, snowshoeing,
    cross-country skiing

⚠ : none
🗑 : adequate throughout
Facilities: benches, interpretive panels,
    picnic tables
Gov't Topo Map: 11L07 (Mount Stewart),
    11L08 (Souris)

Trailhead GPS: N 46° 18.630' W 62° 31.035'

Access: From the junction of Grafton and Water Streets in Charlottetown, cross the Hillsborough Bridge, and drive 12.5 km (7.8 mi). Turn left onto Highway 5 and continue for 27.5 km (17.2 mi). Turn left onto Highway 4 and follow it for 12.9 km (8.1 mi). The trailhead parking area is on the right, just past the fire hall, 1559 Seven Mile Road, Bridgetown.

Introduction: The Boughton River Trail system is one of the Island Trails "Destination Trails," one that they have identified as being most worthy as a day-trip destination.

This series of four stacked loops—each adding to, or "stacked," after the other—enables a hike of up to 9 km (5.6 mi), with shorter distances available for those wishing a briefer walk. The trail fully utilizes the small Boughton River Natural Area, a slender strip of crown land bordering the east bank of the river.

Route Description: There are a number of facilities at the trailhead: a bench, a sheltered picnic table, an interpretive panel, and a large trailhead sign featuring a map. The trail immediately plunges into thick forest, and, surprisingly for PEI, descends a slightly steep little hill. Your path is narrow, on an earthen track worn into the forest floor.

The first junction, for the Dock Station Loop, is reached in about 200 m/yd. To get there, the trail descends a small hill, crosses two small creeks on unrailed bridges, passes another interpretive panel, and climbs a small hill steep enough to have steps cut into the slope. At the junction, where there is a map, keep left, on the inland section. (I prefer to save the best views for later in the hike, when I am tired and might wish to stop and enjoy a few moments of scenery.)

This trail continues uphill, a distinct footpath signed, occasionally, by orange flagging tape. This is a pleasant enough section, traversing several areas of different tree types, including a plantation of pines. The ground is uneven, and you will ascend and descend several small hills, but the only trail feature is a bridge, about 700 m/yd from the junction.

The next junction, with the Wilbur's Creek Loop, is reached after a 1.4 km (0.9 mi) amble through the forest from the previous junction. There was no map here, but a large arrow sign pointing back along your route. Keep left; the map sign is 25 m/yd further.

This trail remains in forest as well, at least for the initial 500 m/yd. After this, it works along the forest edge, a large field to the left; 150 m/yd later, the trail reaches Connector 1. Continue straight, along the field edge, over a small boardwalk, for another 50 m/yd. At post BR 63, the path turns right, and back into the forest.

Immediately the path descends to a small bridged brook. On the far side is the junction with the Ravine Loop. Connector 1 is less than 100 m/yd long. Keep left, on the inland segment. This begins with borders of thick white spruce and moss-covered hillsides, but it soon moves into more mixed woods.

As with the Wilbur's Creek Loop, the ground on the right is lower, sloping toward Boughton River. Though the path remains at a higher level, occasional glimpses of the water can be obtained. However, it is mostly another woodland walk, reaching the junction with Connector 2 after about 1 km (0.6 mi). Again keep left, crossing a deep, steep-sided ravine over a small bridge. Connector 2 works along it for the 85 m/yd to its connection to the final loop, the Pine Tree.

Keep left to remain on the inland loop. This section is less frequently visited, so by late summer ferns may nearly obscure the slender footpath. There are a few small plank boardwalks to cross, and there are increasingly frequent views of the river available, but the trail stays on the higher ground, 5-10 m/yd above water level.

After 600 m/yd of wandering over the rolling ground, mostly surrounded by spruce and fir, the trail reaches a towering white pine. This is just 25 m/yd before the next junction, where sits a rough-hewn bench. Continue straight, along the Trail End Spur, a 215 m/yd extension that leads to a small knoll overlooking a remote section of the Boughton River.

Return to the previous junction; you have trekked about 4.5 km

(2.8 mi) so far, almost all of it surrounded by dense forest. The return trip will be somewhat more scenic. Turn left again, coming from the spur; the trail descends to the top of the bank bordering the river, still under tree cover, and also usually considerably higher than water level.

This is a lovely walk, and the terrain is somewhat more uneven and challenging than the interior section. After nearly 650 m/yd alongside the river, the path reaches a deep ravine, and turns right to climb back to Connector 2. Turn left, and walk back to the Ravine Loop. Keep left; this traces the opposite bank of the ravine back to the river.

Once again, you enjoy a path that remains only a few metres/yards from the river. There are even occasional interpretive panels. After what should be an enjoyable 1 km (0.6 mi) walk, the junction with the Johnston's Island Spur is reached at a viewing platform. This short 200 m/yd branch trail can provide the best views of the river, but it might require getting your feet wet.

From this spur, the Ravine Loop begins to curve right, following a deep indentation into the river bank. The path heads alongside it, returning to the junction with Connector 1, which it reaches about 400 m/yd from Johnston's Island. Retrace the 85 m/yd along Connector 1, and turn left onto the Wilbur's Creek Loop.

Red Pine

Also known as the Norway pine, this tree is favoured for use as wharf and bridge pilings, power poles, and other purposes requiring a sturdy wood that is easily rot-proofed. Red pine was also used for ships' masts, and its heartwood was popular for ships' decks. Because of its commercial value, almost all the old growth trees in the province have been harvested.

Red pine adds one row of spreading branches each year up to 350 years, and grows to heights of 24 m (80 ft). Its bark is reddish-brown with broad, flat, scaly plates. The needles come in bundles of two that are slender, whorled, and dark green year round. Red pines prefer well-drained soils, particularly sand plains, and usually grow in mixed forests rather than pure stands.

This follows the shore of Wilbur's Creek, descending toward Boughton River. Once there it works alongside the waterway, providing more scenic views. The dock is reached at the next junction, 700 m/yd later. It is to the left, and includes several interpretive panels.

The Dock Station Loop is directly ahead, starting up a small wooden staircase. About 150 m/yd later, the trail crosses the deepest gully of the entire route, with a wooden railing on the edge of the path. The trail descends to water level, and 550 m/yd from the gully arrives at a bench situated across the river from the public dock at Bridgetown.

The path follows the river upstream, though with limited views in the dense vegetation. Two small creeks are bridged, 200 m/yd from the bench and 165 m/yd after that, then the path climbs a small steep hill, where it remains to the next junction, 550 m/yd further.

Turn left, and retrace the 200 m/yd back to the trailhead and the completion of this hike.

39. County Line Scenic Heritage Road

◄---► 5 km (3.1 mi) rtn
🕐: 1.5+hrs
🚶: 1
Type of Trail: compacted earth
Uses: walking, biking, ATVing, horseback riding, snowshoeing, cross-country skiing, snowmobiling

⚠: vehicle traffic
🧴: adequate throughout
Facilities: none
Gov't Topo Map: 11L02 (Montague)

Trailhead GPS: N 46° 2.815′ W 62° 42.525′

Access: From the junction of Grafton and Water Streets in Charlottetown, cross the Hillsborough Bridge, and drive 17.2 km (10.75 mi). Turn left onto Highway 3, and continue for 7.6 km (4.75 mi). Turn right onto Highway 24 and follow it for 19 km (11.9 mi), turning left onto Highway 315. After 350 m/yd, turn left onto County Line Road and park.

Introduction: PEI's Scenic Heritage Roads offer an easy manner in which to enjoy a woodland stroll along an old-fashioned country lane. Usually there are few or no houses, and although still a designated Highway, there is rarely any vehicle traffic.

The County Line Road is one of these, where once horse-drawn carriages transported passengers through a road bordered by beautiful hardwood stands that arched overhead, forming a protective natural canopy.

Though County Line Road has been widened somewhat in recent years, and the forest canopy is less complete than in the past, much of the flavour of this bygone era remains along this clay-surfaced back road.

The County Line Road is so named because it follows the boundary of two counties, Kings and Queens.

Route Description: There is a signpost for the County Line Road, but no indication that this is a Scenic Heritage Road. From the intersection with Highway 315, the road immediately begins to climb. This part of PEI is made up of low rolling hills, providing a bit more texture to the walk than in some areas.

As you climb, in the first 200 m/yd, you will see some houses to the left, including an interesting-looking log cabin. Watch for a "Chickens Xing" sign facing the opposite direc-

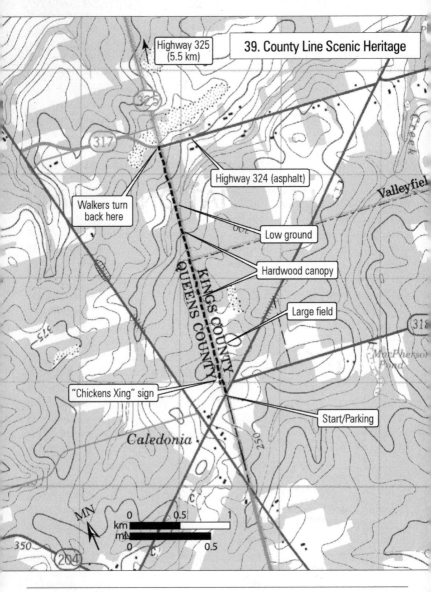

Highway 325
(5.5 km)

39. County Line Scenic Heritage

Highway 324 (asphalt)

Walkers turn
back here

Low ground

Hardwood canopy

KINGS COUNTY
QUEENS COUNTY

Large field

"Chickens Xing" sign

Start/Parking

Valleyfiel

MacPherso
Pond

Caledonia

MN

km
mi

0   0.5   1

0   0.5

tion, also on the left. This is a section with mature trees on both sides, and although there might not be a complete overhead canopy, there should be shade except when the sun is at its peak.

About 300 m/yd from the start, there is a large field on the right, with a vehicle access route into it. Fortunately, a wide buffer of tall trees remains between it and the road. Perhaps 100 m/yd later, you reach the crest of the hill, and begin a gentle descent.

The trees to the left are quite lush. The grassy field on the right continues for almost 450 m/yd, and the ground on that side is slightly higher. After this field ends, trees line both sides of the road, and these are predominantly hardwoods.

The path nearly levels at times, but there is a small rise about 1.25 km (0.8 mi) from the start. After this, the road distinctly descends through the most thickly forested section of this route. There is almost a complete overhead canopy of leaves, and the embankments on either side of the lane are about 1 m/yd high.

The low point of the route is reached about 350 m/yd later, in an area where the ground appears quite soggy, particularly to the left. Don't dawdle here, unless you like mosquitoes. On the other hand, several species of songbirds prefer sheltering

in these dense thickets, so it depends what is most important to you.

This low area extends nearly 200 m/yd before the trail begins to climb again. There is another cleared field, this time to the left, and as the path ascends there are a few places where the embankments are almost as tall as most walkers.

The field accompanies the road only for about 200 m/yd, after which the overhead canopy returns. For the remaining 400 m/yd, all uphill, you should enjoy a pleasantly shaded stroll. About 2.5 km (1.6 mi) from the start, the County Line Road reaches an intersection with Highway 324. This is paved to the right, but clay surface to the left.

Walkers may wish to turn around at this point, while cyclists, might wish to continue along the County

Line Road. From this intersection it becomes much wider, and the attractive overhead canopy disappears. The clay surface continues over the rolling terrain for a further 2.75 km (1.7 mi), until it reaches Highway 316.

For those wishing a longer rural ride, County Line Road actually continues a considerable distance, though it is no longer designated as a Scenic Heritage Road. There is a 900 m/yd paved section after reaching Highway 316, but them the clay surface resumes and lasts for another 5.5 km (3.4 mi), until County Line Road reaches Highway 210.

Whether you turn back at Highway 324, or bike on to Highway 210, you must retrace your route back to the start of County Line Road on Highway 315.

40. Harvey Moore Sanctuary

◄--- ► 2.5 km (1.6 mi) rtn

🕐: 1+hrs

🏃: 1

Type of Trail: natural surface

Uses: walking, snowshoeing

⚠: none

🔋: adequate throughout

Facilities: benches, garbage cans, interpretive panels, picnic tables

Gov't Topo Map: 11L02 (Montague)

Trailhead GPS: N 46° 6.615' W 62° 37.585'

Access: From the junction of Grafton and Water Streets in Charlottetown, cross the Hillsborough Bridge, and drive 17.2 km (10.75 mi). Turning left onto Highway 3, continue for 22.1 km (13.8 mi). Turn right onto Highway 4 and follow it for 11.6 km (7.25 mi). The sanctuary entrance is on the right. Follow the clay road 250 m/yd to the parking area.

Introduction: The Harvey Moore Wildlife Management Area is a wonderful natural area with a fascinating history. Essentially, it grew from the efforts of one remarkable individual, Harvey Moore, who dedicated his life to his love of the outdoors and his affection for birds, particularly waterfowl.

Today, the sanctuary he created has become a facility to educate the public about the natural environment. Its relatively short trail circles two ponds and features numerous excellent interpretive panels describing the sanctuary's flora and fauna. This is a wonderful walk for families, especially those who enjoy observing birds.

The trail is made up of two loops, each circling one of the two ponds that make up the wildlife management area. I have profiled the longer route, around both ponds. If a shorter walk is desired, turn left at the first junction, about 350 m/yd from the trailhead.

Route Description: The trail begins from a large field and parking area, where there are several picnic tables. Look for a "Trail" sign for the start of the path; this is a small opening in the trees, about 20 m/yd to the right of the house with the white picket fence.

As soon as you enter the forest, there is an interpretive panel, and directly ahead is a floating observation deck on the pond. This is a good

spot from which to view the many waterfowl that regularly inhabit the sanctuary.

The trail turns right, a narrow footpath on the forest floor. To the right, quite close, is the large field/picnic area; to the left, the pond, perhaps 10 m/yd away. Almost immediately, the trail passes information post #1 (trail guides may be available at the start). But it is not until you have walked more than 175 m/yd that you reach a sign which features a map.

The path continues, following a small brook after post #2. At 350 m/yd, it reaches another clearing, situated on the edge of the second pond. On the left, there is a small concrete dam, which also has a fish ladder, and the junction with the first loop. This route branches left, crossing a bridge over the dam. Your route heads right,

across the clearing, and past another interpretive panel.

The trail heads into another forested area, and although there are no markers, other than the occasional information posts and interpretive panels, it is extremely well defined, clearly worn into the vegetation. The trees bordering the footpath are mixed, though with softwoods more prominent, and provide fairly good shade.

For the next 450 m/yd, the trail stays close to the pond, which is usually visible through the trees on the left. If not, the incessant honking of Canada geese in the water will reassure you that it is close. Along the way, there are several additional panels and posts.

Then the trail turns right sharply, away from the pond. It continues for

Beaver

The many small lakes and wetlands of Canada are ideal habitat for beaver, and their dams, lodges, and trails of felled trees may be found throughout the country. This largest rodent in North America creates dams as protection against predators and to provide easy access to food during winter. Beavers always work at night and are prolific builders, each gnawing through an average of 216 trees per year.

Hunted almost to extinction for their fur, during the peak of the fur trade era, some 200,000 pelts a year were sold to the European market. Because of recent conservation measures, numbers have increased tremendously and they have returned to many sites where they had disappeared.

37. Beck Trail

43. Roma

44. Singing Sands Beach

46. Valleyfield Demonstration Woodlot

Pileated Woodpecker

Anyone old enough to remember the *Woody Woodpecker* cartoon character will instantly recognize this red-crested bird as it flits between trees in search of the carpenter ants that are its favourite food. The pileated woodpecker is also distinctive because of its size, about as large as a crow and much larger than any other eastern woodpecker.

As these birds require larger, mature trees for nesting, pileated woodpecker populations declined sharply with the harvesting of old-growth forests. However, as regrowth tree populations have matured, so have pileated woodpeckers become more common.

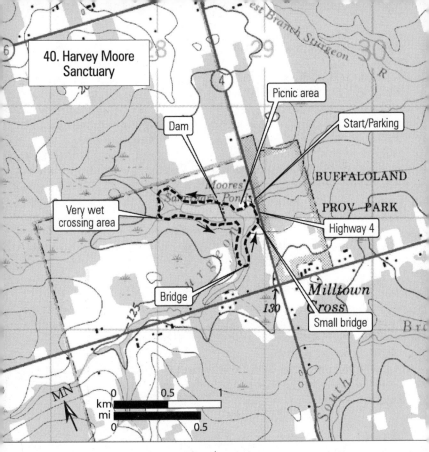

about 100 m/yd before it curves left again, crossing a wet area, and heads back into a more thickly forested area. Now the trail begins to curve and twist somewhat.

The reason for doing so soon becomes obvious, as you will see a large swampy area to the left. This is the end of the second pond, and the trail works around it at the edge of dry, slightly elevated ground, curving left as it does. However, that swampy area eventually must be crossed, and it does so at a bridge/boardwalk. Unfortunately, this does not extend over the entire length of sogginess. Some boards and cut logs have been placed to try to provide dry footing over this muddy area, but I was unable to cross without getting both feet covered in thick black mud up to my ankles.

Once across—whether with dry feet or not—the path ascends a very low knoll, but this is enough to ensure dry footing. The trail soon returns to close proximity to open water, and for the next 750 m/yd, until it reaches the junction with the cross-trail for the first loop, it traces the shoreline. There are frequent opportunities to view the pond, and several interpretive panels and posts.

Keep right at the junction; this trail turns away from the water and plunges into thick spruce forest. The route meanders a little, until it reaches the next interpretive panel and a view of the first pond 175m /yd later. The trail turns almost 90° right, and although you are circling the pond, you will not be able to see it. In fact, the vegetation to the left appears to be alders and other thick vegetation.

It is a pleasant walk, however, along a well-defined pathway. After about 300 m/yd, the trail makes a very sharp turn left, and delivers you onto a very sturdy bridge, though with no railings. This crosses a fairly wide stream and wet area, and turns left again on the opposite bank.

The trail follows this brook back toward the first pond, after which it works along its bank once again. Watch for more interpretive panels, including one nearly hidden by the very ferns about which it explains. Highway 4 is very close, on the right, and not only will you hear passing traffic, but you might also see the vehicles.

About 375 m/yd after crossing the bridge, the trail arrives at another small bridge—this one with railings—that crosses the narrow passage that is the outflow for the ponds. Once across, little more than 100 m/yd remains before you emerge from the forest onto a boardwalk, in the large open area near the picnic grounds. Follow the boardwalk to the large display panel 50 m/yd further, at which point you have finished your hike.

41. Mooneys Pond

◄---► 1.9 km (1.2 mi) rtn
🕐: 1+hrs
🏃🏃: 1
Type of Trail: crushed stone, natural surface
Uses: walking, biking, snowshoeing

⚠: none (road crossing, if connecting to the Confederation Trail)
🗑: adequate throughout
Facilities: benches, garbage cans, interpretive panels, picnic tables, washrooms
Gov't Topo Map: 11L07 (Mount Stewart)

Trailhead GPS: N 46° 17.885′ W 62° 46.440′

Access: From the junction of Grafton and Water Streets in Charlottetown, cross the Hillsborough Bridge, to the junction with Highway 21, about 1.8 km (1.1 mi). Turn left onto Highway 21 and follow it for 25 km (15.6 mi). Turn right onto Highway 22 and follow it for 7.8 km (4.9 mi). The trailhead is on the right and is well signed.

Introduction: Although the walking path is officially named Peggy's Trail, and it passes first near Anderson's Pool, most people appear to know the area best by the name of its largest body of water: Mooneys Pond. As this is even how the trail is listed on the Island Trails Web site, I decided to use that name too. (But it's really Peggy's Trail.)

One of the few small lakes on the island, Mooneys Pond is a popular fishing destination. Throughout the years, as many as seventy thousand salmon have been released into it, and the trail has been designed so that anglers may obtain a good cast. There is also a waterside picnic area and numerous interpretive displays.

This is an attractive but relatively short walk. Those wishing to amble a bit further can extend their hike along the Confederation Trail, to which this connects near the trailhead.

Route Description: Take a minute to examine the trailhead sign, which contains an excellent map—so detailed and precise that distances are listed to the tenth of a metre/yard. From the parking area, head toward the bridge visible from the trailhead. This fairly high structure crosses the outflow from the ponds, and leads directly to the wheelchair ramp and accessible fishing platform at Anderson's Pool.

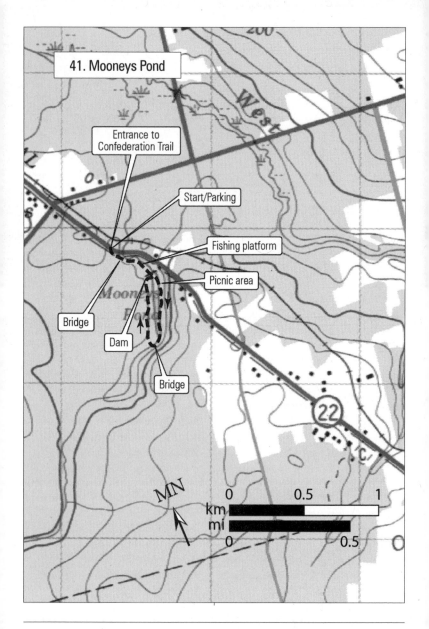

41. Mooneys Pond

Entrance to
Confederation Trail

Start/Parking

Fishing platform

Picnic area

Bridge

Dam

Bridge

22

MN

km
mi

0   0.5   1

0   0.5

This is quite a pleasant area, and there are benches for those who wish to sit and enjoy the tranquil setting, which includes at least one beaver lodge. A boardwalk begins here as well, and continues alongside the pond for the next 150 m/yd (or 158.3 m/yd, if I read their map correctly).

From the end of the boardwalk, there is a well-defined track that leads to an interpretive centre, where there are washrooms—at least, when the building is open. This is also Mooneys Pond, a much larger body of water than Anderson's Pool. From the large grassy area around the interpretive centre, you can see the small dam that has created the pond, and a floating observation dock on which there are benches.

Mooneys Pond is long and narrow, with slightly elevated ground on both banks. There is also a healthy tree cover along its entire length, making it quite attractive. A number of waterfowl, particularly Canada geese, nest in the pond, and will probably be cruising nearby. When I visited, a kingfisher's rattling call echoed across the little basin.

Keep left; the trail heads into the forest, a very wide, level track surfaced with crushed stone and with a wooden retaining wall on the water side. This section is intended for wheelchair use, so it is without any ruts or intruding tree roots. To the right, the pond is visible through a slender buffer of trees, and the trail is a few metres/yards above water level.

About 140 m/yd into the woods there is an elaborate lookoff, with benches, that is also intended as a fishing area. About 100 m/yd after that is a second, but smaller, platform extending out over the water, and 50 m/yd beyond that is a solid bridge crossing a small gully.

After that, the hillside becomes somewhat steeper, which required a fair amount of earth to be removed on the left to keep the trail wide and level. The path also climbs higher above the surface of the water, more than 5 m/yd at some points.

A second, longer bridge is encountered about 175 m/yd later, and is necessary to cross another, deeper gully. Barely 50 m/yd after crossing the bridge, the wheelchair-accessible section ends. The trail turns right and descends a long staircase.

At the bottom of the stairs, there is a long bridge that crosses the head of Mooneys Pond. It emerges from the forest and provides a good view back toward the interpretive centre. You can also see upstream, and there is bench partway across for those who might wish to linger at this peaceful spot.

Once across the bridge, the trail becomes somewhat more natural. It is not as wide, and there are occasional tree roots to trip the unwary. This

Muskrats

There are few large mammals to see in PEI, but you will almost certainly sight some muskrats swimming in one of the ponds or wetlands. Basically a large mouse that has adapted to living in water, the muskrat looks similar to a beaver, but is much smaller, and has a thin, whip-like tail that it uses to propel it. Like the beaver, it is an herbivore.

Perhaps surprisingly, this tiny rodent contributes more income to trappers than any other species in North America. Equally surprising, despite its heavy commercial harvest, and the loss of habitat from marshes drained for agricultural purposes, muskrat populations are considered to be as high as they were when Europeans first arrived.

portion of the pathway, labelled the "Nature Trail," continues down the far side of Mooneys Pond the 400 m/yd back to the dam. Along the way there are several benches and one more lookoff/fishing platform, although in the thicker vegetation on this bank there are fewer views of the water.

Back at the dam, you will see a small bridge behind it that delivers you back to the grassy picnic area by the interpretive centre. To return to the trailhead, retrace the first portion

of your hike back toward Anderson's Pool and over the first bridge.

If you wish to add to the walk by including a portion of the Confederation Trail, from the trailhead walk back toward Highway 22. Cross the road and head into the woods on a small path. Almost immediately, you will reach the Confederation Trail, and there is a sign for Mooneys Pond. If you head to the right, the next road crossing is in 750 m/yd; the next one beyond that is a further 1.4 km (0.9 mi).

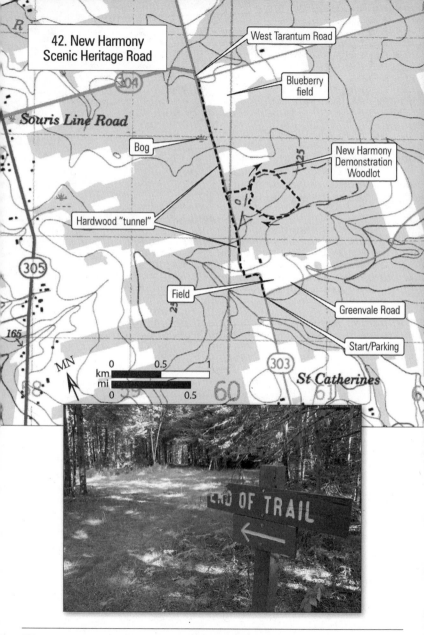

42. New Harmony Scenic Heritage Road

West Tarantum Road

Blueberry field

Souris Line Road

Bog

New Harmony Demonstration Woodlot

Hardwood "tunnel"

Field

Greenvale Road

Start/Parking

St Catherines

km
mi
0   0.5   1
0   0.5

MN

END OF TRAIL

42. New Harmony Scenic Heritage Road

◄---► 7.5 km (4.7 mi) rtn

🕐: 2+hrs

🏃: 2

Type of Trail: compacted earth, natural surface

Uses: walking, biking*, ATVing*, horseback riding*, snowshoeing, cross-country skiing, snowmobiling*

⚠: vehicle traffic

📱: adequate throughout

Facilities: benches, interpretive panels

Gov't Topo Map: 11L08 (Souris)

Trailhead GPS: N 46° 22.815' W 62° 12.860'

Access: From the junction of Grafton and Water Streets in Charlottetown, cross the Hillsborough Bridge, and drive 12.4 km (7.75 mi) on Highway 1 east. Turn left onto Highway 5 and continue for 27.5 km (17.2 mi). Turn right onto Highway 4 and follow it for 36 km (22.5 mi) to Souris. At Highway 305 turn left and drive for 1.4 km (0.9 mi), turning right onto Highway 335. After 2.8 km (1.75 mi), turn left onto Highway 303/New Harmony Road. Continue for 1.3 km (0.8 mi) and park at intersection with Greenvale Road.

Introduction: The New Harmony Scenic Heritage Road is considered to be one of the finest in the province, doubtless because of the thick canopy of hardwoods that provide shade for much of its distance and creates an attractive "green tunnel" through which walkers travel.

Midway along this route sits the New Harmony Demonstration Woodlot. Its self-guided interpretive trail meanders through old white spruce stands, areas of mature hardwoods, and several areas of mixed woods. Adding this to the road nearly doubles the walking distance available, and adds some variety.

Route Description: There is no sign indicating that this is a Scenic Heritage Road, and for the first few hundred metres/yards, little evidence. The road surface is red clay, but there is a large field on the right, and no shade. For the first 200 m/yd, the road is straight, and then it makes an S-curve to the left, then right. It also begins to climb, slightly. From here there are cultivated fields on both sides of the road, and this continues until you reach forest cover 500 m/yd from the start.

For the next 100 m/yd there is still

---

a field to the right, and only a thin strip of trees, and the forest to the left appears to have been harvested fairly recently. But the road begins to narrow, and instead of ditching, there are small embankments rising above road level.

When the field ends on the right, at 600 m/yd, the experience is transformed. Branches from the tall trees lining the road spread overhead, their leaves filtering the sun's light. In summer, everything is suffused with a pale green glow; in autumn, these leaves present a mélange of colours.

At 800 m/yd, there is a large clearing on the right, and this is a popular parking area. This is also where the climb ends, and the road appears to extend straight and level for a considerable distance. Although there are numerous side roads into the forest, none should confuse you as to your route. And remember, most head into private property, so keep to the New Harmony Road.

The first sign for the New Harmony Demonstration Woodlot is on the right about 200 m/yd from the clearing, but there is no access here. That occurs 200 m/yd later, where there is another sign, and a wood road. For now, keep straight, following the road, which still enjoys thick forest cover, even though many of the trees on the right are now softwoods.

The shaded idyll continues for another 250 m/yd, before the trees to the right are replaced by another cultivated field. There is still a buffer of tall trees between field and road, and an awning of leaves, but it is not quite as picturesque. And 200 m/yd after that, at the end of the field, the overhead canopy ends as well.

Over the next 400 m/yd, the road begins to widen again, and the attractive hardwood forest is replaced by more mixed cover, and a large bog populated by black spruce. At 2 km (1.25 mi), a very large blueberry field begins on the right, and this is a constant companion the remaining 400 m/yd to the New Harmony Road's intersection with the West Tarantum Road.

Walkers should probably turn back at this point, though cyclists might wish to continue. The Confederation Trail crosses the New Harmony Road just 1.1 km (0.7 mi) further.

Retrace the 1.25 km (0.8 mi) back to the entrance to the Demonstration Woodlot, turning left onto its access road. Follow this for 200 m/yd to a clearing that is also a parking area. There is no signage and there are several routes available. The road curves left, and there is another wood road joining on the right. Keep straight; you should see several wooden posts. Head toward and past those; in a few metres/yards there is another

intersection, and on the left a sign indicating the trail entrance.

The remainder of the walk should be fairly easy, as the trail is wide and distinct, and there are frequent interpretive and educational signs. This path is more winding than the road, curving through the trees, working in a loop that returns to the clearing. It also frequently crosses wood roads, although in almost every case it is well signed.

Follow the trail as it curves through attractive softwood and hardwood stands, and past dozens of display signs. There is only one place where care is required to stay on the correct route. At 1.7 km (1.1 mi) from the clearing, near post #15, at a stand of Norway spruce—planted in 1960 and thinned in 1984—the trail turns 90° right, and heads into a short section where the vegetation has not been thinned. This leads slightly uphill to a road crossing that is also unsigned. Look for the trail continuation slightly to the left.

The trail remains without signage through an open area, past a small pond, and for nearly 250 m/yd, until you reach post #16. From here, be reassured, it is only another 200 m/yd to the end of trail. Retrace your route back to the New Harmony Road, turn left, and finish the 1.2 km (0.75 mi) back to your car.

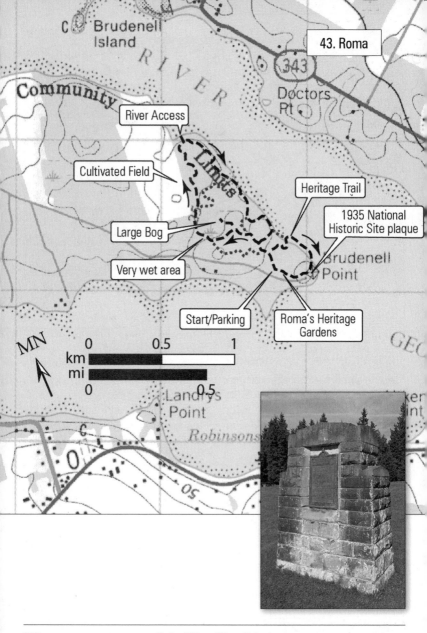

C Brudenell Island

RIVER

343

Doctors Pt

Community

River Access

Cultivated Field

Limits

Heritage Trail

1935 National Historic Site plaque

Large Bog

Brudenell Point

Very wet area

Start/Parking

Roma's Heritage Gardens

MN

0   0.5   1
km
mi
0   0.5

Landrys Point

Robinsons

GE

43. Roma

◀--- ▶ 4.5 km (2.8 mi) rtn

🕐: 1+hrs

👤: 2

Type of Trail: crushed stone, natural surface

Uses: walking, snowshoeing, cross-country skiing*

⚠: cliffs

💧: adequate throughout

Facilities: benches, interpretive panels

Gov't Topo Map: 11L02 (Montague)

Trailhead GPS: N 46° 10.895' W 62° 33.690'

Access: From the junction of Grafton and Water Streets in Charlottetown, cross the Hillsborough Bridge, and drive 17.2 km (10.75 mi). Turn left onto Highway 3, and continue for 22.1 km (13.8 mi). Turn right onto Highway 4 and follow it for 1.6 km (1 mi), turning left onto Highway 319/Brudenell Point Road. After 4.9 km (3.1 mi), Highway 319 turns right. Continue straight on Roma Point Road another 2.5 km (1.6 mi). The parking area is on the left.

Introduction: In 1732, one of Canada's first entrepreneurs landed at Brudenell Point with eighty settlers, determined to create an international trade centre. Within a few years, Jean Pierre Roma and his people had cleared more than 200 acres and erected a number of large buildings. For thirteen years they flourished, until privateers from New England raided, looted, and burnt everything to the ground.

In 1933, the area was recognized as one of the Canada's first National Historic Sites, and in 2004, the Roma at Three Rivers historic park and interpretive centre was established. Today, the park features a number of eighteenth-century style buildings, numerous artifacts and displays, and even costumed historical re-enactors during the summer months.

Route Description: The trail begins in the upper right corner of the parking area. To the right are Roma's Heritage Gardens and some of the buildings. Follow the crushed-stone pathway, keeping to the left of the buildings. About 125 m/yd from the parking lot, there is a large trailhead sign, featuring an excellent map of the property's walking paths.

This is the Heritage Trail, a wide

crushed-stone-surfaced walkway. It immediately heads into the thick forest, where, less than 50 m/yd later, it reaches a junction with the River Trail. There is a smaller map posted here, which conveniently indicates your location.

Turn left; this path is a little more rugged, with a natural surface that includes tree roots jutting into the treadway. The forest is quite thick with trees close to the edge of the trail on both sides. However, by the time you reach the first interpretive panel, Woodland Glades, about

60 m/yd later, many white pines surround you, and there is a small clearing.

In less than 75 m/yd you reach the next junction, where there is another map. Continue straight (or to the right), still on the River Trail, and in 30 m/yd there is the junction with the Bog Run. Turn left, where the very narrow track is marked with blue flagging tape.

This slender footpath snakes among the trees, which include numerous tall pines. There are occasional interpretive panels, and when it reaches the junction with the red-marked side trail, 130 m/yd later, there is another map.

The next section passes through an area of tall pine, and their fallen needles almost obscure the route. At the next junction, in 150 m/yd, along with the map there is an interpretive panel: The Bog. Keep right; the trail descends gently, but distinctly, and reaches the edge of the bog 100 m/yd from the junction.

The maps indicated that there is a viewing platform out in the open area of the bog. However, I found no evidence of it; the trail just stops when it runs out of dry ground. Retrace the 100 m/yd back to the last junction, and turn right onto the red-marked side trail. This short connector, marked by orange flagging tape but nearly hidden by spreading ferns in some places, re-joins the River Trail in 175 m/yd.

The River Trail is marked by white flagging tape, and from the junction it descends toward the bog, quickly moving into an area of black spruce and a ground cover of bright green sphagnum moss. Barely 125 m/yd from the junction, the trail turns sharply right, and enters a very wet area. There are a few scattered logs, and you might notice white Styrofoam floats (used by fishers) hanging in the tree to mark the route instead of flagging tape.

This is a very wet area that extends for more than 100 m/yd, and without knee-high boots it is difficult to cross with dry feet. Once back on dry ground, the treadway is less distinct, and there are fewer trail markings. The bog is on the right, on lower ground. And after about 130 m/yd on dry ground, there is the next junction, where there is another map.

Keep left, on the River Trail. Though in thick spruce forest, you will soon see a cultivated field, not far away on the left. I think that casual walkers will find this section of the trail quite unpleasant. It had not appeared to have been maintained in some time: ferns and other low vegetation nearly hid the treadway, there were only occasional tattered scraps of flagging tape remaining, and there were even numerous fallen trees blocking the path. However, those comfortable with following forest pathways will not be seriously challenged.

Conditions improve once the trail reaches the banks of the Brudenell River, about 700 m/yd later, where a side trail provides access to the water. There is also a map. After a little wandering on the shoreline, resume following the River Trail, which now works through the forest with the river to the left. However, the dense forest rarely permits good views, all the way to the next junction, with another side trail that crosses behind the bog, 500 m/yd later.

The trees are a bit higher here, and older, so there are fewer intervening branches. The river is about 25 m/yd to the left. Less than 100 m/yd from this junction, the trail crosses another wet area, the outflow from the bog. Planks have been spread over the worst spots, a rudimentary solution, but sufficient except in wet weather.

Over the next 250 m/yd, the map shows two side trails connecting to the shoreline. However, even though there are maps posted where they should be, I found them completely blocked with fallen trees.

The River Trail is quite distinct now, and curves right, away from the water. In 100 m/yd it reaches a junction with a side trail that leads to Bog Run, and 20 m/yd past that an interpretive panel, the first in quite some time. Then the trail curves left, into a very twisty section that works back toward the river. There is even some elevation fluctuation.

The next side trail, on the left 250 m/yd from the previous intersection, also did not appear useable. Keep straight, on the River Trail, passing numerous interpretive panels, to the intersection with the Bog Run, 125 m/yd later.

Turn left, and return to the intersection with the Heritage Trail. Turn left again, and follow its wide crushed-stone track. This gentle pathway is easy to follow, featuring frequent interpretive panels and several lookoffs overlooking the river mouth and community of Georgetown. It does, however, pass near the edge of an eroding cliff, so some caution is required.

After a pleasant 450 m/yd, the trail enters a large grass-covered field, strewn with benches and picnic tables. This is Brudenell Point, and in the middle of the field sits a large stone monument, mounting the original 1935 National Historic Site plaque.

Follow the wide road-like track directly ahead; it is 200 m/yd back to the heritage buildings and the end of your hike.

44. Singing Sands Beach

◀ - - - ▶ 11 km (6.9 mi) rtn
🕐 : 3 + hrs
🏃 : 3
Type of Trail: natural surface
Uses: walking

⚠ : wind and waves
💧 : adequate throughout
Facilities: benches, garbage cans,
interpretive panels, picnic tables,
washrooms
Gov't Topo Map: 11L08 (Souris)

Trailhead GPS: N 46° 22.705' W 62° 6.565'

Access: From the junction of Grafton and Water Streets in Charlottetown, cross the Hillsborough Bridge, and drive 12.4 km (7.75 mi) on Highway 1 east. Turn left onto Highway 5 and continue for 27.5 km (17.2 mi). Turn right onto Highway 4 and follow it for 48 km (30 mi). At Basin Head Road turn right, and follow it to end in the parking lot in 1.6 km (1 mi).

Introduction: One of PEI's most popular beaches, Singing Sands frequently appears in lists of the top beaches in Canada. Some claim it is because of the warm water, others because of its many kilometres of clean white sand. The beach gains its name from a peculiar squeaking, or singing, sound produced when the wind blows across it, or even from a person walking.

This is a wonderful beach just to wander along until you run out of room, or desire, to continue any further. For myself, had it been possible to cross the outflow from MacVanes Pond, I would have kept walking. Watch for the ferry to the Magdalen Islands, which leaves from Souris and passes quite close.

Dogs must be on-leash inside the provincial park grounds, but once further down the beach may be permitted to run free. (Not recommended during plover breeding season.)

Route Description: This walk begins at picturesque Basin Head Provincial Park, where there is a great variety of services during tourist season. The massive parking lot provides some clue to the beach's popularity on hot, sunny summer days, and should you choose to walk then, you might face a bit of a trek before you even reach the beach.

Directly ahead is a large complex

Singing Sands

The phenomenon is not completely understood, but some sand "sings." That is, when walked upon, it produces a sound variously described as humming or squeaking — or singing. This condition has been described on a number of beaches throughout the world, including a few in Canada.

But certainly the most well-known in this country is one particular beach near Souris, sufficiently awe-inspiring that it earned a nomination as one of the Seven Wonders of Canada, and a recommendation as one of the ten top beaches in the country.

Best of all, when you get there, just shuffle your feet through the warm, dry, gleaming sand; it really sings!

of low wooden buildings, park services such as washrooms, and the Basin Head Fisheries Museum. Head to this; there is a passage through it that leads to a long boardwalk that descends the low hill toward the beach, and another cluster of small buildings.

This is a very attractive view, as these buildings have been constructed to look hand-built, with shingle roofs and unpainted wooden walls. They sit behind a hedge of grass-covered sand dunes, with the intense blue of the ocean stretching to the distant horizon.

Follow the boardwalk past a modern-looking playground, ignoring the tempting paths over the dunes leading to the beach, to the outflow from Basin Head Harbour. Both sides of this narrow passage have been lined in wooden pilings, creating quays that extend beyond the beach. To the left is a building labelled The Cannery, which is part of the museum.

Crossing this channel, in the middle of the quay, is a very strong metal bridge, which you should cross. On the opposite bank, you step onto the gleaming white sand and begin your beach walk.

The beach at Basin Head is quite broad, perhaps 50 m/yd wide. On the left, there is only a small fringe of beach grasses in front of a thick tangle of white spruce, which are a few metres/yards higher than sand level. Ahead, a tantalizing vista of sand and ocean waves stretches to the limits of your vision.

Trek along the beach, close to the water's edge, where the sand is firmer. After about 600 m/yd, the trees

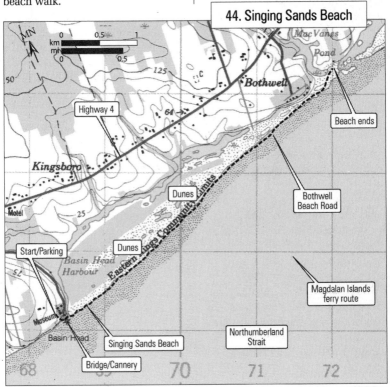

44. Singing Sands Beach

begin to give way on the left, replaced by a barrier of high, steepening dunes. This is a gorgeous, wide beach, exposed wide open to cooling breezes and ceaselessly caressed by lapping waves.

There is both much to see of scenery, but little to mention of detail. When I walked this in October 2013, at 1.8 km (1.1 mi) from the bridge the remains of a small, shipwrecked boat were exposed near the high tide mark. The keel and a few other large wooden beams remained, covered in bright green weeds, as did the engine and several other metal parts. However, the sea is restless and powerful, so by the time you hike, nothing may remain. More likely you will find an occasional lobster trap washed ashore, or some other piece of fishing gear.

As you continue your walk, the beach gradually narrows, and curves to the left. Ahead, you appear to be approaching a forested hill, while to the left a few houses and cultivated fields come into view as the intervening sand dunes decrease in height.

At 3.4 km (2.1 mi), Bothwell Beach Road connects on the left. It is worthwhile walking up about 100 m/yd to a parking area behind the dunes, because from here there is an excellent view of the large pond and salt marsh that extends from this point all the way back to Basin Head Harbour.

The beach continues, though the land on the left gradually increases in elevation, and becomes tree covered. It also converges, until the dunes almost disappear, crowded by the hillside behind. By 500 m/yd after Bothwell Beach Road, there are several houses visible on this hillside, and a few have access paths, and even wooden staircases, permitting beach access.

About 950 m/yd beyond Bothwell Beach Road, about 4.4 km (2.75 mi) from Basin Head, the beach almost completely disappears. Only a thin strip of sand, tree-littered from the eroding bank looming beside it, continues. It would be unwise to continue on a stormy day, but if the weather is calm, you can continue a further 250 m/yd. This brings you to the very end of the beach, across a narrow—but impassable—channel that is the outflow from MacVanes Pond. On the far bank another long stretch of striking beach and sand dunes marches off into the distance.

Retrace the beach back to the parking lot at Basin Head Provincial Park.

45. Souris Striders Trails

◄---► 6.25 km (3.9 mi) rtn
🕐: 2+hrs
🚶: 2
Type of Trail: natural surface
Uses: walking, biking, snowshoeing, cross-country skiing

⚠: none
📱: adequate throughout
Facilities: interpretive panels, picnic table
Gov't Topo Map: 11L08 (Souris)

Trailhead GPS: N 46° 24.155' W 62° 15.155'

Access: From the junction of Grafton and Water Streets in Charlottetown, cross the Hillsborough Bridge, and drive 12.4 km (7.75 mi) on Highway 1 east. Turn left onto Highway 5 and continue for 27.5 km (17.2 mi). Turn right onto Highway 4 and follow it for 35.8 km (22.4 mi) to Souris. At Highway 305/Chapel Avenue, turn left. After 5.8 km (3.6 mi), the clubhouse and parking area are on the left.

Introduction: Since 1988, the Souris Striders ski club has maintained a network of cross-country ski trails. They have also constructed the Harmony Ski Lodge, a full-service facility located at the trailhead. The lodge operates only in the winter, but during the non-snow months the office in the ground floor, used by the Souris and area branch of the PEI Wildlife Federation, might be open.

The trails are not designed or signed for hiking, but walkers are welcome to use them during the non-snow months. The route I have profiled essentially follows the outer perimeter of the network. Exploring some of the interior loops will add distance and a few hills.

Route Description: From the parking lot, two wide tracks have been mown through the grass, with a buffer of tall grass between them; keep to the right. They converge in about 75 m/yd. Notice that small spruce have been planted on either side of the path. Eventually they will grow tall enough to provide wind protection.

The trail works around the edge of a large cultivated field, on the left, and crosses the Confederation Trail at 200 m/yd. There is a cluster of interpretive panels on the far side. In winter, as the Confederation Trail is used by snowmobiles, approach this crossing with caution.

Once across, the trail turns left, as

wide as a forest road and bordered by lights, for nighttime skiing. At about 400 m/yd, the path separates; again, keep to the right. If walking you may ignore the "Wrong Way" sign, but not if you are skiing. In fact, skiers should do this route in the opposite direction I suggest for walkers. Less than 100 m/yd later is a major intersection, with paths seemingly heading in every direction. Again, keep to the far right track.

The trees bordering the trails are mostly hardwoods, making this a colourful walk in the fall. For the next 500 m/yd, the broad path you are on is paralleled by a similar track, with occasional cross-connections. It is not until about 1 km (0.6 mi) from the lodge that the tracks converge, and there is only one path continuing forward.

The trail descends gently, crossing a seasonal stream 150 m/yd later, then curving left to the next junction, at 1.3 km (0.8 mi). Again, keep right. About 50 m/yd further the trail makes a sharp turn right, descending quite distinctly to reach the Souris River, and the Harmony Bridge that crosses it, at 1.5 km (0.9 mi).

About 30 m/yd from the bridge there is a major convergence of routes. If you wish a short, 4 km (2.5 mi) walk, keep left. Otherwise, turn sharply right, and onto a path with

significant vegetation growing in it. This is the Josie Louis Loop.

For nearly 500 m/yd, the path continues along the hillside with the river downslope on the right. It then curves left through more than 90°, reaching an intersection about 150 m/yd later. Again, keep right, climbing to another junction, at 2.2 km (1.4 mi). On the right, only 50 m/yd away, is the Confederation Trail, although a different branch.

Turn left here. The trail quickly drops down to where there is a small pond on the right, boasting a large beaver lodge. Keep straight, climbing up to another prominent junction at 2.3 km (1.4 mi). Turn left; in less than 50 m/yd the trail separates again into two roughly parallel tracks. Keep right, and this will deliver you back down to the major intersection near Harmony Bridge nearly 400 m/yd later.

Again keep right. For the next 650 m/yd the wide, grass-covered trail passes uneventfully through a thickly wooded area, with the Souris River below to the left. At first, the trees are all deciduous, but as the path moves closer toward the river, conifers replace them.

At 3.4 km (2.1 m), the path ends at a clay-surfaced, unnamed road. Turn left, dropping downhill to cross the Souris River 75 m/yd later. Follow this

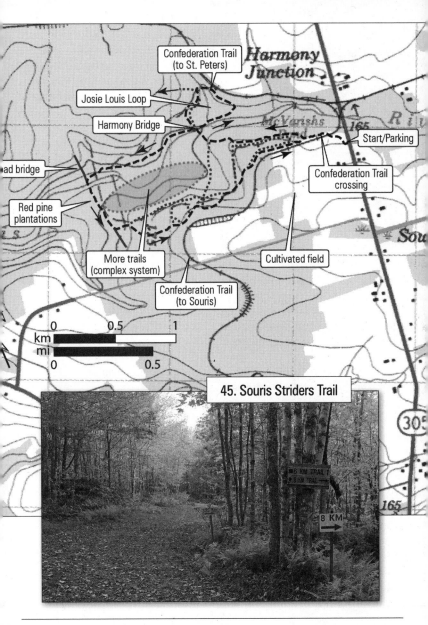

Confederation Trail
(to St. Peters)

Harmony
Junction

Josie Louis Loop

Harmony Bridge

McVarishs

165

R i

Start/Parking

ad bridge

Confederation Trail
crossing

Red pine
plantations

s

Sou

More trails
(complex system)

Cultivated field

Confederation Trail
(to Souris)

0   0.5   1

km

mi

0   0.5

45. Souris Striders Trail

8 KM TRAIL
9 KM TRAIL

8 KM

305

165

at all of them; this is the main path. At the bottom of the steepest hill, a significant (for PEI) drop of perhaps 25 m/yd, is the last junction of this section, connecting, again, from the left. You have walked about 4.8 km (3 mi).

Continue following this route, keeping to the right whenever you encounter a junction. Within 300 m/yd, the trail separates into two roughly parallel tracks, and 100 m/yd later, you should notice that the Confederation Trail is quite close on the right.

The wide pathway continues through the hardwood forests, back into the area with overhead lights. Connections with the parallel track and the Confederation Trail occur, but stay on the the path you're already on. At 5.7 km (3.6 mi), the trail reaches a small warming hut, at another trail intersection.

Continue straight; less than 100 m/yd remains until you reach the very first junction where you kept to the right. Retrace the 400 m/yd back to the club lodge.

road, past plantations of red pine, ignoring several side trails, including a major track on the left about 300 m/yd from the bridge. Continue a further 100 m/yd to an even more distinct junction, and turn left off the road here.

There are a number of routes possible; stay on the widest that heads more or less straight uphill. As the trail climbs, the softwoods are replaced once again by gorgeous maples and beech. The next 900 m/yd may be the most enjoyable of the hike. The ground is undulating, providing some elevation changes, and the bordering trees are magnificent stands of hardwoods, fringed at ground level by ferns.

This section can also be very confusing, as there are many side trails, and plenty of signs. Keep to the right

46. Valleyfield Demonstration Woodlot

◄- - -► 1.7 km (1.1 mi) rtn
🕐: 1+hrs
🏃: 1
Type of Trail: natural surface
Uses: walking, snowshoeing

⚠: none
🌲: adequate throughout
Facilities: benches, interpretive panels
Gov't Topo Map: 11L02 (Montague)

Trailhead GPS: N 46° 8.345′ W 62° 43.190′

Access: From the junction of Grafton and Water Streets in Charlottetown, cross the Hillsborough Bridge, and drive 17.2 km (10.75 mi). Turn left onto Highway 3 and continue for 7.6 km (4.75 mi). Turn right onto Highway 24 and follow it for 10.6 km (6.6 mi). At Highway 326/Valleyfield Road, turn left and drive for 4.6 km (2.9 mi). Turn left onto Highway 354/ Dalmaney Road. The trailhead is on the left in 750 m/yd; watch for the parking sign.

Introduction: Valleyfield Demonstration Woodlot is one of six forest-management properties established by the PEI Department of Environment, Energy, and Forestry. They are intended to provide the public with visible examples of proper forest management and increase public awareness of the forestry industry. Their many interpretive and educational displays offer information on natural history, Island history, wildlife management, and forest ecology.

Perhaps because of the variety of forest types, as well as the different ages in the various stands, Valleyfield Demonstration Woodlot is considered to be one of the best birdwatching locations on PEI, particularly for songbirds.

The interpretive footpath is quite short. Anyone wishing to extend their walk should continue along the forest road leading from the parking area. This does a 1.6 km (1 mi) loop, crossing Dalmaney Road twice, but otherwise remaining under forest cover before returning to the parking area.

Route Description: At the parking area, there are two signs indicating where the walk begins. One is an arrow, pointing toward the Robbins Trail; the other is a map of that route, showing the location of all the interpretive/ educational stations.

The Robbins Trail is fairly wide, with a natural-surface treadway. Just past the trailhead sign is a metal box labelled "Brochures," but none were available when I visited. (I have rarely ever seen a stocked brochure box.)

The forest is thick with the trees densely packed together, and their branches stretch overhead. Within 100 m/yd the first panels are reached, as the trail curves left. Several trees are labelled—beech, sugar maple, and balsam fir (a stand of these)—and there is a sign telling you about a 1.4 ha (3.5 ac) patch cut, though there is no explanation of what that might be.

Nearly 250 m/yd from the start the trail reaches a large board, on which twenty-four pictures of tree needles and leaves are displayed. Soon afterward the path begins a distinct turn to the left, passing posts 4 and 5. At 400 m/yd, there is a large display showing the bark and wood grain of eight different hardwoods.

There is a sign for an emergency exit, pointing left, just 35 m/yd past the hardwood display. The main trail continues to wander along, a dry footpath cut through the forest, passing more signposts and occasional signs. At about 600 m/yd, the next photo display board shows flowers and berries.

Every few steps there seems to be another sign, too many to mention. Not all are valid, such as the sign for a picnic table, beneath a lovely grove of hemlocks—there was no table—but most should be of some interest.

At 950 m/yd, just as the trail reaches another stand of hemlock, it turns sharply left, and after another 100 m/yd it reaches the forestry road that

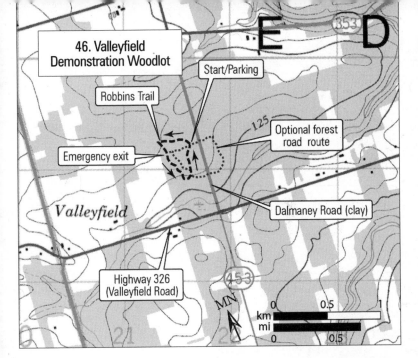

46. Valleyfield Demonstration Woodlot

Start/Parking

Robbins Trail

Emergency exit

Optional forest road route

Valleyfield

Dalmaney Road (clay)

Highway 326 (Valleyfield Road)

MN

km
mi

0   0.5   1

0   0.5

loops around this property. Turn left, and follow this road about 65 m/yd to the next intersection, where you keep to the right. (The sign was hidden by vegetation when I walked it.)

Back under forest canopy, this grass-covered footpath heads gently uphill. The trees are somewhat taller here, and more open. Near the top of the rise, about 100 m/yd later, there is a bench and a display board showing the bark of eight different types of conifers.

The path continues, fairly straight, with maybe fewer signposts than in the first section of the trail. It passes

signposts 14 and 15, and a display for an abandoned woodpile, before reaching a comment box at 1.5 km (0.9 mi). Unlike the brochure box, this was stocked, with both a book and a pen.

Only about 200 m/yd remains, passing a few more displays and a number of bird boxes on nearby trees. The wide path treks through a final stand of spruce to reach the parking area directly across from the trailhead.

PRINCE EDWARD ISLAND
NATIONAL PARK

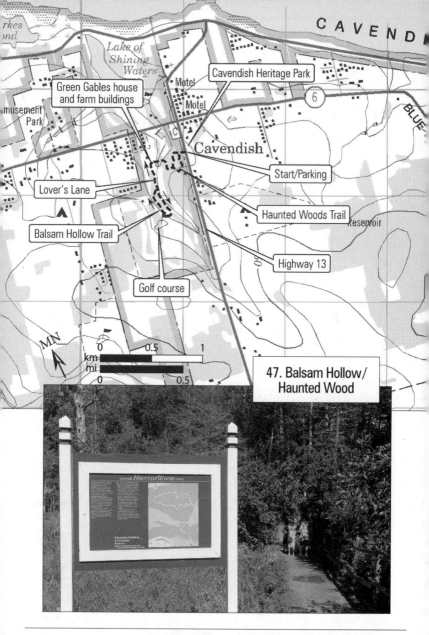

rkes
nd

CAVEND

Lake of Shining Waters

Motel

Cavendish Heritage Park

Green Gables house and farm buildings

6

BLUE

musement Park

Cavendish

Motel

Start/Parking

Lover's Lane

Haunted Woods Trail

Reservoir

Balsam Hollow Trail

Highway 13

Golf course

MN

km
mi

0   0.5   1

0   0.5

47. Balsam Hollow/ Haunted Wood

47. Balsam Hollow / Haunted Wood

◀--- ▶ 2.5 km (1.6 mi) rtn
🕐: 1+hrs
👥: 1
Type of Trail: compacted earth, crushed stone
Uses: walking, snowshoeing

⚠: road crossings
💧: adequate throughout
Facilities: benches, garbage cans, interpretive panels, picnic tables, washrooms, water
Gov't Topo Map: 11L06 (North Rustico)

Trailhead GPS: N 46° 29.375' W 63° 22.655'

Access: From the junction of Highway 1 and Highway 2/Malpeque Road in Charlottetown, follow Highway 2 west for 18.2 km (11.4 mi). Turn right onto Highway 13, driving for 16.2 km (10.1 mi). The parking area is on the right, in Cavendish Heritage Park.

Introduction: Is there any more iconic location in PEI than Green Gables? Since shortly after the publication of *Anne of Green Gables* in 1908, people have been coming to Cavendish to see the site of Lucy Maud Montgomery's inspiration. Today, it is a National Historic Site, restored as it might have appeared in the late 1800s, including a number of farm outbuildings.

In addition to its buildings, Green Gables features two short walking trails, established in areas where Montgomery frequently walked herself. I have combined these into one route, which I begin from a parking area located outside of the exception-

ally busy National Historic Site. The many interpretive panels found along both trails make this ideal for families or slow strolling.

Substantial reconstruction work on the Balsam Hollow Trail in 2014 and afterwards will slightly change my description of the trail as it appeared when I walked it in 2013.

Route Description: From the parking area, walk in the direction of Charlottetown, toward some bronze plaques that overlook a cultivated field. These plaques talk about L.M. Montgomery's Cavendish. Turn right, and cross Highway 13. On the far side, there is a sign saying that this is an entrance to the Haunted Woods Trail.

This easy loop, less than 1 km (0.6 mi) long, works through a forested grove where L.M. Montgomery enjoyed walking, particularly after dark. Then, the thick vegetation, especially in a gully, gave the trees a sinister, menacing quality. Montgomery called it the "Haunted Wood."

Within a few metres/yards of the road sits a bench and the first of many interpretive panels, this marking the site of a former schoolhouse. The path descends, through a series of large, earthen stairs, reaching a junction where a sign indicates that Green Gables is 500 m/yd to the right. Actually, you can head in either direction; both pass through thick forest and a number of interpretive panels, into a gully and across a bridge, then climb to another junction in about 250 m/yd.

At this junction, a sign directs toward Green Gables. The trail soon emerges from the forest to cross a connecting road for the golf course. One green is to your left, another tee on the right. The path returns into forest, where it weaves through the trees, emerging about 250 m/yd from the junction at another bridge, which is at the bottom of a small hill just below the Green Gables house and farm buildings.

A short climb up some earthen steps delivers you into the middle of Green Gables, which is usually a very busy place. Take some time to explore the house and buildings. In addition to the displays, there is a variety of services, including a café and gift shop.

From the top of the stairs exiting the Haunted Woods Trail, continue straight to the front of the house, where a sign indicates that the Balsam Hollow Trail is to the left. Continue past the building and a cluster of picnic tables; on what appears to be an old lane, there is a large sign, which includes a map, for the Balsam Hollow Trail.

This is another short loop, only about 800 m/yd long, which is once again replete with interpretive panels. It is also an exceptionally pleasant little area, quintessentially PEI.

The path, a roadway from an earlier era, descends gently. This is the Lover's Lane of L.M. Montgomery, a space of "green and alluring" beauty capable of repairing "the heartsickness, giving peace and newness of life." A verdant awning of hardwoods frames the wide, clay-surfaced track, sunlight dappling the rich, red earth.

After about 150 m/yd, there is a junction, with the trail keeping right and a maintenance vehicle road heading left. Tiny Balsam Hollow Brook is crossed, and from here the trail meanders for several hundred metres/yard alongside this slow-moving, shallow watercourse, with frequent interpretive panels describing the flora and fauna. There are several benches, and a few small bridges criss-crossing the stream. This is a tranquil, serenely peaceful area.

After crossing the final bridge, about 600 m/yd from the start of Lover's Lane, the trail makes a sharp turn to the right and climbs away from Balsam Hollow Brook. It turns through almost 180°, paralleling Balsam Hollow Brook but several metres/yards above, while to the left, the golf course lies just beyond the edge of the forested area.

About 200 m/yd after the turn, there is a large observation deck overlooking the brook. The trail continues a little further, before turning right, dropping down a long staircase, then crossing an extended boardwalk/bridge one final time across Balsam Hollow Brook. On the far side, the loop closes; turn left, and walk back up Lover's Lane

Green Gables

When Lucy Maud Montgomery wrote *Anne of Green Gables*, it is unlikely that she could have imagined how popular and enduring her character would become. Even now, more than 100 years after its publication, thousands of people come to Prince Edward Island to see the place she loved so much and described so adoringly in nineteen books.

Green Gables House, a National Historic Site, has become the focus of fans of her durable fictional characters, and has been restored to appear as it might have in the late 1800s. Although Montgomery never lived here, she did extensively explore the surrounding woodlands. Walking these trails can help deepen an appreciation of her writing.

to Green Gables, then return on the Haunted Woods Trail to return to Cavendish Heritage Park.

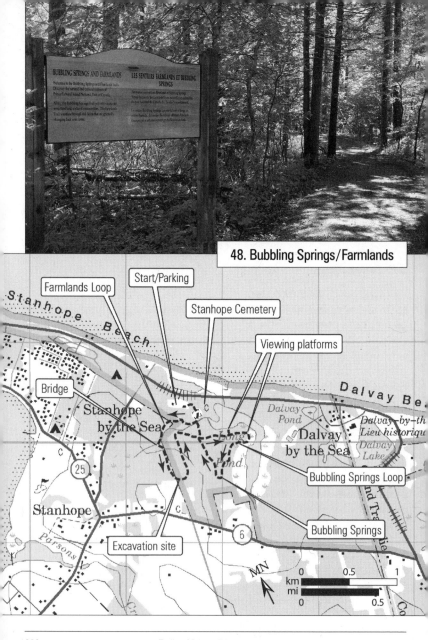

48. Bubbling Springs/Farmlands

Farmlands Loop

Start/Parking

Stanhope Cemetery

Viewing platforms

Bridge

Bubbling Springs Loop

Bubbling Springs

Excavation site

Stanhope Beach

Stanhope by the Sea

Dalvay Beach

Dalvay Pond

Dalvay-by-th
Lieu historiqu
Dalvay
Lake

Dalvay
by the Sea

Long Pond

25

Stanhope

6

Parsons

MN

0   0.5   1
km
mi
0   0.5

48. Bubbling Springs/Farmlands

◄---► 4.5 km (2.8 mi) rtn
🕐: 1+hrs
🏃: 1
Type of Trail: crushed stone
Uses: walking, biking, snowshoeing, cross-country skiing

⚠: none
📷: adequate throughout
Facilities: benches, garbage cans, interpretive panels, picnic tables
Gov't Topo Map: 11L06 (North Rustico)

Trailhead GPS: N 46° 25.000' W 63° 5.745'

Access: From the junction of Highway 1 and Highway 2/Malpeque Road in Charlottetown, follow Highway 1/2/Perimeter Road east for 3.3 km (2.1 mi). Turn left onto Highway 2, driving for 10.2 km (6.4 mi). Turn left on Highway 6, and continue for 9.9 km (6.2 mi) to the junction with the Gulf Shore Parkway East. Keep straight, driving for 3.7 km (2.3 mi). The trailhead and parking area are on the left.

Introduction: This is a pleasant walk that provides a mixture of woodland and wetland viewing. Ironically, the Farmlands Loop is entirely forested, as the former fields have almost completely regrown into woodland. However, the Bubbling Springs Loop includes two covered viewing platforms overlooking Long Pond, home to a wide variety of waterfowl.

As both trails share the same trailhead, and can be walked together

quite easily, I have profiled these two routes as one hike. Each can be walked as a separate loop, should that be desired.

Route Description: The trailhead is well signed, and features a map of both trails. There are also garbage cans, information plaques, and picnic tables inside a shelter—a warm-up hut for winter users. For the first 100 m/yd, both trails share the same track, a wide, crushed-stone pathway that curves through a pleasant, mostly hardwood forest. This provides a leafy canopy overhead—welcome shade on a summer day.

After a few steps, you reach a very large wooden signpost, the first of many. In both English and French, this briefly outlines the type of experience you will find on both trails.

At 100 m/yd, the path reaches the Stanhope Cemetery, which contains graves dating back to 1811. In front of its carefully tended grounds is a low stone wall, which the trail turns to pass alongside.

You also reach the junction where the two routes separate; there is a map. Turn right, onto the Farmlands Loop. This is a little narrower than the first 100 m/yd of pathway, but is still surfaced in crushed stone, with no interfering tree roots or rocks in the treadway.

This is a lovely path, more sinuous than shown on the map. However, it remains wide enough for two and there should never be doubt about your route. The overhead cover persists, and the path is frequently bordered by former hedgerows. There is even a bench.

The ground is noticeably lower to the left, and the trail works along the low slope. Although never much of a climb, the path does move up and down a little. About 650 m/yd from the junction, the trail drops into this modest gully to cross a tiny creek on a sturdy bridge with railings. Another map identifies your current location.

Once across, the trail resumes its twisting route through the forest, which is now mostly young white spruce, commonly the first tree to recolonize abandoned farmland. There is even a modest elevation, perhaps 3-5 m/yd high, which must be climbed. However, the route is fairly straight, and the continuation of the trail is visible through the spruce.

Nearly 700 m/yd from the bridge, the trail makes a distinct curve left, and almost immediately you arrive at an excavation site, which is alongside the path, on the left. This work site is a small ditch, barricaded only by a rope. Just beyond that, also on the left, sits a small pond.

The trail continues its curve left, through thick white spruce, almost all the same age. It is wider now, and descends gently for a few hundred metres/yards, before climbing out of a lower spot. At the top of a low rise there is a bench, nearly 500 m/yd from the excavation. About 100 m/yd further there is actually a small grassy field—the first of this loop.

Shortly after that, the trail swings first right, then left, and passes alongside a small pond, to the left. From here, it climbs out of this low trough, and within 200 m/yd connects once again to the Bubbling Springs Loop at a four-way intersection, where there is a map and a bench.

Keep straight, on a much wider track, past an interpretive sign that describes the formation of Long Pond. This moves through more open forest to the first viewing platform, about 275 m/yd further and 80 m/yd to the left. This covered structure, which shelters a picnic table, provides both views of Long Pond and its surrounding wetlands, but also traffic on the Gulf Shore Parkway.

The trees change, with the tall softwoods being replaced by lower, thicker hardwoods. The path is also completely covered in grass, as the trail curves around Long Pond to the next viewing platform, nearly 300 m/yd later. This is also on the left; there is a bench, map, garbage can, and interpretive panel nearby.

From this lookoff, the trail heads toward the Bubbling Springs, nearly 600 m/yd distant. En route, there are several interpretive panels that speak about the forest today, and the forest that the first settlers found in the early 1800s. The path remains mostly grass surfaced, and although it is no longer very close to Long Pond, occasional glimpses of the water are still possible.

At the spring, where water gurgling to the surface of a small pool is quite apparent, there is another bench, a map, and an interpretive panel. This is a pleasant place to stop and enjoy a snack. From here, the path curves right, and heads through the spruce forest the 500 m/yd back to the four-way junction. Along the way, several more interpretive panels provide additional edification. The treadway also reverts to crushed stone.

Ticks

Ticks are small arachnids — not insects — that attach themselves to mammals and gorge themselves on their blood. Unfed ticks are small, not much larger than a sesame seed, and they move around on the ground, grass, and bushes, waiting to attach themselves to any animal that brushes past.

Ticks are rare on PEI and are usually brought in on migratory birds. Most tick bites cause only skin irritation and swelling, but a small percentage of ticks carry diseases, the most deadly of which is Lyme disease. DEET on clothes is effective at repelling ticks, but other measures are prudent.

At the intersection, continue straight on the wide, former settlement road. After 200 m/yd, the trail crosses a bridge without railings, and less than 50 m/yd later arrives back at the Stanhope Cemetery. Only 110 m/yd remains, along the path on which you first walked, to return to the trailhead.

49. Cavendish Beach

◄---► 11 km (6.9 mi) rtn

🕐: 2.5+hrs

🧍: 3

Type of Trail: asphalt, natural surface

Uses: walking

⚠: poison ivy, motorized vehicles (on road), winds and waves

💧: adequate throughout

Facilities: benches, garbage cans, outhouses, picnic tables

Gov't Topo Map: 11L06 (North Rustico)

Trailhead GPS: N 46° 29.815′ W 63° 24.500′

Access: From the junction of Highway 1 and Highway 2/Malpeque Road in Charlottetown, follow Highway 2 west for 18.2 km (11.4 mi). Turn right onto Highway 13, driving for 16.4 km (10.25 mi). Turn left on Highway 6/Cavendish Road, and continue for 2.6 km (1.6 mi). Turn right onto Grahams Lane. In 1.4 km (0.9 mi), you reach the park entrance. About 300 m/yd past the entrance, turn left toward Cavendish Campground. The parking area is on the left in 150 m/yd.

Introduction: While I was Prince Edward Island, my most frequent walk was this one to the tip of Cavendish Beach and the mouth of New London Harbour. From the first time I ventured over its broad, sandy beach, past its lofty dunes, and into its buffeting breezes, I was deeply affected by its natural beauty.

On a calm summer day, this is the easiest of walks, a stroll along a fragment of paradise. Yet even in winter, when harsh gales drive ice crystals like needles into any exposed skin, Cavendish Beach possesses an ineffable grandeur that may compel you to return.

Route Description: Starting from the same trailhead as the Homestead Trail, walk into the campground along the road. From the entrance building, keep to the left, and continue for 650 m/yd, nearly 100 m/yd beyond the end of the asphalt. To the left is a parking area and picnic shelter; beside it is path heading toward the ocean. Turn left and follow it.

In just a few seconds the trees give way to a field of hardy beaches grasses, and within 100 m/yd, you reach a staircase providing access to the sandy beach. Ahead of you stretches a seemingly limitless horizon of blue (or grey, depending upon weather and season). The crash of the surf, which will be your constant companion for your beach walk, may be loud enough to hinder easy conversation.

Turn left. Ahead extends an arc of beach that dwindles in the distance and blends into far-off hills. On the left, grass-tipped dunes, their faces scoured of vegetation, form a barricade against the unceasing action of the waves. To the right, a rippling line of white, the crests of waves lapping at the edge of the sand.

For the first 400 m/yd, there are no dunes on the left, but a low embankment, and beyond that, trees. The ground is still the distinctive bright red soil of PEI rather than the lighter beige of the sand. About where the trees end, it is possible to walk to the inland edge of the beach and peer over into a salt marsh on the edge of

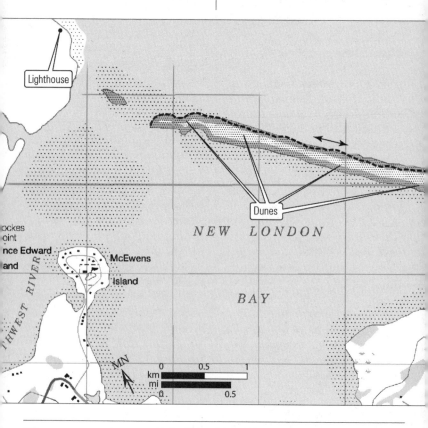

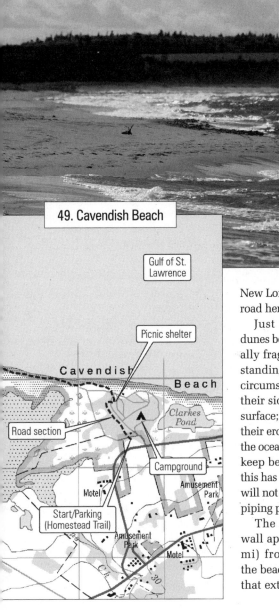

49. Cavendish Beach

Gulf of St. Lawrence

Picnic shelter

C a v e n d i s h

B e a c h

Clarkes Pond

Road section

Campground

Motel

Amusement Park

Start/Parking
(Homestead Trail)

Amusement Park

Motel

New London Bay. There is an old road here as well.

Just past here is where the dunes begin. These are exceptionally fragile structures, notwithstanding their height. Under no circumstances should you climb their sides or disturb their sand surface; this will greatly facilitate their erosion. Instead, walk along the ocean edge of the beach. If you keep below the high-tide mark, this has the added benefit that you will not inadvertently disturb any piping plovers.

The first break in the dune wall appears about 1.5 km (0.9 mi) from where you entered the beach. This is a flat channel that extends to the bay behind,

CC BY-SA 3.0

testament to the power of wind and wave. Actually, the dunes are constantly changing, regularly rearranged by the never-ending winds or suddenly altered by storms. As you walk further along the beach, you will notice rows of wooden posts, the remains of structures intended to support the sand dunes and fix them in place.

Because the dunes are constantly changing, there is little need to elaborate much further about the route. There are no obstructions or sudden changes of direction that require attention; you may concentrate on enjoying the natural beauty surrounding you. Sanderlings and plovers skitter along the forefront of the advancing waves, terns troll the shallow waters for a meal; I even spotted a Peregrine falcon perched on a dune near sunset.

From the staircase to the tip of the beach is about 4.75 km (3 mi). There,

at the mouth of New London Bay, small boats ply the narrow passage. On the opposite bank, the shoreline is sheer cliff, with a lighthouse perched above. The remains of a breakwater, now a perch for cormorants, sits in the middle of the channel. To the left, farms, fields, and the community of Stanley Bridge are visible.

It is possible to extend the walk. The low, broad sand spit curves around to the bay side of the dunes. However, this soon ends in a marshy area. Instead, turn back, and retrace your route along the beach and back to the trailhead at the campground. If you are like me, you will want to return to walk this trail again.

50. Clark's Lane

◄----► 5.25 km (3.3 mi) rtn
🕐: 1.5+hrs
🥾: 2
Type of Trail: asphalt, crushed stone
Uses: walking, biking, snowshoeing, cross-country skiing

⚠: poison ivy, road crossings
💧: adequate throughout
Facilities: benches, garbage cans, interpretive panels, picnic tables, washrooms
Gov't Topo Map: 11L06 (North Rustico)

Trailhead GPS: N 46° 29.402' W 63° 23.604'

Access: From the junction of Highway 1 and Highway 2/Malpeque Road in Charlottetown, follow Highway 2 west for 18.2 km (11.4 mi). Turn right onto Highway 13, driving for 16.4 km (10.25 mi). Turn left onto Highway 6/Cavendish Road, and continue for 1 km (0.6 mi). The trailhead and parking area are on the right, 200 m/yd off the Highway.

Introduction: Although I have labelled this as Clark's Lane, the route profiled includes all of the Cavendish Beach Trail and a significant portion of the Cavendish Dunelands Trail. These trails are connected, and together provide a more enjoyable walk or bike ride than either one alone.

Clark's Lane starts at Cavendish Grove, home to a rare—for PEI—grove of sugar maple and a very pleasant picnic area. After connecting to the Dunelands Trail, the route ends at Oceanview Lookoff, a scenic view-ing platform on the cliffs overlooking Cavendish Beach. On the return, follow the Cavendish Beach Trail back to Cavendish Grove.

Route Description: From the parking area, follow the broad gravel path across a causeway spanning two small ponds and into Cavendish Grove, an exceptionally attractive picnic ground. There are wide grassy areas for play, tables shaded beneath tall hardwoods, and a maze of paths criss-crossing the property.

Unless you wish to explore Cavendish Grove, continue straight (right) along an asphalted path, which climbs a slight rise, winding as it does. About 250 m/yd from the start, there is an interpretive panel near some buildings that advertises the site's new washrooms facilities.

Your route curves left around this cluster of buildings, where the surface reverts to crushed stone, and

continues to the next junction 100 m/yd further. Here, with a gleaming white barn-like building on the right, turn left. The path continues through the well-groomed lawns of Cavendish Grove. In 125 m/yd, with a house to the left and a shelter hosting a number of picnic tables on the right, the path turns 90° right. Flanked by an impressive row of tall conifers, the trail heads to the next junction, 75 m/yd distant, where there is an interpretive panel.

Turn left onto Clark's Lane; the trail leaves Cavendish Grove, and for the next 700 m/yd it passes alongside agricultural lands, curving to work around their borders. For the final 350 m/yd, the pathway is a sunken lane, descending, slightly lower than the ground on either side, and bordered by trees.

The path emerges at a crosswalk over Grahams Lane, a park road. And just 25 m/yd later, Clark's Lane ends at a T-junction with the Cavendish Dunelands Trail, where there is bench and a map.

Turn right, and follow this pleasant, meandering woodland walk, with the ocean visible in glimpses to the left. Within 125 m/yd, there is short side path on the left to an observation area, which provides a good view of the dunes. Then, for the next 425 m/yd, the trail continues through thick forest, with only an occasional interpretive panel for variation.

When it emerges from the trees, the Cavendish Beach complex of buildings is directly ahead, while to the right is a very large parking area. Another 150 m/yd brings you to the

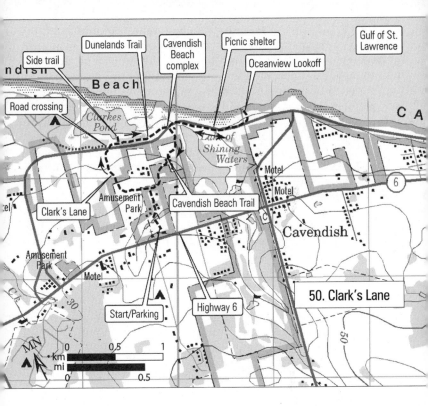

Dunelands Trail | Cavendish Beach complex | Picnic shelter | Gulf of St. Lawrence

Side trail | Oceanview Lookoff

Road crossing

Beach

Clarkes Pond

C A

Lake of Shining Waters

Motel

Motel

Amusement Park | Cavendish Beach Trail

Clark's Lane

Cavendish

Amusement Park

Motel

50. Clark's Lane

Start/Parking | Highway 6

MN

| 0 | 0.5 | 1 |
km
mi
| 0 | 0.5 |

front of the buildings, and the intersection of the trail with a boardwalk.

This is usually a very busy spot, and if biking, you should dismount to navigate your way safely through the crowds. From the intersection, where there is a map, turn left, and walk between the buildings. Behind them, on a large grassy field, is a hefty interpretive panel, and a wooden gate labelled "Dunelands." A distinct track is worn through the grass and heads

in the direction of the dunes towards what proves to be a long, floating boardwalk, 75 m/yd away. The trail crosses this 100 m/yd long bobbing boardwalk—bikers may wish to dismount at this point—across Macneill's Pond: a lovely spot. In the middle is a viewing platform with interpretive panels.

On the far side of the pond, the trail continues across mostly open ground up a gentle hill. On the left, in 275 m/yd, is another picnic area with a modern playground and wash-rooms. The broad trail continues up-hill, turning left in a sweeping curve to arrive at the Oceanview Lookoff parking area in 500 m/yd.

This is another busy spot, as it boasts a beautiful view and is the closest lookoff to the community of Cavendish. However, there are num-erous interpretive panels, two formal lookoffs, situated on the top of low sandstone cliffs, and the opportunity to scramble down to the water's edge. There are also benches and picnic tables, so you might wish to spend a few minutes sightseeing or enjoying a snack.

Once you're finished at the Ocean-view Lookoff, retrace the Dunelands Trail back to the trail junction in front of the Cavendish Beach complex. From here, turn left onto the crushed-stone pathway; this is the Cavendish Beach Trail. (Consult the map if you are uncertain.)

This is an easy stroll intended to permit visitors in Cavendish access to the beach without driving their car into the park. The trail works around the parking lot, which should be on your right, with Macneill's Pond to the left and slightly below. After 250 m/yd, it crosses a gravel road, where there is a map posted. It almost immediately enters the forest, an area of dense young hardwoods.

Less than 100 m/yd later, the trail comes out into a semi-open area, across which it winds, gently climbing, for nearly 300 m/yd before re-entering the forest. This is the grove of sugar maple, a lush belt of towering trees and cooling shade. Unfortunately, after only 200 m/yd of this lovely length of trail you reach the next junction, where there is a map. Turn left, back under the maples. In another 75 m/yd you ar-rive at the junction in Cavendish Grove next to the white barn where you turned left.

From here, retrace the 350 m/yd back through Cavendish Grove to the trailhead.

Raccoon
One of the most highly adaptable of North America's mammals, the raccoon, with its distinctive and disarming black mask, may be found just as often in an urban park as in a backcountry forest. Indeed, raccoons quickly learn that people will feed them if they come out in the open to be photographed.

About the size of a large cat, and plump with a waddling walk, raccoons appear harmless. But, although they are unlikely to attack a human, they sometimes carry a roundworm parasite that is easily transmitted and is thought to have caused twelve deaths — mostly children.

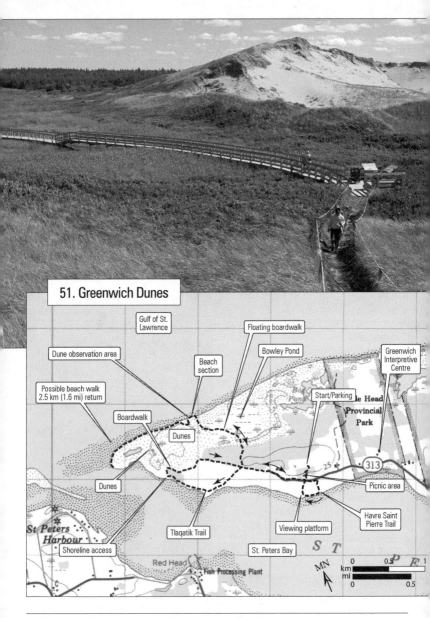

51. Greenwich Dunes

Gulf of St. Lawrence

Floating boardwalk

Dune observation area

Bowley Pond

Greenwich Interpretive Centre

Beach section

Possible beach walk 2.5 km (1.6 mi) return

Start/Parking

le Head Provincial Park

Boardwalk

Dunes

Bo_ Pond

Dunes

313

Tlaqatik Trail

Picnic area

Viewing platform

Havre Saint Pierre Trail

St Peters Harbour

Shoreline access

St. Peters Bay

S T

P F

Red Head

Fish Processing Plant

MN

km

mi

0   0.5   1

0   0.5

51. Greenwich Dunes

◀----▶ 8 km (5 mi) rtn

🕐: 2+hrs

🥾: 2

Type of Trail: boardwalk, crushed stone, natural surface

Uses: walking, biking*, snowshoeing, cross-country skiing*

⚠: none

🧭: adequate throughout

Facilities: benches, garbage cans, interpretive panels, picnic tables, washrooms

Gov't Topo Map: 11L07 (Mount Stewart)

Trailhead GPS: N 46° 26.610′ W 62° 41.640′

Access: From the junction of Highway 1 and Highway 2/Malpeque Road in Charlottetown, follow Highway 1/2/Perimeter Road east for 3.3 km (2.1 mi). Turn left onto Highway 2, driving for 48.7 km (30.4 mi). Keep straight (left), turning onto Highway 16. In 450 m/yd, turn left onto Highway 313/Greenwich Road, and follow the road to its end, at a parking area, in 9.3 km (5.8 mi).

Introduction: Physically separated from the sections of the park with busy Cavendish and Brackley Beaches, and furthest in distance from Charlottetown, Greenwich Dunes retains a more wild and remote flavour. This is enhanced by its extensive and impressive coastal dune system, only accessible through trails longer than those elsewhere in the park.

Although there are officially three distinct hiking trails in the Greenwich

section of the park, all are interconnected and short. Therefore, I have written them as one combined route, and I encourage visitors to this area to spend the time to walk them all. For me, Greenwich Dunes is the one must-see site in the entire province.

Route Description: All of Greenwich's named trails share the same trailhead, starting from the large parking area. The wide, crushed-stone path immediately heads into a forested grove; in 50 m/yd, there is a modern washroom on the left. After this, occasional picnic tables are situated in open ground on both sides of the curving path.

At 200 m/yd, the trail reconnects with the former roadbed, which is also an intersection with the Havre Saint Pierre Trail. Keep right, and follow the wide track through the open former farmland, reading the

---

interpretive panels along the way. After another 950 m/yd, this reaches the junction where the Tlaqatik and Greenwich Dunes Trails separate.

Turn right onto the Greenwich Dunes Trail. Note that neither bicycles nor dogs are permitted on this section. This path heads into thick forest, passing several benches and interpretive panels, before reaching an elevated boardwalk in 300 m/yd. After another 100 m/yd, during which it passes over vegetation-covered but still fragile dunes, the walkway arrives at the edge of Bowley Pond, a large wetland sheltered behind the dune ridges.

This is the start of one of the highlights of hiking in PEI. For the next 550 m/yd, your route is along a boardwalk floating on the surface of Bowley Pond. And as you advance, you draw closer to the large wall of sand dunes lining the ocean shoreline. Along the way, there are observation platforms, benches, and interpretive panels.

On the far side of the pond, the trail, lined with ropes to guide you along the approved route, climbs over the dune wall, down a staircase, and deposits you onto a magnificent wide sandy beach. One solitary sign directs you left, toward an observation area. Walk along the beach for 150 m/yd; another sign directs you left, into a gap in the dunes. A fence-lined route climbs another 50 m/yd to an area

with information panels, where there are the best views of the extensive, elaborate, and nearly unique dune structures that the park was established to protect.

Many people walk along the beach to the tip of the point, a distance of 2.5 km (1.6 mi) return. Others, especially on warm summer days, lounge on the beach. Whatever your choice, when finished, retrace your route the 1.2 km (0.75 mi) back to the junction with the Tlaqatik Trail.

At the junction, keep straight. In a curving route, still wide and surfaced in crushed stone, the path heads through the open landscape toward the waters of St. Peters Bay, which it reaches in 600 m/yd. Along the way are numerous information panels, and the occasional bench. The trail traces the edge of the shoreline, and 200 m/yd later climbs a small hill, where there are more panels, a picnic table, bench, and telescope. On the opposite shore, the busy fishing community of Red Head dominates.

The trail continues through open ground for another 60 m/yd before it enters an area of thick spruce forest. For 200 m/yd, the trail meanders through the dense thicket. It emerges briefly at another viewing area, where there is also access to the waterline.

From here, the trail curves right, back into the spruce, where it remains for another 200 m/yd. There, the path

Hypothermia

Teeth chattering? Shivering uncontrollably? Hands numb? You may be entering Stage 1 hypothermia. Hypothermia is a condition in which a person's temperature drops below that required for normal metabolism and bodily functions, and it can happen in spring and fall as well as winter. If you experience these symptoms, end your hike immediately. A mildly hypothermic person can be effectively rewarmed through close body contact and by drinking warm, sweet liquids.

moves onto an elevated boardwalk, which turns right, emerges from the trees, and climbs along the edge of grass-covered sand dunes. This boardwalk, providing good views of the inland side of Greenwich's dunes, continues for 275 m/yd.

An additional 850 m/yd of the Tlaqatik Trail remains; it is mostly uneventful, with only a few more views of the dunes. The forest to the left is fairly thick, while on the right are the semi-open former farmlands. For the final 350 m/yd, the path is back on the route of the former road.

When you reach the junction with the Greenwich Dunes Trail, keep straight, and retrace the 950 m/yd back to the junction with the Havre Saint Pierre Trail, which is to the right. Although only 750 m/yd long, this can be a pleasant finish to the hike, and features some of the widest and best-tended paths.

This short loop once again heads to the shoreline of St. Peters Bay, and there are good views from a platform there. The trail's interpretive panels also focus on the Acadian heritage of the Greenwich area, just as the Tlaqalik Trail featured the region's Mi'kmaq culture. Once you have completed the Havre Saint Pierre loop, only 200 m/yd of additional walking remains to return to the trailhead.

52. Gulf Shore Way East

◄---► 25 km (15.6 mi) rtn
🕐: 6+hrs (walking), 2+hrs (biking)
🚶: 5 (walking) / 4 (biking)
Type of Trail: asphalt
Uses: walking, biking, inline skating,
  snowshoeing, cross-country skiing

⚠: vehicle traffic
📱: adequate throughout
Facilities: benches, garbage cans,
  interpretive panels, picnic tables,
  washrooms
Gov't Topo Map: 11L06 (North Rustico)

Trailhead GPS: N 46° 25.750' W 63° 12.070'

Access: From the junction of Highway 1 and Highway 2/Malpeque Road in Charlottetown, follow Highway 1/2/Perimeter Road east for 1.7 km (1.1 mi). Turn left onto Highway 15, driving for 18.2 km (11.4 mi). The parking area is on the left, just past the park entrance.

Introduction: This paved bidirectional path extends the entire length of the eastern section of PEI National Park, from the Brackley Beach complex all the way to the park entrance on Highway 6. This parallels the ocean for much of its length and is an exceptionally scenic route.

Although intended primarily for cyclists, several sections of this multi-use trail are very popular with walkers, as it provides pedestrian access between a number of nearby facilities.

Route Description: Your route begins in the parking lot in front of the Brackley Beach complex of buildings. There is a trailhead sign and, to the right of the buildings, a crushed-stone pathway. This avoids the high-traffic areas, and connects to the road at the crosswalk, on the path that leads to the beach.

Cross the road here; on the far side you will find a bidirectional multi-use path, heading only to your right. It is surfaced in asphalt, and has a centre-line stripe down the middle. Follow that, keeping the beach and dunes on your left, the parking area on the right.

The trail reaches the intersection with the main roadway about 350 m/yd later, and turns left. You continue riding facing traffic for another 450 m/yd, until the next parking area for beach access, when the trail crosses the Highway on a crosswalk. (Dismounting is recommended.) There is a bench here, as well as a rack for bikes.

For the next 600 m/yd, trees line

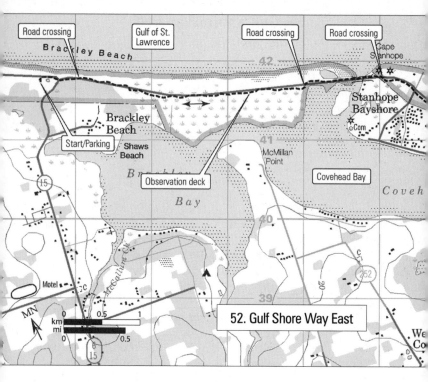

Road crossing

Gulf of St. Lawrence

Road crossing

Road crossing

Brackley Beach

Cape Stanhope

Stanhope Bayshore

Brackley Beach

Start/Parking

Shaws Beach

cCom

15

Observation deck

McMillan Point

Covehead Bay

Coveh

Brackley Bay

Coveh

Motel

McCallum Bk

252

MN

km
mi

0   0.5   1

0   0.5

52. Gulf Shore Way East

We
Co

15

the trail both left and right, though to your left there will be glimpses of dunes. After that, the trees fade away, and you face an extended stretch with no wind barrier whatsoever. For nearly 3 km (1.9 mi), on the right is a large open salt marsh with views of Brackley Bay, Covehead Bay, McMillan Point, and the lands on the far bank. Along the way, at about 3.25 km (2 mi) from the start, there is an observation deck with benches and interpretive panels.

The land on which the road is situated continues to narrow, and about 950 m/yd from the viewing platform, the trail once again crosses the road, in order to cross the bridge over Covehead Harbour. This is quite a scenic area, but it is also potentially dangerous. The bridge is narrow, and everyone — including you, probably — will be looking around at the ocean, beaches, and bustling harbour.

The trail stays on the left of the road only about 450 m/yd, until just

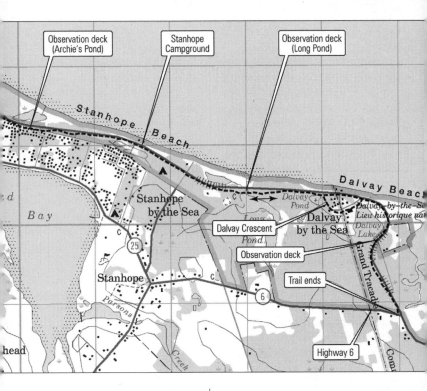

after the turnoff to Covehead Harbour. Then, on another crosswalk, next to a small lighthouse, it recrosses to the right side. The road then begins a long, gradual turn to the right, uninterrupted until it reaches, and crosses, Bayshore Road 500 m/yd later. A sign directs left to Stanhope Cape Beach.

The next few hundred metres/ yards are forested on both sides, but soon houses, then driveways, appear on the right, then another pond on the left. At 6 km (3.75 mi), the trail crosses Ross Lane. On the opposite side of the road is another observation deck, this one overlooking Archie's Pond.

The trail moves away from the houses, into areas with a dense tree cover, and gradually comes closer again to the ocean. About 1.3 km (0.8 mi) from Ross Lane, the trail crosses the entrance to Stanhope Campground, its closest point to the water. About 800 m/yd after that, Stanhope Lane crosses the trail, with the Stanhope Beach parking area to the left.

For much of its remaining distance, the trail passes through wooded terrain, with frequent ocean views on the left. About 500 m/yd beyond Stanhope Lane, it passes the trailhead for the Bubbling Springs and Farmlands Trails. And 300 m/yd after that there is another observation platform, this one overlooking Long Pond.

After another 1 km (0.6 mi), you reach Dalvay Crescent, where the path branches. Turn right, and head onto the Dalvay House grounds. (You might also want to play a round of golf.) The trail takes a 650 m/yd detour before it rejoins the main Highway.

This might be a good spot to turn left, and head back to Brackley Beach. However, still more of the trail remains, if you wish to finish it all. Turn right. The road and trail make a long curve right, working around Dalvay Pond. At 800 m/yd,

opposite Winter Road, there is a final observation platform on the shore of Dalvay Pond with an excellent view of Dalvay House.

This would make another good spot to turn around, but for those who need to complete the trail, it continues another 1.1 km (0.7 mi), past the park entrance and all the way to the parkway intersection with Highway 6. Here it ends abruptly, without fanfare or signage. You have travelled 12.5 km (7.8 mi); retrace your route back to Brackley Beach.

Common Loon

The loon's eerie, beautiful call is one of the most recognizable sounds of Canada's forests, a sound that instantly evokes a sense of wilderness in the listener. Loons prefer to breed on quiet, remote lakes, and are sensitive to disturbance by humans. Powerful swimmers, loons slide beneath the water's surface to chase the fish on which they feed.

In summer, common loons are fairly distinctive: black heads, white breast, and black-and-white backs. For the rest of the year they are a pale grey, with a white throat, and can be mistaken for a number of similar species.

In Prince Edward Island, loons are most frequently seen in coastal waters, during migratory season.

53. Gulf Shore Way West

◀- - -▶ 17 km (10.6 mi) rtn
🕐: 4+hrs (walking), 2+hrs (biking)
🚶: 5 (walking) / 2 (biking)
Type of Trail: asphalt
Uses: walking, biking, inline skating, snowshoeing, cross-country skiing

⚠️: vehicle traffic, poison ivy
🚻: adequate throughout
Facilities: benches, garbage cans, interpretive panels, picnic tables, washrooms
Gov't Topo Map: 11L06 (North Rustico)

Trailhead GPS: N 46° 27.835' W 63° 17.990'

Access: From the junction of Highway 1 and Highway 2/Malpeque Road in Charlottetown, follow Highway 2 west for 6 km (3.75 mi). Turn right onto Highway 7, driving for 10 km (6.25 mi). Continue straight on Highway 6, for 11.7 km (7.3 mi) to North Rustico. Turn right onto Harbourview Drive, the left in 100 m/yd onto Church Hill Avenue. Continue for 1 km (0.6 mi) to the park entrance. The parking area is on the right on Beach Lane.

Introduction: This paved bidirectional path runs from the North Rustico park entrance as far as the Oceanview parking area near Cavendish. It provides frequent views of the ocean and access to all the park facilities along its length. At Oceanview, there are benches, viewing platforms, and interpretive panels—a good location for a picnic.

Although intended primarily for cyclists, several sections of this multi-use trail are used by walkers, as it provides pedestrian access between a number of parking areas, beaches, and picnic sites. It is also one of the few long-distance walking routes available inside the park.

Route Description: The trail begins just to the left of the parking area on Beach Lane. There are benches and a bike rack, and a sign indicating that Cape Turner is 3 km (1.9 mi) distant and Cavendish East is 9 km (5.6 mi). To the left, on the other side of the road, is small Rollings Pond.

The trail is in excellent condition, a 3 m/yd wide asphalt strip with a painted centre line. There is also a grass buffer between the road and its paralleling path. The route begins by climbing a low hill over a headland. Red coastal cliffs line the water's edge.

About 650 m/yd from the start, near the crest of the hill, Macneill

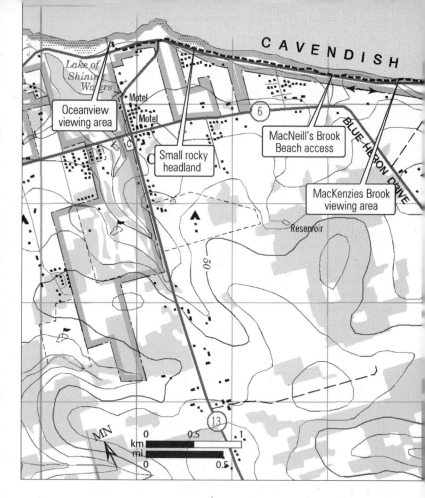

Lane connects to the road on the left, location of the Gulf View Cottages and other lodgings. Thick trees, almost all spruce, line the trail on the right, restricting views of the ocean.

A pleasant downhill follows, ending in 1.3 km (0.8 mi) at Doyles Cove, where there is a viewing area, complete with bike rack and benches. There is also a small beach here, which you can access. Cottages are clustered around the cove.

Another hill follows, climbing for the next 700 m/yd. By the time you

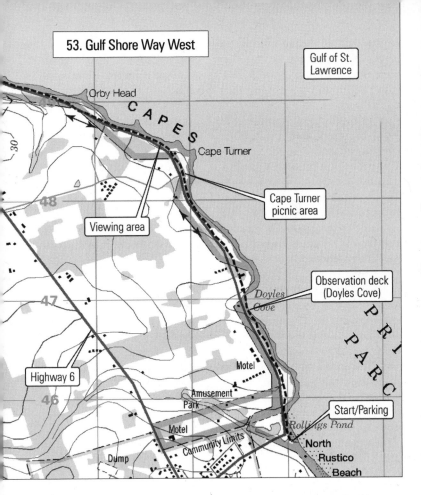

53. Gulf Shore Way West

Gulf of St. Lawrence

Orby Head

C A P E S

Cape Turner

Cape Turner picnic area

Viewing area

Observation deck (Doyles Cove)

Doyles Cove

P R I

P A R C

Highway 6

Motel

Amusement Park

Start/Parking

Motel

Rollings Pond

Community Limits

North

Dump

Rustico

Beach

reach the top, there is once again thick tree cover on the right, and only cultivated fields to the left. This is how the trail continues, except for the occasional private driveway, until at 2.9 km (1.8 mi), when there is the turnoff—to the right—for Cape

Turner. Here you will find covered picnic tables, washrooms, garbage cans, and a view of the ocean from the top of a headland. This might be a good destination for walkers.

The path continues, descending while curving to the left. As it does, an expanded view of the ocean opens up. Just 400 m/yd from Cape Turner, there is an unnamed viewing area, with a bench. Any tree cover is now all on the left.

Another long, gradual climb is required, but at least the ocean is visible through most of it. At this crest, at about 4.2 km (2.6 mi), there is a turnoff to Orby Head. This is an interesting viewing area, high above the water. Fences limit access to the edge of the high coastal cliffs, but you can walk around the grass-covered headland and obtain excellent views of a cormorant perch.

The trail descends again, and as it does the road moves very close toward the water's edge. At 5.2 km (3.25 mi), there is the MacKenzies Brook viewing area, where there is a bench and bike rack. There is also access to a small beach.

The trail now is only a few metres/yards higher than the ocean, and will remain mostly level for the remainder of its distance. About 1 km (0.6 mi) later, you reach the larger, and more popular, MacNeill's Brook Beach access. As with all these viewing areas, the trail detours around the parking spaces, and cyclists need to be observant of pedestrians crossing from their cars to the beach.

The entire ocean side of the trail has been open since Orby Head, although there are occasional stands

of densely packed spruce. After MacNeill's Brook, there are more cottages and cultivated fields on the left.

No official viewing areas remain, but at 7.4 km (4.6 mi) there is a parking area, on the right, that seems quite popular. It allows access to a small rocky headland and a tiny beach.

Only 400 m/yd past this, the trail separates from the Gulf Shore Parkway Road, which curves left and heads into the community of Cavendish. The trail keeps straight, and soon reconnects with the access road to Oceanview: Terre Rouge Lane.

At 8.4 km (5.25 mi), the trail makes its only road crossing, on a crosswalk, just before Terre Rouge Lane curves right into the large parking area. The path continues straight another 100 m/yd, then reach an intersection with the Dunelands Trail. Keep right; your trail ends 50 m/yd later, where there is bike parking, and foot access to the viewing platforms.

Retrace your route to return to the North Rustico trailhead.

54. Homestead

◀ - - - ▶ 8.5 km (5.3 mi) rtn

⏱: 2+hrs

🏃: 2

Type of Trail: compacted earth, crushed stone

Uses: walking, biking, snowshoeing, cross-country skiing

⚠: poison ivy

🚻: adequate throughout

Facilities: benches, garbage cans, interpretive panels, picnic tables, washrooms

Gov't Topo Map: 11L06 (North Rustico)

Trailhead GPS: N 46° 29.815′ W 63° 24.500′

Access: From the junction of Highway 1 and Highway 2/Malpeque Road in Charlottetown, follow Highway 2 west for 18.2 km (11.4 mi). Turn right onto Highway 13, driving for 16.4 km (10.25 mi). Turn left onto Highway 6/Cavendish Road, and continue for 2.6 km (1.6 mi). Turn right onto Grahams Lane. In 1.4 km (0.9 mi) you will reach the park entrance. About 300 m/yd past the entrance, turn left toward Cavendish Campground. The parking area is on the left in 150 m/yd.

Introduction: The Homestead Trail is one of the more varied walking experiences available in PEI National Park. It touches the shore of New London Bay, providing views of the sand dunes near Cavendish, but it also heads through woodland, and alongside both active and abandoned farmlands. It features a number of picnic sites and is ideal for families and casual walkers or hikers.

Homestead is also one of the longer walking paths available in the park, requiring at least two hours to complete. However, it is designed with two loops, the shorter permitting a walk of 6.3 km (3.9 mi) if you do not wish to complete the full 8.7 km (5.5 mi).

Route Description: From the trailhead, where there is a large sign featuring a map, Homestead begins with a pleasant 350 m/yd walk along a wooded lane. This extends to a four-way junction, where there is also a map. Continue straight along the path where there is an Entrance sign.

For the next 1.2 km (0.75 mi), this path, wide and resembling a settlement cart track, passes through thick forest, with only very occasional views—to the right—of more distant terrain. Then, at 1.5 km (0.9 mi), the trail emerges from the forest onto a small grassy field at the edge of New London Bay. There is a picnic table here, and a garbage can—and a wonderful view.

The trail turns left, following the water's edge, the trees giving way to tall beach grasses (and poison ivy—stay on the trail). About 200 m/yd later, it crosses a long, very sturdy bridge over the outflow from a tidal pond and salt marsh, which is on the left.

Once across this bridge, the path climbs back into a patch of spruce. On the left is a cultivated field, while the treadway is a grass carpet mown through the tall vegetation. After about 200 m/yd, the trail comes back into open ground, next to a small rivulet. It turns back toward New London Bay, and crosses this brook on another, slightly smaller, bridge.

The trail continues alongside the ocean for another 200 m/yd, before turning left and arriving at another picnic area. This is also the junction for the shorter loop, and that path heads to the left. To complete the longer loop, turn right. What follows is a very pleasant 650 m/yd where the path traces the shoreline through a grassy field. On the left, cultivated fields; to the right, New London Bay and easy access to the water's edge.

At 2.8 km (1.75 mi), there is an-

other attractive picnic area, which is also where the trail turns away from the ocean. For the next 1 km (0.6 mi), the path works around the edges of a number of cultivated fields, these at first on the left, then on the right. As it does so, the trail climbs slightly, providing better views of New London Bay.

At 3.9 km (2.4 mi), your route turns sharply left and once again into a thickly forested section. (Watch for an Exit sign.) About 150 m/yd later you reach the next picnic area, where there is a map, situated beside the crumbling remains of an old farmhouse. The trail continues straight, through farmland regenerating into woodland, for another 450 m/yd, until it reaches another area of cultivated fields.

Once again, an Exit sign directs you left, although you can probably see cars travelling on Highway 6 directly ahead. For the next 250 m/yd there is still wooded land on the left, but then the trail turns sharply right, and the only trees remaining are a narrow strip lining one side of the lane. After 200 m/yd, the route turns left again, and continues more or less straight for the next 500 m/yd. Here it makes a little curve to the left and crosses an area of lower ground.

On the far side, at 5.5 km (3.4 mi), there is another picnic area, this one set amongst some old farming

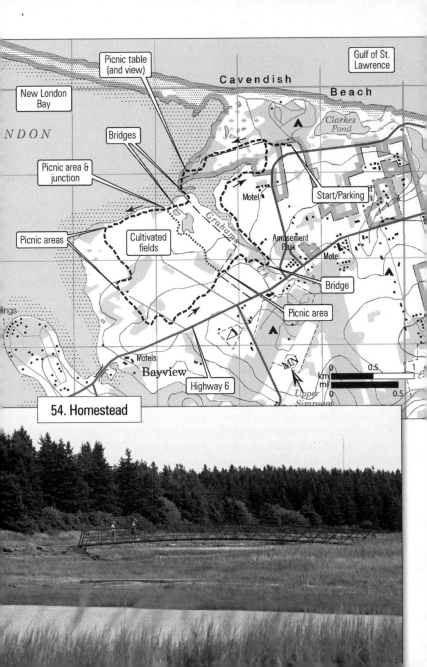

Gulf of St. Lawrence

Picnic table (and view)

Cavendish   Beach

New London Bay

NDON

Clarkes Pond

Bridges

Picnic area & junction

Start/Parking

Motel

Picnic areas

Cultivated fields

Grahams

Amusement Park

Motel

Bridge

Picnic area

ings t

Motels

Bayview

Highway 6

Cr

MN

Upper Simpsons

0   0.5   1
km
mi
0   0.5

54. Homestead

artifacts. In addition to the tables and garbage can, there is also an outhouse. This is where the short loop trail again reconnects, and there is another map at that junction.

The main trail continues straight, alongside a cultivated field, for another 250 m/yd before it turns right again. It follows the edge of this field for a final 150 m/yd before reaching, and heading into, a thickly wooded section. Once inside the forest, the path drops to cross a small stream, on a bridge, 250 m/yd later.

Once across, the trail climbs the steepest—but very short—hill of the walk. And 60 m/yd from the bridge, the path turns through more than 90° to the left. After a further 100 m/yd among the trees, the path comes up to another cultivated field, and keeps this on its right for the next 450 m/yd, as it heads back in the direction of the ocean.

The trail enters another mostly wooded section, and begins a series of turns for the next 250 m/yd, after which the trees give way to large grassy fields. To the left is a large pond; to the right is another cultivated field.

For the next 1 km (0.6 mi), the trail follows along the edge of the pond, an excellent shelter for waterfowl. You might even notice the large bridge at the pond's outflow into New London Bay, or other hikers and bikers. Along this section, there are benches and the final picnic area.

Once the path reaches another area of trees, it turns left, and only 300 m/yd remains before it reaches the initial four-way junction. Turn right, and retrace the 350 m/yd final back to the trailhead.

47. Balsam Hollow / Haunted Wood

47. Balsam Hollow / Haunted Wood

Dunes

Dunes are sand deposits on beaches that develop into a series of one or more ridges through wind and wave action and become stabilized by the growth of American beach grass. New dune ridges develop on the seaward side depending upon the sediment supply, the pace of erosion, and the rate of sea level rise.

All sand beaches have some measure of dune systems, although beaches on the Atlantic coast of the mainland tend to be retreating landward too rapidly for full successional series development.

The fragile grasses that populate the dunes are essential to their survival. Boardwalks are designed to prevent human passage that can quickly kill the plants, causing more rapid sand erosion. Stay on boardwalks at all times.

49. Cavendish Beach

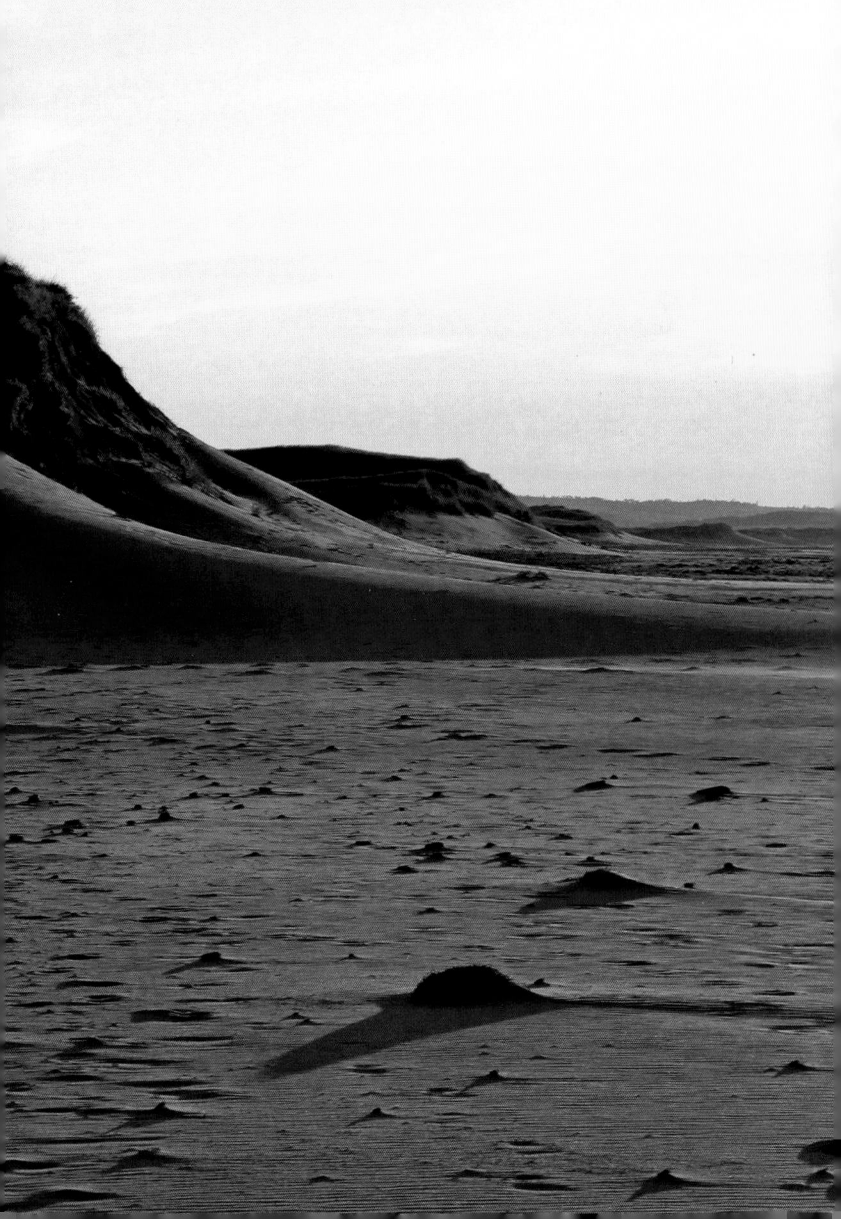

50. Clark's Lane

50. Clark's Lane

51. Greenwich Dunes

Don't Leave the Trail
Prince Edward Island has the smallest percentage of public land of any province in Canada, less than 10%. Most trails pass close to working agricultural properties; respect that and do not leave the public pathway. Even in parks you should stay on the defined track, because the surrounding land, such as the Greenwich Dunes, may be environmentally sensitive.

Ring-necked Pheasants

Native to Asia, ring-necked pheasants were introduced in the United States in the 1800s and have long been one of North America's most sought-after game birds, renowned for its succulent meat.

A ground dweller, pheasants prefer agricultural landscapes, where waste grains from crop fields provide a substantial percentage of their diet, although ring-necks require nesting cover of grasses and stubble high enough to conceal nests but allow for easy ground travel.

The male is particularly colourful, and is one of the most distinctive bird species. It is often seen running alongside the road, or flying away in a low-altitude near-glide.

53. Gulf Shore Way West

54. Homestead

Red Fox

The red fox is a member of the dog family and is indigenous to PEI. Adult red foxes range in weight from 4 to 6.5 kg (9 to 14 lb), although their long-haired coats make them appear to be much larger.

With the arrival of coyotes in the 1980s, foxes have been driven from their customary woodland habitat into closer association with humans. As a result, they are seen far more often than in earlier times, even though their numbers have significantly declined.

55. Reeds & Rushes/Woodlands

55. Reeds & Rushes/Woodlands

55. Reeds & Rushes/Woodlands

◄----► 7.5 km (4.7 mi) rtn

🕐: 2+hrs

🏃: 2

Type of Trail: asphalt, compacted earth, crushed stone, natural surface

Uses: walking, biking*, snowshoeing, cross-country skiing*

⚠: none

🐾: adequate throughout

Facilities: benches, garbage cans, interpretive panels, picnic tables, washrooms

Gov't Topo Map: 11L06 (North Rustico)

Trailhead GPS: N 46° 24.915' W 63° 4.530'

Access: From the junction of Highway 1 and Highway 2/Malpeque Road in Charlottetown, follow Highway 1/2/Perimeter Road east for 3.3 km (2.1 mi). Turn left onto Highway 2, driving for 10.2 km (6.4 mi). Turn left on Highway 6, and continue for 9.9 km (6.2 mi) to the junction with the Gulf Shore Parkway East. Keep straight, driving for 1.9 km (1.2 mi). Turn left onto Dalvay Crescent. The parking area is on the left in 300 m/ yd at the Dalvay Trail House.

Introduction: The Woodlands Trail provides the opportunity for one of the longest walks in the park. However, as it occurs entirely in thick tree cover, it is probably one of the least varied routes available. (It also is home to some truly ravenous mosquitoes.) It is, however, an excellent facility for cross-country skiing, with multiple loops providing various trail options.

On the other hand, Reeds & Rushes, though short, is quite scenic, providing views of the fauna in Dalvay Pond and accompanied by detailed interpretive signage. Together, these two trails deliver worthwhile exercise with some scenic attractions.

Note: Parks Canada closed these two trails in 2014 in order to upgrade the park's nearby wastewater facilities. This work might have created some minor changes to the path.

Route Description: From the Dalvay Trail House, walk to the road and onto the multi-use pathway, turning right. Follow this for 200 m/yd; it will take you to the start of the off-road portion of these trails, where you turn left. There are trail maps, but there is no parking here.

The path is surfaced in crushed stone, and it is wide enough for two to

---

walk side by side. On the left are some old buildings, and in less than 100 m/yd Dalvay Pond comes into view on the right. After another 100 m/yd, you reach the junction where the Reeds & Rushes Trail branches off to the right. There are signs, maps, and a bench.

Keep straight on the Woodlands Trail, on what appears to be a woodland road. The tall trees flanking the path, mostly spruce, appear to have been planted at the same time as they are nearly a uniform height. Within 150 m/yd, the trail splits left from the road, which is barricaded. Another map is provided to assist correct navigation. The crushed stone ends here, and the treadway is compacted earth, mostly grass covered. The path is still wide, but it narrows somewhat, and there are some low shrubs that extend their branches into the trail.

After 350 m/yd, you reach the next junction, where there is another map. There is also an Exit sign directing back toward the trailhead. Keep left, as this provides the quickest route to the next intersection, in case you wish to shorten the walk.

It is 360 m/yd to the next junction. (The maps are very precise, providing the distance between each intersection.) Except for a small pond on the right, the entire route is shrouded by tall trees, with the only variation being their species. At the next junction,

where there is another map, keep left again.

This 560 m/yd segment is a pleasantly meandering grass-covered track bordered by quite tall trees. There is even a small hill—okay, a very small mound. It continues through the next junction—keep left—and all the way until the trail makes a sharp turn to the right, at about 2.5 km (1.6 mi). At this point, you are actually only a few metres/yards from Highway 6, and you might be able to hear, or even see, cars travelling along it.

For the next 1.5 km (0.9 mi), the trail runs nearly parallel to Highway 6, sometimes close enough to see houses, always near enough to hear traffic. Along the way, there are two more path junctions, both with maps. Throughout the entire route, you are shaded by a high canopy of tree branches; the only clearings are the small areas at each junction.

Around 500 m/yd from the second junction, the trail turns sharply right, heading back in the direction of the trailhead. I enjoyed this section the most of the Woodlands, as it was somewhat more open, and there was a greater variety of tree species, although spruce still dominate. After 800 m/yd, you reach the end of the loop, back at the first junction. Turn left, and retrace the 500 m/yd back to the Reeds & Rushes Trail junction.

This is a very different experience

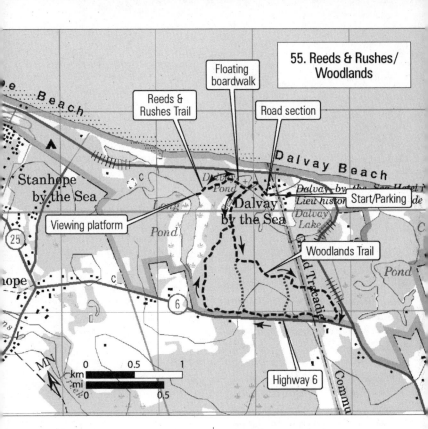

Floating boardwalk

Reeds & Rushes Trail

Road section

Stanhope by the Sea

Viewing platform

Dalvay Pond

Long Pond

Dalvay by the Sea

Start/Parking

Dalvay by the Sea Hotel

Lieut histor

Dalvay Lake

Woodlands Trail

Pond

Highway 6

25

6

MN

0   0.5   1
km
mi
0   0.5

from Woodlands, and is for walkers only. (Cyclists must leave their bikes at the intersection.) The former had few views; Reeds & Rushes enjoys a great deal, and in a very small area. Indeed, less than 125 m/yd from the junction, the trail reaches a long floating boardwalk, which contains viewing platforms with benches and interpretive panels.

Numerous waterfowl inhabit Dal-

vay Pond, and there is an old beaver lodge virtually built into the boardwalk. Herons ply the pond's edge, and although they are shy of humans they will occasionally ignore us if they're concentrating on a potential meal. Kingfishers scold with their distinctive chittering.

The boardwalk makes several turns, with frequent interpretive panels to encourage dawdling, and con-

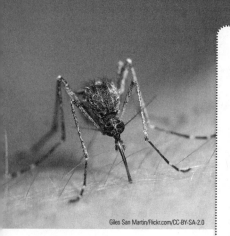

Mosquitoes

Between May and first frost, no hike will be entirely free of these tiny, annoying, blood-sucking pests. Forget wild animals; mosquitoes are the most common threat. Without adequate precautions your walk can turn into a running battle where scenery is forgotten while you slap frantically and flail the air trying to drive them away.

Though their primary food source is nectar from flowers, mosquitoes prefer blood to develop eggs. Some species carry diseases such as St. Louis encephalitis and the West Nile virus, which they can transmit to humans.

To limit your exposure to these ubiquitous nuisances, wear long sleeves and pants, especially during dawn and dusk (and a hat for those of us follicly challenged), and use insect repellents with up to 35 percent DEET for adults and 20 percent for children over six months of age.

tinues along the edge of Dalvay Pond. It also extends into the forest, through an area of soggy ground, for more than 200 m/yd before it reaches dry ground.

Once the boardwalk ends, the path heads along a compacted earth surface for another 650 m/yd, once again enclosed by thick forest. Though still wide enough for two, this is the narrowest section of the trail. Quite suddenly, an elevated viewing platform comes into view on the left. From it you can view Long Pond, another favourite of waterfowl. However, the platform is set back a short distance from the water, so binoculars will definitely be helpful.

This is the end of Reeds & Rushes. Retrace your route back to the Dalvay Trail House to complete the hike.

56. Robinsons Island

◀----▶ 4 km (2.5 mi) rtn
🕐: 1+hrs
🚶🚶: 1
Type of Trail: crushed stone
Uses: walking, biking, snowshoeing,
cross-country skiing

⚠: none
🗑: adequate throughout
Facilities: benches, garbage cans,
interpretive panels, picnic tables,
washrooms
Gov't Topo Map: 11L06 (North Rustico)

Trailhead GPS: N 46° 26.205' W 63° 14.610'

Access: From the junction of Highway 1 and Highway 2/Malpeque Road in Charlottetown, follow Highway 1/2/Perimeter Road east for 1.7 km (1.1 mi). Turn left onto Highway 15, driving for 18.2 km (11.4 mi). Turn left onto Robinsons Island Road, and continue for 3.6 km (2.25 mi) to its end, at the trailhead.

Introduction: The newest trail in PEI National Park, Robinsons Island is an ambitious combination of mountain biking, walking, and recreational cycling, will all users sharing one track. There is even a Pump Track near the trailhead. Once the site of a campground that closed in 2005, Robinsons Island sits opposite North Rustico Harbour and separates Rustico Bay from the Gulf of St. Lawrence.

In addition to the principal pathway, about 3 m/yd wide and surfaced with crushed stone, there are frequent diversions for mountain bikers that

employ a variety of obstacles, including teeter-totters. Hikers can access the beach and add a considerable distance of off-trail walking along the sandy shoreline.

Cyclists are required to ride the trail in a clockwise direction. Unless otherwise directed, I recommend that walkers negotiate the paths counterclockwise, in order to be facing oncoming bicycle traffic.

Dogs are permitted, on-leash, along the trail, but are not permitted on the beach.

When I visited the trail, in late September 2014, the trail surface had been laid and no signage had been installed.

Route Description: From the trailhead, walk to the first junction 60 m/yd (or, as the map lists, very precisely, 57.2 m/yd) away and turn right. In the first curve you will notice how this trail has been built keeping mountain

Great Blue Heron

One of the most distinctive and stately birds that you might sight is the great blue heron. Standing over 1 m/yd high, it is Canada's largest heron, and is the most widely distributed across the country. It is usually sighted perched motionless in areas of calm water, its long neck bent, waiting for a fish to venture into range for a lightning-fast strike with its sharp beak, or flying majestically overhead with deep, slow wingbeats.

Herons are migratory, generally arriving in April and heading south from mid-September to late October.

bikes in mind, as the outer edge has been built up. Most of the tree cover is white spruce, and all nearly the same age, as if they had been planted to help recover what had been farmland and help stabilize the island against erosion.

The meandering path twists its way among the trees, arriving in about 425 m/yd in sight of the Gulf of St. Lawrence. The first lookoff, where there is a bench, is on a 25 m/yd side trail to the right. There is also access to the beach here.

The main trail, however, turns left almost 180°, and heads away from the water, passing through a stand of younger, more densely packed spruce. Just 200 m/yd further it reaches an intersection with a former road. Turn right, and follow it to the beach, 150 m/yd away. This is another attractive spot, and a good place to start a stroll on the sand to the tip of the island, nearly 2 km (1.25 mi) distant.

Return to the main trail and turn right; the trail continues through spruce forest. Just 60 m/yd later is the first mountain-bike obstacle: on the left, a series of rocks and a narrow boardwalk. And only 50 m/yd after that is the junction with the first cross-trail; keep right.

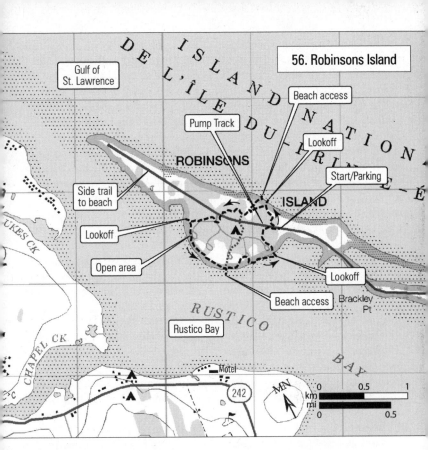

Gulf of
St. Lawrence

DE L'ÎLE DU PRINCE-É

ISLAND NATION...

Beach access

Pump Track

Lookoff

ROBINSONS

Start/Parking

ISLAND

Side trail
to beach

Lookoff

Open area

Lookoff

Beach access

Brackley
Pt

RUSTICO

Rustico Bay

BAY

ILUKES CK

CHAPEL CK

Motel

242

MN

km
mi

0   0.5   1

0   0.5

The sinuous pathway coils through
tall spruce. The next mountain-
bike hurdle, a teeter-totter, is on the
left 125 m/yd from the junction. Two
banked corners follow, then the next
obstacle 60 m/yd later. Just 75 m/yd
after this, the path reaches what was
formerly the end of the road, and it
will be an intersection with a new
trail running along its route. To the
left is a 685 m/yd direct return route
to the trailhead; to the right, a 500 m/
yd footpath leading to the beach.

You have walked about 1.3 km
(0.8 mi) to this point. Unless you
choose the detour to the beach, continue straight. The trail resumes its
winding course, rarely straight for
more than a few metres/yards. The
next mountain-bike diversion is en-

countered 200 m/yd later, a simple series of earthen mounds. The next, a series of posts and rocks, is less than 75 m/yd after that.

The trail appears to be gently descending, and soon you will be able to see Rustico Bay through the spruce ahead. About 150 m/yd from the last mountain-bike obstacle, there is a junction. To the right, 40 m/yd away, is a lookoff, where there is another bench. This provides a very attractive view of a salt marsh on the bay side of Robinsons Island, where great blue herons frequently wade in the shallow waters, searching for their meal.

The main trail turns left here, and within 75 m/yd it emerges from tree cover to enter a grassy field. To the right is Rustico Bay, where you might see fishers collecting their harvest in traps placed nearby. After only 200 m/yd in the open, the trail enters another thick stand of white spruce. This is a much straighter section of trail, and the trees are taller and larger.

You re-emerge into the open about 250 m/yd later, having passed another mountain-bike section and just after another banked turn. However, the ocean is further to the right, and the area is covered by shrubs, rather than grass, so your view is somewhat obscured.

The trail remains in this semi-open area slightly more than 350 m/yd, to the next junction, which is with a cross-path and a beach-access track. Turn right, and walk the 90 m/yd to the shore of Rustico Bay. Again, from here it is possible to walk along the beach for some distance.

Return to the main trail. It continues across semi-open ground for another 150 m/yd, and then heads back into forest. The trail becomes very tortuous, curving around considerably. Over the next 500 m/yd, there are three more mountain-bike obstacles, including another teeter-totter, and one more banked turn. During this snaking run, the trail works its way back toward the ocean, reaching it at the final lookoff, at 3.5 km (2.2 mi).

The trail curves left here, once again turning away from the water. And for the first time, there are more hardwoods than softwoods in the trees bordering the path. In this final 415 m/yd there are two more mountain-bike hurdles, including the first one to the right, rather than the left.

The trail reaches an intersection with the centre path next to the Pump Track. Turn right; the trailhead is only 100 m/yd (well, 95.8 exactly) away.

Acknowledgements

Prince Edward Island is not my home province, so I relied heavily on obtaining my starting information from the local trail community. Fortunately, it is an active and enthusiastic group that offered exceptional support and encouragement.

The Island Trails website is modern and informative, and provided a solid base from which to begin my explorations. Ruth DeLong, the province's Trails Community Relations Coordinator, was always available to answer my questions, was eager to hear about current trail conditions, and was always looking for suggestions on how to improve the province's trails. Doug Murray, a long-time volunteer and former director of PEI's Provincial Parks, generously volunteered information gained from his lifetime of accumulated knowledge. (This knowledge included the only known location on the Confederation Trail where showy lady's slippers bloom—and in time for me to view them.)

Many others provided assistance, including Bryson Guptill, President of Island Trails; Leo Gill, Manager—Confederation Trail Maintenance; Dan McAskill, Provincial Forests Manager; Brian Thompson, Director—Land & Environment Division, PEI Transportation & Infrastructure Renewal; Kevin MacLaren, Tourism PEI; Trent Williams, City of Summerside; and André Laurin and Jennifer Stewart, Parks Canada. In addition to all the individuals named, I also wish to extend my thanks to the hundreds of people I met and spoke to while hiking and biking on Prince Edward Island. Everyone I met was interested in my project, pleasant to chat with, and invariably eager to see the upcoming book.

To all of you, and to any others who I—with sincere apologies—missed mentioning, please accept my thanks. It is also my earnest wish that you may find this book to be helpful, and one that does justice to the enjoyment of the outdoors in your beautiful province.

Indian Head Lighthouse

Web Pages

The URLs listed below were current as of December 2014. However, organizations and even governments occasionally change their Web addresses. If you find a listed link that does not work, I recommend that you copy the site's name and paste it into your preferred Internet search engine. This should direct you to the new link.

A. Parks, Trails, and Outdoor Associations:
Beck Trail: http://www.becktrail.com/
Confederation Trail: http://www.tourismpei.com/pei-confederation-trail
Cycling PEI: http://cpei.ca/
Go PEI: http://www.gopei.ca/
Harvey Moore Sanctuary: http://www.historicplaces.ca/en/rep-reg/place-lieu.
    aspx?id=12361
Island Trails: http://islandtrails.ca
PEI Provincial Parks: http://www.tourismpei.com/pei-provincial-parks
Port-la-Joye—Fort Amherst National Historic Site of Canada: http://www.
    pc.gc.ca/eng/lhn-nhs/pe/amherst/index.aspx
Prince Edward Island National Park: http://www.pc.gc.ca/eng/pn-np/pe/pei-
    ipe/visit.aspx
Roma: http://www.roma3rivers.com/
Souris Stiders: http://www.sourisskilodge.com/
Town of Summerside: http://www.city.summerside.pe.ca/community-
    services/pages/2011/12/trails/
Trans Canada Trail: www.tctrail.ca

B. General Interest:
Geocaching: http://www.tourismpei.com/pei-geocaching
Leave No Trace Canada: www.leavenotrace.ca
Pet Friendly Travel: www.petfriendlytravel.com/dog_parks_canada

Scenic Heritage Roads: http://www.tourismpei.com/pei-scenic-heritage-
    roads
Tourism PEI: http://www.gov.pe.ca/tourism/index.php3
Weather Information: https://weather.gc.ca/forecast/canada/index_e.
    html?id=PE

C. Animals/Plants:

Coyote Information: www.pc.gc.ca/eng/pn-np/ns/cbreton/natcul/natcul1/c/
    i/a.aspx
PEI Plants and Animals: http://www.gov.pe.ca/infopei/index.
    php3?number=1032079&lang=E
Poison Ivy: http://www.pc.gc.ca/eng/pn-np/pe/pei-ipe/visit/visit4/visit4b.
    aspx
Raccoon: http://www.gov.pe.ca/photos/original/raccoonproblem.pdf
Red Fox: http://www.gov.pe.ca/photos/original/redfox2007.pdf
Ticks: http://www.gov.pe.ca/health/LymeDisease

D. Cellphone Coverage

Bell: www.bell.ca/support/PrsCSrvWls_Cvg_Travel.page
Rogers: www.rogers.com/business/on/en/smallbusiness/rogers/coverage/
Telus: http://www.telus.com/en/pe/mobility/network/coverage-map.
    jsp?&eVar35=http://www.telus.com/en/mobility/network/coverage-map.
    jsp

Index of Hiking and Cycling Tips and Sidebars

22. North Cape/Black Marsh Nature Trail

Index